The Apocalyptic Dimensions of Climate Change

Culture & Conflict

Edited by
Isabel Capeloa Gil, Catherine Nesci and
Paulo de Medeiros

Editorial Board
Arjun Appadurai · Claudia Benthien · Elisabeth Bronfen · Joyce Goggin
Bishnupriya Ghosh · Lawrence Grossberg · Andreas Huyssen
Ansgar Nünning · Naomi Segal · Márcio Seligmann-Silva
António Sousa Ribeiro · Roberto Vecchi · Samuel Weber · Liliane Weissberg
Christoph Wulf · Longxi Zhang

Volume 19

The Apocalyptic Dimensions of Climate Change

Edited by
Jan Alber

DE GRUYTER

ISBN 978-3-11-126976-4
e-ISBN (PDF) 978-3-11-073020-3
e-ISBN (EPUB) 978-3-11-073028-9
ISSN 2194-7104

Library of Congress Control Number: 2021937994

Bibliographic information published by the Deutsche Nationalbibliothek
The Deutsche Nationalbibliothek lists this publication in the Deutsche Nationalbibliografie;
detailed bibliographic data are available on the Internet at http://dnb.dnb.de.

© 2023 Walter de Gruyter GmbH, Berlin/Boston
This volume is text- and page-identical with the hardback published in 2021.
Cover image: Photo by Ian @greystorm on Unsplash.
Typesetting: Integra Software Services Pvt. Ltd.
Printing and binding: CPI books GmbH, Leck

www.degruyter.com

Acknowledgments

The editor would like to thank Myrto Aspioti, Stella Diedrich, and the anonymous reader for their perceptive comments on the manuscript. My gratitude also extends to Anne Stroka for expertly guiding this collection to the finish line. Furthermore, I would like to thank Anna Horstmann, Bianca Schüller, Zoë Takvorian, Kathrin Vaßen, and Linda Wetzel for editorial assistance and help with the proofreading. Finally, I want to mention that the great photograph on the cover was taken by Stormseeker, who can be found at: https://unsplash.com/@sseeker.

Contents

Acknowledgments —— V

Jan Alber, Steffen Jöris, and Wolfgang Römer
The Apocalyptic Dimensions of Climate Change between the Disciplines —— 1

Wolfgang Römer
Scenarios of Human-Induced Climate and Environmental Changes at Different Spatial and Temporal Scales —— 11

Gerbern S. Oegema
The Apocalyptic Imagination and Climate Change —— 49

Marco Caracciolo
Narrative and the Texture of Catastrophe —— 63

Diana Dimitrova
Hindu Apocalyptic Notions, Cultural Discourses, and Climate Change —— 81

Judith Eckenhoff
The Desert Wasteland and Climate Change in *Mad Max: Fury Road* —— 93

Jon Hegglund
Drawing (on) the Future: Narration, Animation, and the Partially Human —— 109

Axel Siegemund
Environmental Sciences, Apocalyptic Thought, and the Proxy of God —— 125

Carlos A. Segovia
Four Cosmopolitical Ideas for an Unworlded World —— 137

Jan Alber and Zoë Takvorian
Climate Change, the Apocalypse, and Other Ideologies in *The Day after Tomorrow* —— 157

Biographical Information —— 175

Subject Index —— 177

Name Index —— 181

Jan Alber, Steffen Jöris, and Wolfgang Römer
The Apocalyptic Dimensions of Climate Change between the Disciplines

1 Introduction

A simple google search already demonstrates that climate change and the apocalypse are frequently connected in the popular imagination of the twenty-first century (see also Gardner 2015, Haker et al. 2014, and Horn 2014). There is even a Wikipedia entry on the 'climate apocalypse,' where the phenomenon is described as follows:

> [. . .] a hypothetical scenario involving the global collapse of human civilization and potential human extinction as either a direct or indirect result of anthropogenic climate change and ecological breakdown. Under a global catastrophe of this scale, some or all of the Earth may be rendered uninhabitable as a result of extreme temperatures, severe weather events, an inability to grow crops, and an altered composition of the Earth's atmosphere. (https://en.wikipedia.org/wiki/Climate_apocalypse, accessed 15 April 2021)

This collection brings together climatologists, theologians, literary scholars, and philosophers to address and critically assess this connection, i.e., the apocalyptic dimensions of climate change in scientific models and cultural discourses. The chapters all deal with the following questions:
- How and why do fictional, philosophical, and religious narratives negotiate climate change in relation to the apocalypse?
- How are (or can) these narrative representations (be) related to the scientific models developed by climatologists?
- To what degree are the depicted scenarios or events realistic and to what degree do they involve instances of fictionalization? And why is this so?
- Can one observe any kind of influence of scientific knowledge on cultural productions?
- How do cultural narratives and scientific models influence attitudes regarding climate change?[1]

---

[1] The papers collected here were presented at a conference on the apocalyptic dimensions of climate change at RWTH Aachen University between November 15 and 16, 2018. We would like to thank the Exploratory Research Space (ERS) at RWTH Aachen University for funding our conference in the context of the ERS Seed Fund OPSF405.

https://doi.org/10.1515/9783110730203-001

Among other things, we are interested in the narrative strategies that the mentioned text types or genres use in order to depict climate change as one example of a fluctuating environment.[2] In particular, we zoom in on the interaction between the setting and the characters to illustrate how the represented figures deal with climate change. Some analyses of this kind already exist in the discipline of literary studies (see, e.g., Chakrabarty 2012, Kluwick 2014, Trexler 2015, and Mehnert 2016), and we want to build on them.

Furthermore, our main focus will be on the ideological underpinnings of these textual representations (see also Alber 2019). More specifically, we wish to determine what the narratives in question want their recipients to get or do. In this connection, Louis Althusser writes that for him, the term "ideology" denotes "imaginary [. . .] world outlooks," that is, worldviews that do not "correspond to reality" (2001: 1498). From this perspective, ideologies are distorting worldviews. As examples of such imaginary distortions, Althusser mentions the belief in God (or gods), duty, justice, the family, the trade union, and the party. These beliefs are all ideological because they involve a certain degree of subjectivism: there can be no absolute reason why one should take a specific belief system for granted. Along similar lines, Stuart Hall explains that

> [. . .] we experience ideology as if it emanates freely and spontaneously from within us, as if we were its free subjects, 'working by ourselves.' Actually, we are spoken by and spoken for, in the ideological discourses which await us even at our birth, into which we are born and find our place. (1985: 109)

As Matthew B. Arbuckle has shown (2017: 177–194), discussions of climate change are obviously also influenced by underlying ideologies or worldviews (see also Faust 2011). In this collection, we are particularly interested in the role of *apocalyptic* images in relation to representations of climate change.

The climate is one of the fundamental control mechanisms in the environmental system of the Earth. It enables a habitable globe for different species – including humans. In the context of the joint initiative of the World Meteorological Organization (WMO) and the United Nations Environmental Programme (UNEP) in 1988, the Intergovernmental Panel on Climate Change (IPCC) was set up. The IPCC has already published several reports on climate change (see, e.g., IPCC 2013a) that also provide guidelines for policymakers (IPCC 2013b). In the

---

[2] Narrative strategies involve the dialectical relationship between form and content: in other words, they cut across the distinction between story (*fabula*), the 'what' of narrative, and discourse (*syuzhet*), the 'how' of narrative. Narrative techniques are representational modes that carry meaning. Authors use them for specific purposes. These choices are thus "highly semanticized and engaged in the process of cultural construction" (Nünning 2000: 360).

last three decades, various studies provided further evidence of global warming and climate change. The rate and direction of climate change is controlled by a number of feedbacks of the Earth's environmental system. Most of the changes (in the climate and the environment) result from the increasing human interference in terrestrial and marine ecosystems which are influencing the fluxes of sensible and latent heat, material turnovers, and directly and indirectly the release of greenhouse gases and the carbon storage capacity.

Although the physical aspects of climate and environmental change form the basis for the detection of the effects of human interference and constitute the basis for scenarios, projections, and predictions of future climatic conditions, there is an imbalance in the debates on the effects of climate change, as this issue concerns various aspects of human coexistence, civilization, culture and views on nature. These issues are closely associated with the behavior of societies, economies, cultural developments and spiritual imaginations. The humanities and the social sciences provide new perspectives on these issues and new visions regarding the role of humankind in nature. These points of view are often neglected by both natural scientists and engineers. In addition, they may contribute to new ideas, visions, and solutions to the issues associated with climate and environmental change by means of a perspective shift.

For example, the hazardous effects of land degradation (due to natural or human-induced climate and environmental change) have also been realized in past cultures and civilizations, though the interpretation of the causal and functional relationships often differ from contemporary ones. This collection contains several examples of the apocalyptic dimensions of changes in the Earth's climate and environment viewed from different perspectives of the humanities and the social sciences on catastrophic and apocalyptic events as well as on questions related to the vulnerability of the planet. The ideas, visions, and perspectives are an important part in the discussion and search for solutions of issues related to climate change, and demonstrate the central role of a creative transdisciplinary debate in the search for new ideas and visions. This collection attempts to provide a more comprehensive view on climate and environmental change and to stimulate further debates.

2 Definitions of Terms

2.1 Climate, Climate Change, and Environmental Conditions

According to the WMO, the term 'climate' describes the average weather conditions for a particular location and over longer stretches of time (Weischet and Endlicher 2012). Thus, climatologists study the atmospheric conditions over a period of time (usually 30 years, e.g., from the years 1901 to 1930; 1930 to 1960; 1961 to 1990; and 1991 to 2020) in order to calculate average atmospheric conditions or an 'average weather.' Since the weather varies strongly in a year, between different years and decades, and since there are also seasonal influences, the period of 30 years is usually long enough to balance out the influence of short-term fluctuations (e.g., of temperature or precipitation) and to calculate averages and variabilities of relevant quantities. By means of the comparison of different 30-year periods, small fluctuations of climatic elements (temperature, precipitation, wind, pressure, and solar radiation) or tendencies and trends can be detected.

On a longer temporal scale, studies on climate change also encompass analyses of historical archives and geological records to reconstruct past climatic conditions. Systematic changes, the persistence of anomalous conditions, and statistically significant trends on a global or regional scale such as an increase in temperature, a change in mean precipitation, or a change in the frequency of extreme events or of the seasonality of rainfall indicate changes in climate. With respect to climate change, certain parameters have to be compared over periods of time, ranging from months, years, decades, centuries to thousands or millions of years. The term 'global warming' is often used as a synonym for climate change. It may in fact induce climate change as global warming affects other factors such as the moisture content in the atmosphere, rainfall, and the development of air pressure systems and is associated with complex feedbacks in the atmospheric circulation system and at the surface of our planet. In other words, global warming, i.e., the rise of the average temperature of the Earth's climate system, is one dimension of climate change, which, apart from rising global surface temperatures, also includes its effects, such as changes in precipitation.

Generally speaking, environmental conditions result from the interplay of physical factors such as climate, soil, relief, rock, hydrology, biological processes, and anthropogenic factors such as land use. Environmental conditions in ecozones and ecological systems tend to vary during different seasons and fluctuate between the years and decades. The variability of the relevant quantities may swing about a large range within or between the years and decades. However, depending on the temporal and spatial scale, the relevant quantities may vary about an average condition, a state which characterizes a dynamic equilibrium. A change is indicated in the persistence of anomalous conditions such as continuous decrease in biodiversity, or an increasing rate of soil loss by soil erosion.

2.2 The Apocalypse

The religious connotations of the ancient Greek term 'apocalypse' become apparent through its etymological meaning; the term translates as 'revelation' and it is used as a title for the last book of the New Testament. It is thus not surprising that the term is highly debated within theological studies. Scholars usually use the term 'apocalypse' as a designation for a specific genre that encompasses certain ancient biblical and non-biblical texts, although the characteristics of this genre as well as its attributed texts or even the question of whether such a fixed genre existed in the ancient world are both still a matter of debate. Nonetheless, the designation of 'apocalyptic' in conjunction with certain ancient texts has become a *terminus technicus* among theological scholars.

In order to appreciate the designation 'apocalyptic,' it is noteworthy to reflect upon the belief system (or worldview) that is usually conveyed by these texts. Generally speaking, apocalyptic literature encompasses "a narrative framework, in which a revelation is mediated by an otherworldly being to a human recipient, disclosing a transcendent reality which is both temporal, insofar as it envisages eschatological salvation, and spatial, as it involves another, supernatural world" (Collins 1979: 9). More importantly, this narrative framework within apocalyptic literature provides meaning for the addressed reader in that it situates certain events within a larger divine plan of salvation. In this way, "an apocalypse is an imaginative response to a specific historical and social situation" (Collins 2011: 457).

Simultaneously, apocalyptic texts create a sense of collective identity that usually attempts to raise awareness for a specific crisis situation. This can be an actual historical crisis, such as a greater war and its accompanying destructions, or simply a perceived crisis situation that the author wants to call attention to. In other words, apocalyptic texts often insinuate that a certain group, which the author associates himself with, experiences a crisis that is part of salvation history with a teleological outlook. It is this teleological outlook, mostly expressed in eschatological images which concern humanity's ultimate destiny and provide assurance for the group that the current crisis situation can be overcome and a bettering in line with a final salvation is at hand, provided the group remains steadfast in their beliefs (and associated behavior). Therefore, the individual apocalyptic text can also function as consolation or exhortation for proper behavior.

Lastly, it should be noted that these general observations on the definition of apocalypse stem from the analysis of what modern scholarship attributes to this genre (see, e.g., Wolter 2005: 171–178). The label 'apocalyptic' is no longer attributed to ancient texts only (see Fried 2001); rather, it has become a general concept that is used in several scholarly disciplines and popular culture. Nonetheless, most of the characteristics mentioned above do still apply in one way or the other (Becker and Jöris 2016). It is important to see that many of the narratives analyzed in this collection represent climate change as involving some kind of cleansing that will ultimately lead to salvation.

3 The Contents of this Collection

What about the specific foci of the individual chapters? Wolfgang Römer begins this collection by providing a climatological basis for the discussions that follow, namely an overview of different reaction paths of environmental systems on human-induced climate change in different climatic zones. He shows that these issues closely correlate with the future behavior of societies in terms of changes in lifestyle, consumption patterns, and economic decisions. The intricate pattern of the interaction of societies, economics, and global environmental changes shows that the search for a solution to these problems is an interdisciplinary issue that can only be resolved through the collaboration of various disciplines. Some geo-engineering options and technological advances may support a striving of a more sustainable development. However, besides the problem that technological solutions suffer too often from the risk of unknown side-effects, future challenges appear to be closely related to developments in societies and economics.

In his chapter, Gerbern Oegema shows that the recent revival of apocalypticism in cultural discourses has been spurred by the growing discontent with climate change. The prevalence of apocalyptic discourse, which can be observed in different forms of texts and media, underscores changes in people's outlook. Even though the value of apocalyptic discourse has typically been dismissed by the more established Christian and Jewish theologies, this chapter contends that apocalyptic language carries in it existential and theological messages that are highly relevant for our fight against climate change. Such language, Oegema argues in this chapter, can positively direct people to acknowledge their own responsibility to address climate issues and thereby take on an active role to locate solutions and improve climate conditions.

Marco Caracciolo deals with the question of how fictional narratives may render the lived experience of catastrophe in ways that reduce the physical distance associated with mediatic representation and visual experience more generally. In a second step, he zooms in on Jeff VanderMeer's 2014 Southern Reach trilogy, which comprises the novels *Annihilation*, *Authority*, and *Acceptance* and has been hailed as a prime example of contemporary fiction that deals with climate change in the 'weird' mode. Caracciolo demonstrates that by adopting haptic ways of imagining catastrophe through narrative representation, stories can offer a highly embodied route into human-nonhuman enmeshments (such as the climate crisis).

In her chapter, Diana Dimitrova discusses questions of climate change, power, and the Anthropocene in relation to Hindu traditions and indigenous ecological consciousnesses. In doing so, she explores the complex links between Hindu eco-religious and eco-cultural traditions, the connections between myth and nature, and the mythologizing of contemporary cultural and religious discourses on climate change. Dimitrova considers Hindu apocalyptic notions in the Vedas, the Upaniṣads, in the epics, and in the Vaiṣṇava and Śaiva-Śākta Paurāṇi traditions. Furthermore, Dimitrova reflects on modern environmental discourses and activist movements to shed light on the fact that modern scholars have turned anew to Hindu texts in order to alert people to the pressing issues of climate change.

Judith Eckenhoff examines the postapocalyptic storyworld of *Mad Max: Fury Road* (2015) against the background of climate change and land degradation. As a product of mainstream popular culture and speculative engagement with ecological devastation, this action movie makes use of the 'wasteland' trope to represent a possible future in which civilized societies and ecosystems have collapsed. Eckenhoff analyses the film's ideological implications in the context of climate change, particularly regarding its ecofeminist politics and its ambivalent negotiation of car culture. It also addresses the functions of *Fury Road*'s spectacular action and the highly aestheticized desert environment from the perspective of ecocriticism and cognitive narratology. Eckenhoff argues that the film's depiction of the wasteland and its environmental themes confront the audience with anthropogenic environmental destruction and the exploitative and unsustainable systems at its root, while also expressing a sense of solastalgia and grief for a world inalterably changed.

John Hegglund addresses one mode through which narratives – such as Richard McGuire's graphic novel *Here* (2014) and Don Hertzfeldt's animated film *World of Tomorrow* (2015) – can express the limits and transformations of a human future on the planet. This sense of futurity is based in a view not of the anthropocentric, non-human, or post-human, but of what he calls 'the partially human.' The partially human differs from the post-human because it acknowledges that, while we are newly aware of an interconnected enmeshment between humans and world, we are stuck with certain human traits, most notably at the level of a consciousness and cognition that is singularly capable of producing narrative. Where the post-human (in its more optimistic visions, at least) wishes to push through the clouds of anthropocentrism to the shining light a brave new world, the partially human admits that such wishes amount to a futile attempt to outrun our own shadows.

Axel Siegemund deals with questions that have to be placed on the overlap between theology, natural science, and technology. More specifically, he brings a theological perspective to the topic of climate change in his chapter about the notion of apocalyptic thought. At the center of Siegemund's reflections is the consideration that ecology and apocalypticism are reflected in the fact that a collective fundamental awareness of their existence is bestowed upon them. Here, he takes a position that confronts climate change and the biblical apocalypse in a perspective that in both cases expects something that seems inevitable. Starting from this, Siegemund focuses on the transformative power of today's apocalyptic thinking and the concept of feasibility, taking into account the modern expectations towards religion and technology in equal measure.

In his chapter, Carlos A. Segovia delves into the idea of our world being subjected to a social and ecological collapse that gradually leads to the ultimate extinction of life as we know it. Subsuming this under the term "unworlding," he elaborates on three different examples, illustrating how to approach this apocalyptic scenario from an ontological perspective. In connection to this, the role of technological advances concerning this process receives special attention, for example, when addressing the question of how artificial intelligence affects our life on earth. Finally, Segovia sheds some light on the ontological fluctuance of our natural and social environments as well as the importance of cosmopolitical relations for escaping this apocalyptic future.

Last but not least, Jan Alber and Zoë Takvorian analyze the interwoven ideologies in Roland Emmerich's well-known film *The Day after Tomorrow* (2004). This movie is about the dawn of a new ice age, and it is apocalyptic because it does not end in total disaster (or with the complete disintegration of the planet) but with the hope for a renewal. They demonstrate that the film clearly argues in favor of science and rationality as well as the idea of learning from our mistakes. At the same time, however, it proposes a reactionary rather than a radical new start, while clearly zooming in on the white, male, and heterosexual middle class, i.e., a privileged societal group whose supremacy it reproduces and stabilizes. Ultimately, the nostalgic renewal of the old western order could (or perhaps rather should?) be seen as being the main problem behind climate change – rather than a possible solution.

Taken together, the chapters of this collection seek to shed light on the question of how and why narratives of various historical and cultural backgrounds (as well as in different media) associate climate change with the apocalypse. In addition, our contributors try to demonstrate how these representations relate to the actual problem of climate change as it is discussed in the models developed by climatologists.

Bibliography

Alber, Jan (2019) "Introduction: The Ideological Ramifications of Narrative Strategies," *Storyworlds: A Journal of Narrative Studies* 9.1–2, 3–25.

Althusser, Louis (2001 [1970]) "Ideology and Ideological State Apparatuses," in *The Norton Anthology of Theory and Criticism*, ed. Vincent B. Leitch (New York: Norton), 1483–1509.

Arbuckle, Matthew B. (2017) "The Interaction of Religion, Political Ideology, and Concern About Climate Change in the United States," *Society & Natural Resources: An International Journal* 30.2, 177–194.

Becker, Patrick and Steffen Jöris (2016) "Toward a Scientific Designation: *Apocalypticism* in Biblical and Modern Studies – A Comparative Approach," *Horizons in Biblical Theology* 38.1, 22–44.

Chakrabarty, Dipesh (2012) "Postcolonial Studies and the Challenge of Climate Change," *New Literary History* 43.1, 1–18.

"Climate Apocalypse," <https://en.wikipedia.org/wiki/Climate_apocalypse> (accessed 15 April 2021)

Collins, Adela Y. (2011) "Apocalypse Now: The State of Apocalyptic Studies Near the End of the First Decade of the Twenty-First Century," *Harvard Theological Review* 104.4, 447–457.

Collins, John J. (1979) "Apocalypse: The Morphology of a Genre," *Semeia* 14, 1–217.

Faust, Eberhard (2011) "Globaler Klimawandel, globale Klimakatastrophe: mythische Elemente in der kulturwissenschaftlichen und medialen Diskussion," in *Neutestamentliche Grenzgänge: Symposium zur kritischen Rezeption der Arbeiten Gerd Theißens*, ed. Peter Lampe and Helmut Schwier (Göttingen: Vandenhoeck und Ruprecht), 202–227.

Fried, Johannes (2001) *Aufstieg aus dem Untergang: Apokalyptisches Denken und die Entstehung der modernen Naturwissenschaft im Mittelalter* (München: Beck).

Gardner, Claire (2015) "The Apocalypse Is Easy: Limitations of Our Climate Change Imaginings," *Demos Journal* 1, no pag.

Haker, Hille, Andrés Torres Queiruga, and Marie-Theres Wacker (2014) "Die Wiederkehr des apokalyptischen Bewusstseins," *Concilium: Internationale Zeitschrift für Theologie* 50.3 (2014), 237–244.

Horn, Eva (2014) *Zukunft als Katastrophe* (Frankfurt am Main: Fischer).

IPCC (2013a) Climate Change 2013: The Physical Science Basis. Contribution of Working Group I to the Fifth Assessment Report of the Intergovernmental Panel on Climate Change (Cambridge: Cambridge University Press).

IPCC (2013b) "Summary for Policymakers," in: Climate Change 2013: The Physical Science Basis. Contribution of Working Group I to the Fifth Assessment Report of the Intergovernmental Panel on Climate Change (Cambridge: Cambridge University Press), 1–30.

Kluwick, Ursula (2014) "Talking About Climate Change: The Ecological Crisis and Narrative Form," in *The Oxford Handbook of Ecocriticism*, ed. Greg Garrard and Cheryll Glotfelty (Oxford: Oxford University Press), 502–516.

Mehnert, Antonia (2016) *Climate Change Fictions: Representations of Global Warming in American Literature* (London: Palgrave Macmillan).

Nünning, Ansgar (2000) "Towards a Cultural and Historical Narratology: A Survey of Diachronic Approaches, Concepts, and Research Projects," in *Anglistentag 1999 Mainz: Proceedings*, ed. Bernhard Reitz and Sigrid Rieuwerts (Trier: WVT), 345–373.

Trexler, Adam (2015) *Anthropocene Fictions: The Novel in a Time of Climate Change* (Charlottesville: University of Virginia Press).

Webb, Robert L. (1990) "'Apocalyptic': Observations on a Slippery Term," *Journal of Near Eastern Studies* 49, 115–126.

Weischet, Wolfgang and Wilfried Endlicher (2012) *Einführung in die Allgemeine Klimatologie* (Stuttgart: Borntraeger).

Wolter, Michael (2005) „Apokalyptik als Redeform im Neuen Testament," *New Testament Studies* 51.2, 171–191.

Wolfgang Römer
Scenarios of Human-Induced Climate and Environmental Changes at Different Spatial and Temporal Scales

1 Introduction

This chapter provides an overview of different reaction paths of environmental systems on human induced climate change in different climatic zones. Climate change influences several environmental systems on earth, encompassing the dynamics of the atmosphere, biosphere, hydrosphere, pedosphere, and their associated subsystems. The interaction of the processes in different environments depends on the state of the natural process-response system. However, natural process-response systems in nearly all parts of the world have been changed to various degrees by agriculture, mining, industry, and the associated infrastructure. The superimposition of climate change and human interference in natural process-response systems in different climatic zones results in a spatially and temporally non-uniform response of the process dynamics with different reaction and relaxation patterns at various spatial and temporal scales. On a global scale, human-induced climate warming resulted in an increase of temperature of about 1 °C in the last 100 years. However, the increase in temperature has not been uniform.

Environmental effects of climate warming vary in individual regions as a function of the process realms and the temporal and spatial scales considered. The rate of temperature increase in arctic regions is higher than in mid-latitude, sub-tropical, and tropical climate zones and appears to have influenced the processes in the biosphere, pedosphere, and the rate of surface denudation processes. Reduced amounts in rainfall are predicted for subtropical areas whereas some mid-latitude regions are likely to experience an increase in rainfall. This tendency results in an increasing contrast between regions with high and low rainfall amounts as well as in changes of the seasonal distribution of rainfalls. These changes may strongly influence the fluvial system and the hydrologic balance. Although, sea-level change threatens coastal areas globally, the sensitivity to sea-level rise and climate warming of coastal areas depends on a complex set of factors. The response on an increasing sea-level varies with coastal type, the intensity of human interference in the coastal environment, and the climate setting.

https://doi.org/10.1515/9783110730203-002

The results of this overview show that human interference in the process dynamics of the different ecosystems affects different process systems in different regions and climatic zones. Climate change is likely to become an additional factor that interacts with the changed environmental dynamics of the natural processes. The combined effects of changed environmental conditions tend to increase the frequency of hazardous events as the natural process-response-systems will adjust constantly to the changing conditions.

One of the biggest issues facing the Earth's environments is the anthropogenic induced climate change. The human induced global warming results mostly from the release of greenhouse gases. As climate is a major controlling factor in terrestrial and marine ecosystems, climate change will affect numerous processes at the earth surface and may induce profound effects on future environments. Human induced climate change is often closely allied with human interference in natural environments. Human interferences include various forms of land use, raw material extraction, the development of infrastructure, waste disposal, and pollution. The interplay of the combined effects of changed environmental conditions and the increasing rate of anthropogenic land transformation has affected the feedback-controlled interaction of the natural processes. This has resulted in an increasing frequency of extreme events such as floods, landslides, heavy rainfall, or droughts.

The scenarios and projections of the IPCC clearly indicate that in several regions of the world climate change will increase the intensity and frequency of extreme events in the future (IPCC 2007). However, the effects of climate change will vary regionally and locally as a function of the environmental setting and the intensity of the changes in climate variables whilst, at the same time, the intensity of the impact and sensitivity to changes is also controlled by the different degrees of human landscape modifications. The objective of this chapter is to show that both, climate change and human interference into earth surface systems, has affected the process dynamics in different regions and climatic zones, and that the superimposition of human interferences often results in a higher sensitivity to climate change.

However, a comprehensive evaluation and description of all effects at all temporal and spatial scales of environmental and climatic changes is beyond the scope of this chapter. Alone the reports of the IPCC are based on a contribution of more than 230 authors and co-authors whilst the reports often include more than 600 references from various fields of research and there are numerous detailed studies in scientific journals and books concerning environmental and climate change which cover nearly all parts of the world.

2 Anthropogenic Climate Change and Greenhouse Effect

2.1 Global Warming and Greenhouse Gases

Global warming is often used as a synonym for climate change though it induces climate change as global warming affects other factors such as the moisture content in the atmosphere, rainfall, and the development of air pressure systems and is associated with complex feedbacks in the atmospheric circulation system and at the earth surface.

Global warming has been proved by empirical data from instrumental sources, proxy data, statistical analyses, and results of climate modeling. According to these studies, the principal contributors to atmospheric warming are carbon dioxide (CO_2), methane (CH_4), nitrous oxide (N_2O), a number of trace gases, such as chlorofluorocarbons (CFCs), as well as other pollutants including dust (Huddart and Stott 2020). Although geologic records of the past indicate that climate has changed during various times in earth history, data from archives in polar ice sheets show that the rise in most greenhouse gases in the post-industrial period is higher than at least in the past 800,000 years (Glaser 2014). In the last 10,000 years, the global mean concentration of CO_2 in the atmosphere was at about 280 ppmv (parts per million by volume, 1 ppmv = 0.0001 % of the volume). Since the 1950s, the CO_2 concentration increased continuously from about 320 ppmv to 400 ppmv in the year 2013 (Dlugokencky et al. 2019) and 407.5 ± 0.1 ppmv in 2018.

Global warming is a function of the complex interplay of solar radiation, dynamic processes, and variable gases in the atmosphere such as CO_2, CH_4, N_2O, water vapor ($H2O$), and CFCs. The dynamic processes include the energy received by absorption of direct solar radiation and earth radiation as well as the fluxes of sensible and latent heat resulting from conduction of heat at the surface, heat transfer by condensation and turbulent transport, and various feedbacks between the hydrosphere and the earth surface. The most important process for global warming is the anthropogenic increased greenhouse effect. In the atmosphere, variable gases such as CO_2, CH_4, N_2O, and H_2O, including suspended water droplets and ice crystals in clouds, are effective absorbers of infrared radiation. As each of these gases has characteristic absorption ranges, a different proportion is filtered out from the incoming solar radiation as a function of wavelength. The spectrum of the radiation emitted from the sun, on the other hand, ranges from long radio waves down to extremely short wave length radiation with a length of less than 10^{-10} m, with a maximum emission at 10 μm

(Hidore and Oliver 1993; Weischet and Endlicher 2012). Most greenhouse gases except ozone (O_3) and nitrogen (N), which absorb at 0.01 to 0.38 µm and 0.5 µm respectively, are virtually transparent for the incoming ultraviolet and visible range of the solar radiation (Fig. 2). As a consequence, radiation of this wavelength penetrates through the atmosphere and is virtually unaffected by greenhouse gases. The passage of the solar radiation through the atmosphere to the Earth surface is controlled by various processes. Part of the solar radiation is scattered and reflected in the atmosphere on molecules, particulate matter, and clouds whilst another part is transmitted. At the earth surface, a part of the radiation is reflected while another part is absorbed. On a global scale, the sum of radiation reflected in the atmosphere and at the earth's surface (global albedo) is in the range of 30 % of the total incoming solar radiation (Fig. 1). This portion of the radiation cannot contribute to the warming.

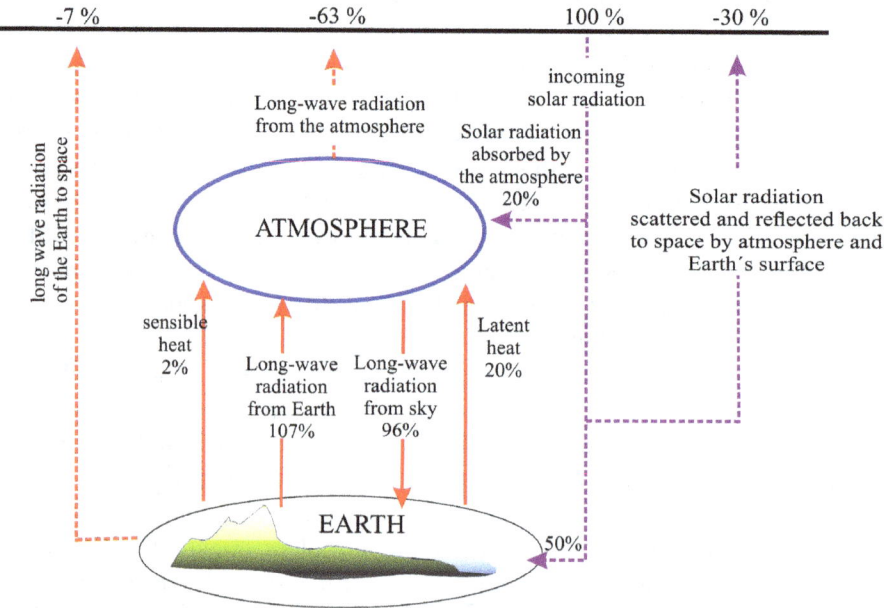

Fig. 1: Simplified energy balance of the Earth. (Modified after Hidore and Oliver, 1993: 34, and Weischet and Endlicher, 2012).

The absorption of the solar radiation at the earth surface, on the other hand, converts the radiation to other forms of energy. At the Earth's surface, the solar radiation is converted to sensible heat and latent heat and the surplus of energy is reradiated as infrared radiation. As the Earth's surface is colder than the sun, the energy increase resulting from absorption is radiated at longer wavelengths in the infrared bands, ranging from about 3 to 30 μm. CO_2, CH_4, N_2O, water vapor, and other trace gases are able to absorb this infrared radiation. CO_2, which has the greatest influence on global warming due to its high concentration in the atmosphere as compared to other greenhouse gases, absorbs this radiation in the bands between 2.3 and 3.0 μm, 4.2 and 4.4 μm, and 12 to 16 μm (Weischet and Endlicher 2012). Water vapor absorbs in the bands 2.5 to 3.0 μm, 5 to 8 μm, and beyond 14 μm and acts as a weaker absorber in the bands between 1 and 2 μm (Fig. 2) whilst methane and nitrous oxide are effective absorbers in the bands around 7.7 to 8 μm. As a result of the different absorption bands of the gases, an extremely important atmospheric window occurs in a range between about 8 and 13 μm where gases in the atmosphere do not absorb the longwave radiation emitted from the earth surface. This window corresponds with the wavelength of maximum emission of the terrestrial radiation at about 10 μm. In this atmospheric window greenhouse gases are transparent to infrared radiation and terrestrial radiation can escape to space. However, within the window ozone (O_3) tends to absorb in the bands at 9.5 μm (Weischet and Endlicher 2012) and clouds, which are very effective absorbers, also tend to absorb radiation in the range between 8 to 13 μm (Fig. 2).

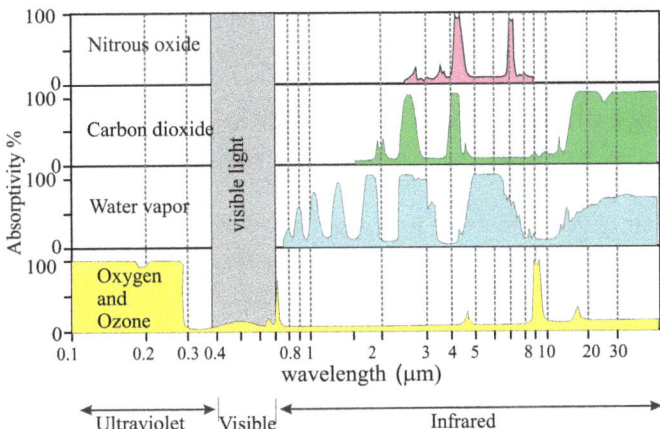

Fig. 2: Selective absorptivity of some greenhous gases and water vapor. (Modified after Weischet and Endlicher, 2012).

The effect of the greenhouse gases is that through the process of absorption the atmosphere gains heat and the atmosphere itself acts as a radiator. The increase in energy by absorption is re-radiated from the greenhouse gases, water vapor, and clouds into space but also back to the Earth's surface (Fig. 1). At the Earth's surface, this results in an additional source of energy, leading to a higher temperature compared to a planet without an atmosphere with greenhouse gases and increases the mean temperature at the Earth's surface (Oliver and Hidore 1993; Weischet and Endlicher, 2012, Goudie 2019).

Calculations of the anthropogenic climate forcing, resulting from changes in the albedo (reflectivity) of the Earth's surface due to changes in land cover and coverage of ice and snow, the anthropogenic release of greenhouse gases and aerosols range from 0.6 to 2.4 Wm^{-2}. In a study on the human-induced changes in temperature in Europe, Schönwiese et al. (2004) calculated that the increase in temperature by greenhouse gases and aerosols is in the range of +1.5 °C and +0.6 °C. On the other hand, there are the cooling effects of volcanic eruptions which range from −0.2 to −0.3 °C, whilst fluctuations in the activity of the sun and of the North Atlantic Oscillation are in the range of ± 0.5 °C. On a global scale, the increase in temperature due to the emission of greenhouse gases is about 1 °C compared to the preindustrial period. However, this global average masks the temperature changes in the different regions on the globe. Regions experiencing the highest temperature increase are the Arctic regions, where average temperatures are about 2 to 3 °C higher than 50 years ago (French 2007) whilst in temperate latitudes, the temperature increase corresponds roughly with the global average of 1 °C as compared with the preindustrial period.

2.2 Climate Change and Tipping Points: Possible Changes at Timescales of Several Decades to Centuries

In addition to the human-induced increase in greenhouse gases, several other processes contribute to global warming as the atmospheric processes interact with the land surface. Of major importance are changes of the land surface resulting in changes in the cover of snow and ice and vegetation. Since the radiation from the sun and the atmosphere is partly absorbed and partly reflected at the Earth's surface, changes in the reflectivity of the surface due to land use and urbanization tend to influence the delicate energy balance on the Earth's surface. These changes are associated with various feedbacks concerning the evaporation and transpiration, soil moisture regimes, and atmospheric moisture. Energy is also transferred through ocean currents. Different scenarios of future climate change have indicated different "tipping elements" (Lenton et al. 2008, 2019). These are points or thresholds where changes in the environment will inevitably and irreversible enhance global warming within the time scale of human life, once they are crossed. Some tipping points may be achieved within decades whilst others in centuries if global warming continues at high rates. The links and feedbacks between the different tipping points are indicated in Fig. 3.

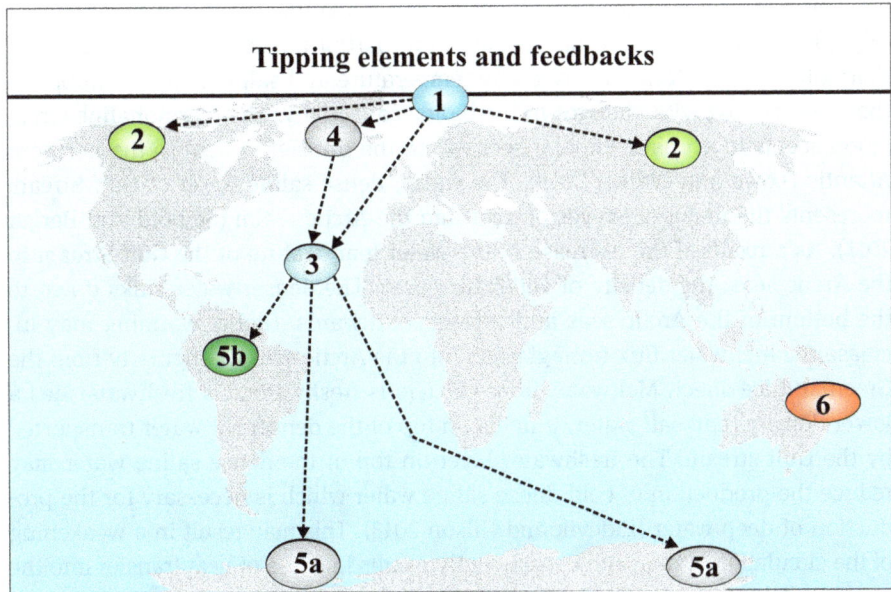

Fig. 3: Simplified map of tipping elements and feedbacks (modified after Lenton et al., 2008, 2019). 1 – melting of the Arctic sea ice, 2 – Thawing of permafrost and shift of the bundaries of the tundra zone and boreal zone, 3 – Changes in the thermohaline circulation (i. e. the Gulf stream), 4- Melting of the Greenland ice sheet. 5a Melting of the west and east Antarctic ice sheet and ice shelves, 5b – higher frequency of severe drought due to changes in the thermohaline circulation, 6 – Coral reefs.

An important tipping point is the extent of the Arctic sea ice (Fig. 3). Once the areal extent of the sea ice diminishes below a critical point, the reflectivity (albedo) of the earth surface will be reduced which results in more absorption and hence, enhanced global warming. However, the reduced areal extend of sea ice is also linked with an increase of fresh water in the surface water of the Arctic ocean which in turn, may affect the thermohaline circulation (Fig. 3). The changes in the regions of the boreal forests and the Arctic play also an important role as warming results in the degradation of permafrost and the release of huge amounts of greenhouse gases, such as CO_2 and CH_4. Global warming induces a northward movement of the boreal forest at the expense of the tundra regions and there is increasing evidence that these areas will become subject to fires, which may enhance the melting of permafrost and increase the thickness of the active layer, whilst warmer conditions may induce the likelihood of forests to insect infections (Calef 2010).

An important and central role for the current climate as well as for future climate may be played by the behavior of the thermohaline circulation in the oceans (Fig. 3). The Gulf stream forms an important part of this circulation system. The thermohaline circulation is driven by temperature and salt density variations in the oceans along with changes in the biological activity. The thermohaline circulation seems to act as a "bipolar seesaw" in the transfer of heat to the northern Atlantic (Lowe and Walker 2015). The warm, dense saline water of Gulf Stream represents the major conveyor of heat into the Arctic realm (Seibold and Berger 2017). As a result of the decrease in the water temperature of the Gulf Stream in the Arctic seas, the density of water increases. The denser water sinks down to the bottom of the Arctic seas and travels southwards. Global warming may increase the meltwater flux from glaciers into the Arctic seas, particularly from the Greenland ice sheet. Meltwater from glaciers is freshwater. As freshwater has a lower density than salt water, it floats on top of the denser saltwater transported by the Gulf stream. The freshwater layer on top of the dense saline water may reduce the production of cold dense saline water which is necessary for the production of deep water (Eldevik and Nilson 2013). This may result in a weakening of the circulation system and consequently results in a loss of heat transfer into the northern Atlantic and to severe cooling. The lower heat transfer towards the northern hemisphere, in turn, results in an increase in temperatures in the southern hemisphere. This will affect the ice sheet and shelve ice in the West and East Antarctic (Fig. 3). However, a shutdown of the circulation is unlikely if the global temperature increase remains at 2 °C (Hoegh-Guldberg et al. 2018). Much of the current thermohaline circulation appears to depend on the future melting rate of the Greenland ice sheet. This melting rate depends on the warming effects resulting from the melting of the Arctic sea ice and the thawing of the permafrost (Fig. 3).

In the global warming scenarios of the IPCC (2007), the Greenland ice sheet may lose 19–28 % of its volume by 2100 if warming continues at the current high rates (Machguth et al. 2013). Currently, the melting of Greenland ice sheet contributes to about 43 % of the sea-level rise (Noel et al. 2017). As a result of the increase in temperature, the ice sheet loses mass year after year which is associated with a concomitant rise in sea-level. However, as long as the accumulation of ice and snow enables the maintenance of an accumulation area that is large enough to produce new glacier ice, the ice sheet may achieve a new mass balance, though it will diminish in size. With respect to global warming, the question arises at what temperature the Greenland ice sheet will inevitably diminish further in size and will eventually disappear.

The threshold temperature at which the Greenland ice shield will irreversibly decline and disappear is subject to controversial discussions and ranges from about 1 to 2 °C above the present temperature level up to about 6 °C (IPCC 2007; Bamber et al. 2009; Pattyn et al. 2018). The large differences in these estimates are also an expression of the great uncertainty in the different models which run at different resolutions and use different descriptions of the energy balance. Recent studies show that the runoff from the Greenland ice sheet has increased to a volume that exceeds that of the twentieth century by about 33 %. A warning signal is the reduction in the refreezing capacity of the peripheral ice caps of Greenland ice sheet due to the loss of pore space in the firn layer. This layer usually forms a porous layer between the snow layer and the ice of the glacier and reduces the runoff of melt water from the glacier surface. Noel et al. (2017) emphasize that the reduced freezing capacity of the peripheral ice caps of Greenland results from the melt water percolation into this layer. Particularly, in the last decades high amounts of meltwater percolated into the firn layer and reduced the pore space by the refreezing of the water. As a result of the reduced pore space the percolation and the refreezing of the meltwater is reduced which is associated with a higher meltwater runoff and hence, with a higher long-term mass loss of the peripheral ice caps. In the extensive inland of the Greenland ice sheet, however, the firn layer has retained most of its refreezing capacity (Noel et al. 2017).

The complex processual linkage between the Greenland ice sheet, the tundra area, and the boreal zone and the thermohaline circulation can be summarized by some few effects. The reduced areal extend of sea ice results in the warming of the Arctic. The molten sea ice produces a freshwater layer above the Arctic saltwater which causes a weakening of the thermohaline circulation whilst the warming induces further degradation of the permafrost, which results in an increased release of greenhouse gases such as CO_2 and CH_4. Consequently, this results in enhanced warming. The increased warming enhances the further melting of the Greenland ice sheet. This increases the freshwater influx into the Arctic ocean and causes further weakening of the thermohaline circulation. The weakened thermohaline circulation results in a reduced heat transfer to the northern hemisphere. At the same time, this leads to a warming of the southern hemisphere which, in turn, accelerates the melting of the west and east Antarctic ice sheet and ice shelf.

Some clues on the effects of a longer prevailing global higher temperature may be inferred from the past. About 130,000 years ago, the mean global temperature exceeded the current temperature by about 1 °C (about 2 °C for the pre-industrial time), and Greenland temperatures appear to have been about 4 to 5 °C warmer (Huddart and Stott 2020). During this time, the global sea-level was about 4 to 6 m or even 9 m higher than today, though a complete collapse of the

Greenland ice sheet in this time is not documented (Dutton et al. 2015). About 3 to 5 million years ago, before the onset of the extensive glaciation of Greenland, the average global temperature exceeded the current ones by about 3 °C. During this period mean sea-level was about 15 to 35 m higher than today (Stanley 2005; Robert and Bousquet 2018). However, such comparisons neglect several important factors, constraining the simple transfer of such comparison for forecasting future sea-level rise. On the other hand, such figures may provide information on significant thresholds as they show that the long-term effects often involve further interactions that cannot be inferred from short term effects.

Further feedbacks resulting from a weaker thermohaline circulation may affect the tropical rain forests as warming of the southern hemisphere may result in a shift of the intertropical convergence zone (Fig. 3). The tropical rain forests store enormous amounts of carbon. Deforestation, drainage of peatlands, and changes in soil moisture due to unsustainable agriculture have changed the carbon fluxes and reduced their function as a sink for greenhouse gases. Possible effects of a weaker thermohaline circulation may be an increase of droughts in the Amazon rainforest, leading to further degradation of the rain forest which, in turn, reduces the function of carbon storage and contributes to a further increase in greenhouse gases. The studies of Lenton et al. (2019) suggest that a weakening of the thermohaline circulation would affect further atmospheric circulation patterns, which could induce droughts in the Sahel region in Africa and a destabilization of the East African monsoon.

The likely degradation of numerous coral reefs represents a further tipping point (Fig. 3). Global warming affects coral reefs in several ways. Firstly, by the rise of the sea-level; secondly, by the increase in water temperature; thirdly, by the acidification of the ocean water; fourthly, by the possible increase in the frequency of severe storms, and by changes in the frequency of atmospheric decadal variations and ocean circulation systems, such as the El Niño Southern Oscillation (ENSO) or the Indian Ocean Dipole (IOD) (Hughes et al. 2003, Lenton et al. 2019). Superimposed on these changes are human interferences due to mining, fishery, tourism, and pollution, and the removal of key reef organisms that control the outcome of competition between coral and large algae (Seibold and Berger 2017). As coral reefs are the habitat for several thousand of species and play an important role in ecosystems and in coastal protection, the degradation of coral reefs will influence the aquatic life and the coasts in several ways, including the uptake of carbon in the form of a carbonate which is used for building the calciumcarbonate skeletons of the corals.

In a study about the current state of the Earth, Boysen and Schellnhuber (2007) presented further hazards and tipping elements and compared the potential hazards with the current state of the environment (Fig. 4, Tab. 1). Since

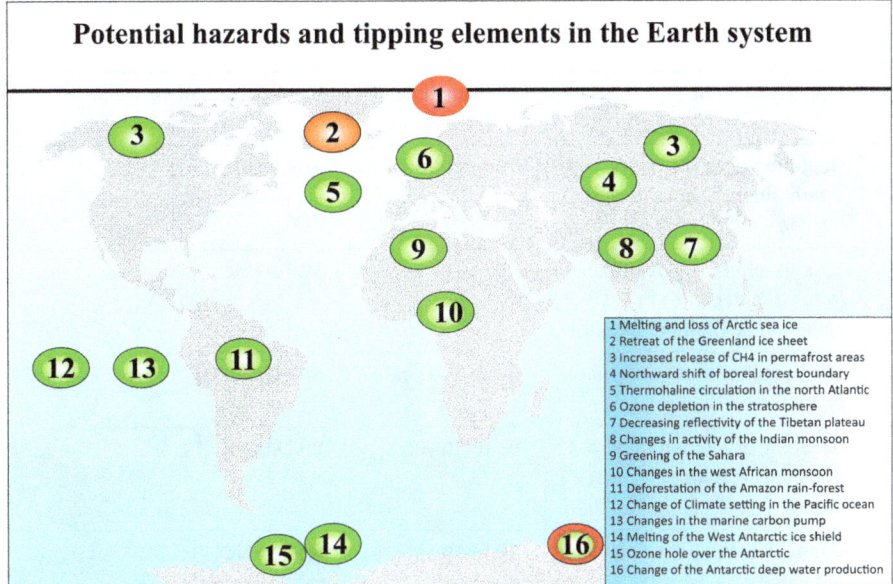

Fig. 4: Simplified map of hazards and tipping elements (modified after Boysen and Schellnhuber, 2007 and Glaser, 2014). Numbers to hazards and tipping elements in the map are explained in table 1.

Tab. 1: Hazards and tipping elements in the Earth system (compare with Fig. 4). (Modified after Boysen and Schellnhuber, 2007, Glaser 2014).

No.	Tipping Element	Time scale of change	Current state of environment
1	Melting and loss of Arctic sea ice	up to 100 years	Instable, and increasing in the last decade, presumably already tipped
2	Retreat of the Greenland ice sheet	300 to 1000 years	Initiated. Several feedbacks
3	Increased release of CH_4 in permafrost areas	up to 1000 years	Still stable
4	Northward shift of boreal forest boundary	50 to 100 years	Still stable. Recent studies provide indicates of species shift and changes in ecodynamics
5	Thermohaline circulation in the north Atlantic	100 to 500 years	Still stable

Tab. 1 (continued)

No.	Tipping Element	Time scale of change	Current state of environment
6	Depletion of ozone in the stratosphere over northern Europe	10 to 1000 years	Still stable
7	Loss of reflectivity due to dust influx and decrease in snow cover at the Tibetan plateau	50 to 1000 years	Still stable
8	Changes in activity of the Indian monsoon	30 to 100 years	Still stable
9	Greening of the Sahara and decrease of sources of dust supply	up to 50 years	Still stable
10	Changes in the west African monsoon	50 to 100 years	Still stable
11	Deforestation of the Amazon rain-forest	50 to 100 years	Still stable. Enhanced loss of forested areas in the last years
12	Changes in the climate setting of the Pacific ocean	10 to 100 years	Still stable
13	Changes in the marine carbon pump	unknown	Still stable
14	Melting of the West Antarctic ice shield	300 to 1000 years	Still stable
15	Ozone hole over the Antarctic	10 to 100 years	Already tipped
16	Weakening of the Antarctic deep water production	Up to 100 years	Relatively stable

the year 2007, more evidences concerning the possible hazards, which are associated with the tipping elements and on the current state of the environment, have been provided. New observations on the shifts of species in the permafrost regions and in the boreal forests as well as on the decreasing thickness of the arctic sea ice are better understood, and the significant effects of these changes are now indisputable.

2.3 Human Interference on the Earth Surface Systems and Climate

Human interferences on the earth surface resulting from the expansion of rural land, agriculture, urbanization, the quest for raw materials, and processes related to the production and consumption of energy have substantially contributed to environmental changes. Although humans have interfered in the natural environment since they used fire, the increasing use of new technologies in the last 100 to 150 years has increased the impacts to a degree that they are able to modify the energy interchange of the Earth's surface and of the earth surface systems. The growing human population and the increasing demand for resources is indicated in the enormous consumption of land for agriculture and urban areas and in the movement of vast quantities of soil, sediments, and rocks for building-materials, extraction of ores and fuels, energy, and infrastructure. The changes in the land surface have affected various components of the natural environment and range from the fragmentation of habitats of animals and changes of the vegetation cover to changes in soils and soil moisture regimes, from the hydrologic behavior of rivers to changes in the frequency and magnitude of geomorphic processes, acting at the earth surface – to name only a few (Hooke 2012). Changes of the land surfaces often affect the albedo (proportion of the reflected incident light) of the Earth's surface, thereby, altering the fluxes of sensible and latent heat. Human interference has altered not only the rates of surface processes on the earth but also the connectivity of the environmental systems and their reaction times by creating different thresholds and energy fluxes. This may result in unpredictable changes and in an increase of the sensitivity of the natural process-response systems.

Difficulties arise when attempts are made to quantify the effects of these changes on the environment on a global scale and to determine the intensity of the impacts as compared to rates of pre-human intervention. In a study on the geomorphological role of humans on earth, Hooke (1994) has shown that human activities on the earth surface move about 40 to 45 Gt/year (1 Gt = 1 giga ton = 1 billion tons) when including the inputs of agriculture on the sediment budget of rivers. Accordingly, the vast quantities of material moved by humans have been raised to a level that is in the range of natural denudation processes. Therefore, Hooke (1994: 224) concluded that humans have become "geomorphic agents" on the earth surface. This also appears to be valid for the changes in the land cover. Vitousek et al. (1997) demonstrated that about 45 % of the earth surface has been transformed for land use and that about 50 % of the global freshwater resources, excluding freshwater in glaciers, are currently used for various purposes by humans. The same study has shown that humans are responsible for about 60 % of the terrestrial nitrogen fixation (Vitousek et al. 1997). In concert with these findings are the analyses of Ellis and Ramankutty (2008). They demonstrated that 75 % of the ice-free continental area cannot be considered anymore to be wild, and Hooke (2012) estimated that more than 50 % of the land surface has been transformed by various degrees by humans. Examples of the increasing rates and the growing areal extent of land surface transformations in the last decades for mining, building, or land reclamation purposes are the lignite open mining in western and eastern Germany, mountaintop removal mining for coal in the eastern USA, surface leveling projects in loess landscapes in China for urban construction, or the building of offshore island complexes in the United Arab Emirates (Glaser 2014; Li et al. 2014, Goudie 2019). The direct impacts of land surface transformations for mining purposes range from changes in groundwater levels and increased dust pollution to significant biological impairment downstream of mountaintop mines and from valley fills to alkaline or acid mine drainage due to the placing mine spoil in the path of streams. These changes are accompanied by changes in aquatic ecology and overall aquatic ecosystem health but tend also to enhance hazards by land sliding, land subsidence, and in increased flooding. The rapid growth of cities in several countries has increased the need for building materials. An example of the impact of these tendencies is the Shaanxi province in China. In this area loess hills 100 to 150 m in height are flattened in a leveling project in order to create an area of more than 70 km^2 of flat ground (Li et al. 2014). The removed material is used as infill for urban construction. Besides the associated destruction of forests, plants, the effects on wild animals, and the losses of farmlands, this land transformation alters also, watercourses and water discharge and is associated with several geological and ecological hazards such as soil erosion, land sliding, land surface subsidence, and water pollution (Li et al. 2014). All these changes appear to result in increasing consumption of land, soil, and raw material and in an increased erosion of material.

However, at a first sight, less dramatic but through its areal extent highly significant is the increase of areas that have been transformed for agricultural land use, particularly for agricultural intensification. In the last three centuries, the area of global croplands increased from about 3,000,000 km^2 in 1700 AD to 15,000,000 km^2 in 2000 AD (Klein Goldewijk et al. 2011). Most of the increase was at the expense of grasslands and to a lesser proportion of forests. A similar increase in area is also reported for pasture lands, which covered about 34,000,000 km^2 in 2000 AD. These data show that the impact of humans on the landscape has increased more strongly in the last 300 years than ever before, and Kaplan et al. (2010) inferred from modeling land use changes that in the last 8,000 years carbon emissions due to land use, even in preindustrial times, might have had a strong impact on the global carbon cycle. In addition, agricultural activities ppear to be associated with an increase in the release of CH_4. CH_4 is a very active greenhouse gas as it absorbs long wave radiation several times more effective than CO2. Studies of Ruddiman (2014) have shown that since the 1950s the CH_4-concentration in the atmosphere increased from 1,300 ppbv to 1,840 ppbv (parts per billion and volume, 1ppbv = 0.0000001 %). Compared to the long-term background level of the CH_4 concentration of about 600 ppbv, this corresponds with a threefold increase. Although the increase of intensified agricultural land use and pasture lands differ among regions, the effects are considered to influence the global biogeochemical cycles and sediment discharges, which both tend to contribute to environmental and global climate changes, to a considerable degree (Klein Goldewijk et al. 2011).

Calculations of pre-human sediment discharges on a global scale by McLennan (1993) provided a quantity of sediment discharge of about 12.6 Gt /a, which is about 60 % of the current rate. Comparing long-term (deep-time) geologic sedimentation rates with recent erosion rates from agricultural land (pasture + cropland) suggests that human-induced erosion is likely to be 28 times higher than the long-term natural erosion rates (Wilkinson 2005). More recent studies on soil erosion rates in cropland regions provided rates of 35 Gt/a (Borrelli et al. 2013). There is consensus that agricultural practices in most cropland regions in the world have increased soil erosion and hence, soil losses. Climate change may exacerbate the pressure on agricultural land use and thereby, increasing rates of soil erosion. However, several of the effects appear to remain unpredictable as rates of global erosion represent an average of soil erosion rates. As natural environments are very different with respect to the factors controlling the dynamics of earth surface processes, such as relief, vegetation, soils, rocks, climate, and hydrology, it is unlikely that different ecozones will respond to climate change in a similar way.

Global rates cannot provide detailed information on processes and erosion rates of the "hot spots" of soil erosion regions, due to differences in the spatial and temporal resolution of the models compared to regional and local studies and the different methodological approaches. Major difficulties arise from evaluating the degree to which the agricultural practices have augmented erosion as different methods of measuring soil erosion may have different outcomes and soil erosion measurements depend highly on spatial and temporal scales. Whilst small soil erosion test plots tend to produce soil erosion rates that are much higher than actual net losses from hillsides, estimates of erosion rates at the scale of drainage basin have a different temporal and spatial resolution (Stocking 1987, 1999). This also applies to the calculation of soil loss by wind when rates are estimated from field studies or satellite images. Different methodologies are faced with the problem of the transfer of the results, as the rates may differ greatly, even within the same landscape and climatic zone. The comparison of the impacts of human-induced erosion rates with the pre-human erosion rates faces similar problems. However, even with respect to the problems associated with the different methods of measuring soil erosion, soil erosion rates have been clearly increased by human interference on a global scale.

The principle of onsite effects of soil erosion is the reduction of both, the soil fertility, soil water storage, and on steeper hillslopes, a change in the stability against landsliding, whilst the offsite effects are the export of large volumes of eroded material to the rivers which affects the suspended load and aquatic biota and the sediment balance, the quality of water and eventually the frequency of flooding (Goudie 2019). In addition, soil erosion may be associated with an increase of water discharge in rivers due to the reduction of soil water storage resulting from erosion of the permeable humus layer which increases the runoff on sloping land surfaces. The reduced water permeability of the soils and the higher runoff may be also associated with a lowering of the groundwater table.

The losses of soil are irreversible and most of the eroded soil material is irretrievably lost within the human timescale as the processes of weathering and soil development act on a timescale of hundreds to thousands of years. Soils play a pivotal role in the growth of vegetation, as carbon sink, and as the foundation of ecological habitats (White et al. 1984). Therefore, the degradation of soils affects several ecological processes including processes such as the turnover of nutrients as well as the carbon fluxes from the soil to the atmosphere and vice versa.

In addition, the use of soil fertilizers is associated with several issues that may affect the global environment. Every year, between 8.5 to 9.5 million tonnes of phosphorus are transported into the oceans. These amounts exceed the natural background influx into the oceans by about eight times (Rockström et al. 2009). An increase in the content of phosphorus in the ocean water results in increased growth of algae and plankton. This induces a chain reaction which ends with a decrease of the dissolved oxygen levels in the water. In geological records from the past, the crossing of a critical threshold of phosphorus influxes into the ocean was often associated with anoxic events, high extinction rates and reduced biodiversity (Elicki and Breitkreuz 2016). As changes in biodiversity affect the function of ecosystems, the crossing of such a critical threshold will also result in an alternation of the oceanic ecosystem. Nitrogen is another element used in fertilizers. Nitrogen is mostly obtained from the atmosphere. However, for its use in fertilizers, the nitrogen has to be converted into a reactive form. In this form, it is often transported into the environment by soil erosion or by water flow and induces the pollution of freshwater, coastal waters, and it becomes a greenhouse gas after oxidation to N_2O (laughing gas) (Rockström et al. 2009).

In the last centuries, the rapid transformation of land surfaces for land use often affects important carbon storages such as peatlands which after drainage release of CO_2 and CH_4. According to Green and Page (2017) about 15 % of the peatlands in Europe and Southeast Asia have been drained which accounts for about 5 % of the human CO_2 emissions. In rainforest environments, the peatlands store about the same amount of carbon as the rain forest. Future changes in land cover due to burning and land use associated with deforestation may result in the release of huge amounts of CO_2 and CH_4 (Schultz 2005; Draper et al. 2014). Thus, it can be inferred that the sculpting and transformation of the land surface by humans for various purposes in the last centuries has influenced increasingly the interactions between different process systems. The changes are associated with higher erosion rates and changes in the material turnovers and tend to affect also the climatic system. As the different systems and subsystems are coupled, they are not independent of one another and a change of one component of the system is propagated and transferred to another system as function of the coupling strength, the state of the land surface, and the intensity of the impact (Slaymaker 2000). The high areal extent of the land surface transformations results from technological developments in the last century and the expansion of human population, which is closely associated with a higher demand on food, raw materials, and areas for agriculture and urban growth.

2.4 Human-Induced Climate Change and Environmental Change

Changes in climatic conditions will affect nearly all areas of the world. At a temporal scale of decades, some regions of the world may experience more favorable climatic conditions. However, without reducing the current trend of the increase of CO_2, a shift in climate zones is likely within the next centuries (Seneviratne et al. 2012). An increase in the likelihood of extreme rainfall and runoff events coupled with a higher variability of rainfalls and risks of flooding are expected for many regions of world at the end of the century (Hoegh-Guldberg et al. 2018, Huddart and Stott 2020). In those parts of the world which become more prone to serious droughts, such as the Mediterranean, a decline of up to 50 % of hydropower potential can be expected. The decline and disappearance of glaciers will also influence the hydropower potential in areas such as northern and western Europe. Drier climatic conditions and a higher likelihood of more frequent droughts are expected for the Mediterranean, parts of Africa, the Middle East, and the south western America (Hoegh-Guldberg et al. 2018). These changes will result in a reduction of the fresh-water resources, particularly in regions where the demand of fresh-water is increasing due to a rising population and the higher individual demand. However, changes at a specific site may be also controlled by more far-reaching effects. In countries such as the Sudan and Egypt agriculture depends also on water for irrigation. The water for irrigation is supplied through the tributary rivers of Nile and the Nile from highlands of Eastern and Central Africa. Changes in hydrologic conditions of these headwater areas may have profound effects on further land use in the lowlands (Taylor 1999).

However, even the boundaries and the spatial extent of ecozones will be affected if global warming continues. If the emission of greenhouse gases is not reduced, the results of most scenarios suggest that at the scale of several decades to centuries most of the world's ecozones are likely to be subjected to marked changes (Seneviratne et al. 2012). West Africa appears to experience negative impacts from climate change on crop yields, and a high increase in temperature is likely for parts of South Africa, Namibia, and Botswana. Reduced rainfalls are expected to occur in the regions of the Limpopo basin, parts of the Zambezi basin in Zambia, and parts of Western Cape in South Africa and, on the other hand, rainfall may increase over central and western South Africa and southern Namibia (Seneviratne et al. 2012). In northern Africa, an increase in temperature by about 1.5 °C will result in a decrease in precipitation particularly during the summer months. This is associated with a higher water deficit in the summer and with more frequent edaphic drought. The changes in rainfall are expected to be associated with the replacement of the deciduous forests by shrubland vegetation and the decline of the alpine forests as deciduous forest vegetation invades into the mountain areas (Huddart and Stott 2020).

Where the ecozonal distribution of the vegetation is constrained by temperature, such as in case of the boreal forests, a poleward shift of the forest boundary is likely, and the extent of the tundra vegetation will be reduced (Goudie 2019). Large parts of the arctic will be affected by a milder winter and a delayed winter onset, presumably accompanied by an increase in fire disturbances (Bring et al. 2016). The melting of permafrost will be associated with accelerated coastal erosion whilst at the same time, methane and carbon dioxide will be released from the formerly frozen ground. In mountain areas, warming will result in a replacement of the alpine vegetation by forests. Although an accurate prediction of far-reaching effects of climate change at the scale of several decades and centuries remains difficult as several processes and feedbacks in earth surface systems and ecosystems are not always fully understood, it is now clear that climate change will cause shifts of vegetation and animal populations and will result in an alternation of the distribution of species and the interaction among the different species. As an increase in temperature also affects microbial activity levels, it also influences residue decomposition rates and processes controlling soil dynamics, growing conditions for the vegetation and carbon storage processes.

However, species are able to migrate with the changing conditions, unless they are near the limit of their geographical range (White et al. 1984). An example is the vegetation in mountain areas, where the decreasing areal extent of suitable environments at higher elevations limits migration. Besides natural barriers that may delay or inhibit the migration, the fragmentation of habitats by the human modification of the landscape has led to new barriers and a reduction of possible habitats. In addition, the migration routes are not necessarily similar to the requirements of different species on environmental factors differ. With respect to the maintenance of biodiversity, the rate of migration and availability of suitable habitats are important factors. As the rate migration of the vegetation depends on the production of propagules, their quantity, and dispersal rates, it appears unlikely that all species will respond in similar ways and with similar rates on environmental changes (White et al. 1984; Classen et al. 2015). Therefore, it seems plausible that the combined effects of human interferences and climate change will result in a rapid decrease in biodiversity as the species have different migration rates and tolerances against environmental change. As a consequence of different dispersal, migration, and establishment rates, the interactions between the different species may be affected which alters the biodiversity and the function of terrestrial ecosystems (Walther et al. 2002).

3 The Response of Landscapes and Earth Surface Processes on Climate and Environmental Change

3.1 Differences in Response

The effects of all changes in climate, vegetation, soils, and hydrologic components will be mediated by erosional and depositional processes at the earth surface. For these processes, the climate is only one driver as their reaction depends also on landscape forms and materials which have evolved over longer time spans and which now serve as a further set of boundary conditions that control the thresholds and rates of their reaction. As landforms reflect local conditions of climate, topography, geology, hydrology, and land-use, the changes in climate and environmental conditions may be exacerbated or reduced by other factors acting at the local scale (Jones 1993; Brunsden 2001; Ritter et al. 2011). Thus, some landforms may react highly sensitive to environmental changes whilst others show a retarded response or a slight increase or no response. Landforms that are prone to cross crucial thresholds of temperature, precipitation, and changes in vegetation will respond more rapidly when the change affects just those components of the process-response system that are strongly coupled and if there is a low resistance against a change (Brunsden 2001; Goudie 2019). A simple example of the differences in the sensitivities to changes by rainfall is landslide processes. In regions with steep hillslopes, highly weathered, deep soils and densely vegetated hillslopes the frequency of landsliding may be increased by heavy rainfalls due to the more frequent occurrence of high pore-water pressures in the soils and weathering layers which reduce the shear strength. A similar change in rainfall in another region may result in an increased density of deep rooting trees and a higher evapotranspiration rate which stabilizes hillslopes against landsliding. A further factor is that landscape forms and materials are often inherited from very different past environmental conditions. Landscapes have a long history and hence have experienced various changes in climate and environmental conditions (Chorley et al. 1984; Brunsden 2001).

Simple examples are the changed conditions during the last ice age about 20,000 years ago. During this time, climate zones of the earth changed markedly, and cold climatic conditions on the northern hemisphere expanded southwards towards the temperate latitudes whilst large regions in the tropics and subtropics became much drier than today (Thomas 2006). Drier conditions in sub-tropical and tropical areas resulted in an increased mobility of sand and in the formation of dune sands. At the end of the last ice age when climate became warmer and wetter, dunes were stabilized by soils and vegetation. However, the dune sands are prone to erosion by wind and water once the soil and vegetation cover is removed either by unsustainable land use or by climate change.

During the last ice age, slopes in many mountain ranges were steepened by glacial erosion. After the last glaciations (about 11700 years ago), the retreat and lowering of the glaciers exposed over-steepened hillslopes and rock walls. Erosion of rocks by glaciers and the reduced buttressing of the over-steepened, newly exposed rock slopes after the lowering and retreat of the glaciers resulted in a change of the stress state in the rocks. The rocks in rock walls reacted on the reduced buttressing by the glaciers by the opening of preexisting fracture sets and the development of pressure release fractures. These fracture patterns have grown in size in the following millennia and have caused the development of unstable hillslopes several thousand years after the end of the ice age. This induced the development of huge landslides which result from processes of fracturing which were inherited from the last ice age and are acting as zones of weakness into the recent time.

Earth surface process systems often show a cascading behavior. The material removed from one slope has to be transported or deposited downslope to the river. The river, in turn, responds by a change of its gradient or channel bed form in order to adjust the stream power and to enable the downstream transport of the material. However, downstream conditions are also exerting control on the transport and erosion processes upstream, and, with longer delay time, they also control the rate of hillslope processes at the slope foot, which itself, in turn, controls the rate of the upslope propagation of the erosion and deposition processes. The up- and downstream propagation of erosional and depositional zones within the catchments results in various feedbacks in the river channel and on hillslopes and different thresholds are crossed at various temporal and spatial scales until all components of the process-response system are mutually adjusted to the prevailing environmental conditions. The different temporal and spatial scales involved in the process to achieve the adjustment, and frequent changes of environmental conditions are competing components in the process-response systems and complicate the adjustment to a dynamic equilibrium which is often not achieved.

The superimposition of climate change will affect not only the absolute amount of material removed from the slopes but also the frequency and magnitude of the processes with marked consequences on erosion, deposition, and sediment transport. Particularly in formerly glaciated mountain areas, such as the Alps, the changes resulting from global warming affect different process systems (Reynard et al. 2012). Soil development by weathering and the rate at which the vegetation is able to react on climate change and to colonize new suitable areas differ significantly (Parola and Rossi 2008). The increase in temperature will potentially cause a retreat of the permafrost. As the permanently frozen ground beneath the thawing near the surface layer (the active layer) impedes drainage, a change in the thickness of the active layer may result in a higher pore water pressure. This encourages the mobilization of the soils and sediments and increases the supply of coarse material to the rivers. The rivers will react by changes in gradient or as a function of the increase in meltwater by changes in the magnitude of water discharge. Although several studies indicate that climate warming is accompanied with an upward migration of vegetation, the majority of these primary colonizers on the formerly non-vegetated hillslopes appear to be unable to control hillslope stability (Clague et al. 2012; Reynard et al. 2012). At the same time the melting of the interstitial ice in the fractures of the rocks reduces their cohesion and contributes to the development of loose rock blocks of various sizes. Rock walls composed of rocks which have lost their cohesion due to the melting of the interstitial ice in the fractures, and the large fracture patterns that started to grow shortly after the retreat of the glaciers at the end of the last ice age are potentially prone to huge rockfalls. The results of a monitoring program of Kellerer-Pirklbauer et al. (2012) suggest that such a combination of processes is also responsible for the increase in landslide activity in the Austrian Alps after the Little Ice Age. The Little Ice Age was a period of colder climatic conditions which followed a relatively warm period (Medieval Warm Period). In the European Alps, a marked increase in glacier volumes occurred between the sixteenth and nineteenth century. Since the 1840s and the 1860s temperatures increased slightly. This increase appears to represent the end of the Little Ice Age (Schönwiese 1994, Glaser, 2001). In the area of the Mittlerer Burgstall (Austrian Alps) Kellerer-Pirklbauer et al. (2012) have shown that since the Little Ice Age the surfaces of the glacier tongues were lowered by about 70 to 250 m and that the reduced buttressing of the rockwalls and melting of interstitial ice resulted in a loss of cohesion. These processes induced rock slope instability. The ultimate trigger leading to the collapse of the weakened rockwalls was associated with a set of factors that were controlled by the conditions in the warm winter of the year 2006/07 (Kellerer-Pirkkbauer et al. 2012). However, in complex systems climate remains only one driver of landslide activity as several other processes are involved. Huggel et al. (2012) suggest that after the period of warming landslides may evolve independently of climate change and that in alpine environments the storage of sediments and ice from past periods may induce significant lag time effects which tend to influence the frequency and the magnitude of landslide events.

Changes in magnitude and frequency of events are not necessarily proportional to the changes in climate. In small catchments, the size and frequency of river floods is not directly proportional to the changes in rainfall, whilst even small changes in rainfall and temperature can trigger significant changes in the recurrence intervals and the effects of floods as a function of catchment properties (Blum 2007). The increasing areal extent of both, human transformed and artificial landscapes (cuttings and embankments for traffic and other purposes), is associated with changes in drainage systems, flow directions, and in the stability of slopes. These changes potentially affect the magnitude and frequency of events – even without climate change – but the superimposition of climate change may increase the risks of soil erosion, flooding, and landsliding, though, for some mountain regions in Europe, the effect of climate change on landslide activity is subject to controversial debates.

3.2 Desertification and Climate Change

The complex response of the combined effects of human interference and the coupling of various earth systems and their subsystems is clearly indicated in phenomena associated with desertification. Desertification is a process driven by human interferences in drylands and encompasses the degradation of soils and vegetation due to unsuitable management practices in eco-climatic zones characterized by severe droughts. The overexploitation of drylands results from economic and social pressures and is associated with degradation phenomena due to overgrazing, deforestation, over-cultivation, and unsuitable as well as poor irrigation practices (Yang 2010). The interferences lead to changes of the properties of soils and in the density and composition of vegetation cover and affect local and regional climate conditions through changes in soil moisture, loss of soil retention, and changes in soil water and groundwater storage thereby increasing the effects of droughts. These changes affect via various feedbacks the generation of overland flow in the wetter seasons and tend to exacerbate the effects of heavy rainfalls but are also altering the response of rivers and other the hydrologic sub-systems (Goudie and Viles 2010). Even without human induced climate change, dry land areas are highly sensitive to changes. These environments often suffer from inter-annual variations of rainfall and also experience rainfall variations at the scale of decades (Mensching 1990). A period of several dry years may be followed by a period with high rainfall amounts or extreme rainfall events, which results in intense soil erosion as the sheltering ground cover has been reduced during the dry spells before (Goudie and Viles 2010). The varying availability of moisture and the varying ground and vegetation cover is one factor which enables erosion by water and wind.

Regions currently most threatened by desertification are the Sahel zone, the Kalahari, parts of the Mediterranean, regions in Southern America such as northeastern Brazil, south- western Argentina, parts of Australia and Asia, particularly Mongolia, parts of north eastern China, and parts of the sub-Himalayan India (Huddart and Stott 2020). Although drylands on all continents show common impacts of human interference, the causes of desertification are complex and vary even within the same eco-climatic zone from one part of the world to another.

Most drylands affected by land degradation are located in the ecozones of the summer wet savannas and the winter wet steppes in the subtropical and tropical climate zone (Schultz 2005). During the Pleistocene, when the glaciers had their greatest extend, deserts expended also, and the tropical and subtropical savannas and winter dry steppe zones were subject to more arid conditions. In Africa, south of the Sahara, arid conditions enabled intense sand transport by wind and the formation of dunes and the accumulation of sand fields, even in areas which are today receiving annually more than 600 mm rainfall and are covered by savanna vegetation (Völkel and Grunert 1990). The amelioration of the climate at the end of the last ice age (Pleistocene) resulted in a warming and in an increasing supply of moisture by rainfall. The new environmental conditions enabled the development of savanna vegetation and soils and dunes became fixed. Inherited from these past climatic conditions are sandy deposits which formed formerly sand dunes. The sandy deposits are now weathered in their upper parts to soils. However, the dune sands are easily remobilized by wind once the vegetation cover is reduced and the soils are eroded. The soils themselves are liable to the disturbances of the biological crust and have a high erodibility, which enhances erosion by both, water and wind (Römer 2012).

An example of the complex response of surface processes on human interference and relatively small changes in the rainfall pattern has been documented by Mensching (1984, 1990). In the Sahel zone in Darfur (Sudan), a continuous decline of rainfall-levels is documented for the time from the 1960s to the 1970s, followed by a second rainfall minimum in the 1980s. The decline in rainfall clearly triggered the crisis-situation in this area, though the growth of the population and the extension of intensive agronomic activities into an area of formerly fixed dunes belonging to Ooz-belt resulted in irreversible changes in the ecosystem. The dunes of the Ooz-belt have formed under drier climatic conditions about 20,000 to 10,000 years ago (Mensching 1984). This dune activity period was interrupted by a humid period which enabled the development of soils under a denser vegetation cover. Soil development resulted in an encrusting of soil particles which became less permeable for water flow. In addition, the encrusted sand grains were less prone to the attack by winds. A further shift to drier climatic conditions resulted in a supply of new sands and the development of a new generation of sand dunes (younger dunes) which covered the older sand dunes and the encrusted soils. In the last 10,000 to 8,000 years, the climate became wetter and the dunes stabilized and were covered with vegetation (Mensching 1984).

In the 1970s and 1980s, intensive agricultural land-use, overgrazing, and a change in rainfall patterns as well as a decrease in rainfall amounts resulted in a strong degradation of the vegetation cover. The consequences were soil erosion and remobilization of the younger dune generation and the exposure of the encrusted soils. The lower water permeability of the exposed encrusted soils led to an increased rate of water flow during heavy rainfalls and resulted in intense soil erosion (Mensching 1984). Exposure of encrusted soils and soil erosion provided only poor material for agricultural use and resulted in a decline of harvest. As a counteraction to this situation, areas for cultivation and grazing were enlarged which has increased land degradation and soil erosion. The combined effects of a change in rainfall amounts, which was coupled with a high sensitivity of the landscape due to the properties of the inherited material, has increased the vulnerability against unsustainable human interference.

Complex responses to a change in climate are likely in the future in several regions threatened by desertification. In the Kalahari (southern Africa), stabilized dunes systems are threatened by expanding agricultural land use and human-induced climate change is suggested to exacerbate the process of land degradation (Lancaster 1999). Desertification is also associated with several risks such as salinization of soils, sand encroachment, deflation. Particularly dust storms which are allied with desertification processes are expected to affect geochemical cycles (Yang, 2010).

3.3 Changing Ecological Conditions in Arctic Areas

The most drastic effects of global warming are supposed to occur in the sub-arctic and arctic areas. Predictions suggest that until 2050 about 50 % of the permafrost areas will experience thawing (French 2007). Similar tendencies are proposed by Seneviratne et al. (2012). Allied with these changes might be changes in the precipitation patterns, and the combined effects of higher temperatures and changes in precipitation will be associated with changes in zonation of the vegetation. If temperature continue to increase by about 4 to 5 °C, the northern boundary of the boreal forest will move northward by about 100 to 700 km whilst the southern boundary will shift at a higher rate of about 200 to 900 km (French 2007).

Recent observations show that woody shrubs have replaced grasses and forbs in several regions of the Arctic indicating that it is likely that the changing vegetation cover is influencing the carbon feedbacks (French 2007; Goudie 2019). With respect to the effects of global warming, one has to distinguish between terrains covered with continuous and discontinuous permafrost (French 2007). Here, the latter includes also sporadic permafrost. In continuous permafrost terrains, the ground is frozen at nearly all sites except beneath lakes and rivers whilst in discontinuous permafrost terrains areas of unfrozen ground separate bodies of frozen ground (Chorley et al. 1984; French 2007). The thickness of the continuous permafrost ranges from several meters to several hundred meters, up to 400 m at some sites in Canada and Alaska and up to 600 m in Russia (French 2007). In northern America, the southern boundary of the continuous permafrost follows the mean annual isotherm of −6 to −8 °C, whilst the southern boundary of the discontinuous permafrost roughly coincides with the mean annual isotherm of −1 °C. Continuous and discontinuous permafrost areas encompass about 20 % of the earth's surface (Ritter et al. 2011). Common to all permafrost areas is the development of an active layer, which represents a near-surface layer that thaws when temperatures in summer exceed 0 °C. The seasonally developing active layer over the permafrost has a thickness of 0.4 to 0.5 m in northern Greenland at latitudes of 75 to 80 °N and 1.5 m in Canada at a latitude of about 60 °N (Ahnert 1998; Seneviratne et al. 2012).

The reason for the distinction between continuous and discontinuous permafrost is that global warming in these areas occurs at different rates and induces different effects. Several studies indicate that the arctic areas underlain by continuous permafrost experienced the highest increase in temperature by global warming ranging to about 3 °C (French 2007; Seneviratne et al. 2012), whilst the temperature increase in areas underlain by discontinuous permafrost ranges to about 1 °C (Osterkamp and Jorgenson 2006). Therefore, the impact of climate changes is quite different.

Areas underlain by continuous permafrost will mostly remain at or below the freezing point even if the temperature increases by 4 to 5 °C. However, global warming will induce higher snowfall, an earlier onset of snowfall, a longer duration of the snow cover, and higher cloudiness. At first glance, these changes tend to induce cooling. However, under conditions of continued global warming, these areas will retreat towards the north and hence, their areal extent will decrease. In the longer term, it appears unlikely that the feedbacks involved by increasing the reflectivity through a longer snow cover and more cloudiness will be able to balance the effects of the warming as several other processes interact to enhance the warming (French 2007). The earlier snowfall and the presumably thicker snow cover will lead to stronger insulation of the permafrost and to warmer permafrost temperatures than air temperatures (Seneviratne et al. 2012). Higher temperatures in the summer months will result in a thickening of the active layer and in changes in the hydrologic system.

Marked changes are expected to occur in areas underlain with discontinuous permafrost. The increased duration of the thaw period reduces the snow cover and the albedo, which in turn, increases the absorption and hence, the warming of the ground surface. The earlier onset of thawing and of the snow melting as well as the change in the proportion and amount of snow and rainfall will affect soil-hydrology and the hydrologic systems. The increased thickness of the active layer is associated with an increased thaw-subsidence which affects buildings, roads, and other structures as ice-rich soils and sediments are prone to consolidation during melting (French 2007). In addition, the delayed water drainage of the pores of the soils and sediments contributes also to a high pore-water pressure which tends to destabilize the ground surface and hillslopes. However, thaw-subsidence not solely result from consolidation. As ice has a greater volume than water, the thawing of ice-rich in the porous soils and sediments is associated with the development of depressions that may fill with water (Ritter et al. 2011). If larger areas are subject to the thawing of ice-rich soils, the depressions develop into thaw lakes, a process which might be reinforced by heat transfer from the water (temperature > 0 °C) into the surrounding ice-rich material, once a critical quantity of water has accumulated (Yoshikawa and Harada 1995; French 2007). The thawing of the soils, and particularly of peat bog, is associated with a release of greenhouse gases (methane and carbon dioxide) thereby enhancing global warming and changes soil chemical and physical properties are likely to influence the arctic ecosystems via feedbacks between the nutrient cycle (e. g. nitrates) soil moisture and water quality.

3.4 Changing Environments at Coasts

The scenarios of the IPCC have calculated an increase of sea-level rise in the range of 0.5 to about 1.0 m at a rate of 8 to 16 mm/year until the year 2100 due to the warming of the ocean water (steric effect) and the melting of ice from glaciers and large ice caps (Seneviratne et al. 2012). The estimates of the annual sea-level rise range from 3 to 4 mm/a (Yi et al. 2015, Watson et al. 2015). Although sea-level rise is a global phenomenon, the actual rise at a specific site of a coast may be lower or higher than the global rise. Factors contributing to these differences are uplift or subsidence, either by tectonic processes or due to glacial-isostatic rebound. The latter is a consequence of the deglaciation following the last ice age when ice sheets with a thickness of thousands of meters covered both, northern Europe and parts of northern America. The weight of the ice sheets deflected the Earth's crust downward. The deglaciation results in uplift and often prevails into the present (Ahnert 1998). Variation in sea-level is also caused by different rates of thermal expansion of the ocean water, by the melting of large masses of land-ice, and by climatic influences such as high rainfalls and high discharge from rivers, though the effects vary interannually.

The strongest impacts of sea-level rise are expected to occur at low-lying coasts and low-lying subsiding coasts, consisting of loose material (beaches and dunes, marshes, mudflats, mangrove swamps, deltas) and subsiding coral reef islands (Goudie and Viles 2010). Subsiding coasts occur along the eastern seaboard of the USA, south eastern England, and at some of the world's greatest river deltas, e. g. Indus, Ganges, Nile, Mississippi, Mekong, Tigris-Euphrates, Zambesi (Goudie and Viles 2016; Goudie 2019), though even rising coasts may be affected by sea-level rise. In several cases, the rate of sea-level rise is comparable or exceeds the rate of coastal uplift which results in a smaller relative rate of sea-level rise but also affects the coasts. Even cliff coasts, consisting of bedrock, may be affected. In England, the rise in sea-level at AD 1100 to 1200 resulted in a rapid retreat of soft rocks cliffs and the surplus of material has affected the distribution of accumulation areas along the coasts (Brunsden 2001).

Coasts are experiencing constantly alternating water levels due to the action of tides, waves, and storms. Coastal settings are highly variable and their reaction on changes in sea- level depends on factors such as the coastal topography, the geomorphic type of coast, the material forming the coast (loose material or rock), the role of vertical crustal movements, the exposure to severe storm tracks, the influence of coastal defense structures, and the sensitivity of the coast to changes, just to name a few factors. Human interferences in the coastal processes have changed the mutual adjustment of the natural processes of erosion and deposition through the building of defense structures, dams, and various forms of land use (Hails 1977). Dams along the rivers retain sediments, thereby interrupting the supply of sediments to coasts which often results in beach erosion. Coastal defense structures, such as groins, breakwaters, and other engineering structures, not only inhibiting coastal erosion but also inducing deposition at a particular site with the consequence that other parts of the coast become undernourished with sediments (Hails 1977; Bird 2001, Goudie 2019). Even small interferences such as the narrowing of tidal channels at the East Frisian Barrier Islands along the German North Sea coast for shipping with ferryboats have resulted in increased erosion of the beaches and an alteration of the deposition sites (Hempel 1983).

The East Frisian Barrier Islands at the German North Sea coast are characterized by dynamic changes which are associated with the sediment transport into the North Sea, the erosion and deposition by longshore coastal currents, and wave attack during storms. However, human defense and protection structures often interact with these processes. The sediment budget in this area depends largely on the amount of sediments transported by the rivers into the North Sea and on the transport of this material by longshore currents towards the east (Fig. 5). The transport processes are comparable with a west-east acting "conveyor-band" where material losses on an island in the east are compensated by sediment which has been removed from the next island in the west. Ideally, this would result in the migration of the barrier island without any net loss of material. The maintenance of these islands depends on an intricate pattern of coastal sediment transport and erosion and deposition, and a perturbation of sediment supply results in a change of the size of the barrier islands. The narrowing of the tidal channel between the islands Spiekeroog and Wangerooge was associated with an increased water flow velocity at low tide in the tidal channel (Hempel 1983). This resulted in a northward deflection of the longshore current and a change in the sites of sand bar deposition (Fig. 5a,b). As a consequence, the east coast of Wangerooge experienced severe erosion of beaches whilst its western coast experienced deposition (Fig. 5b).

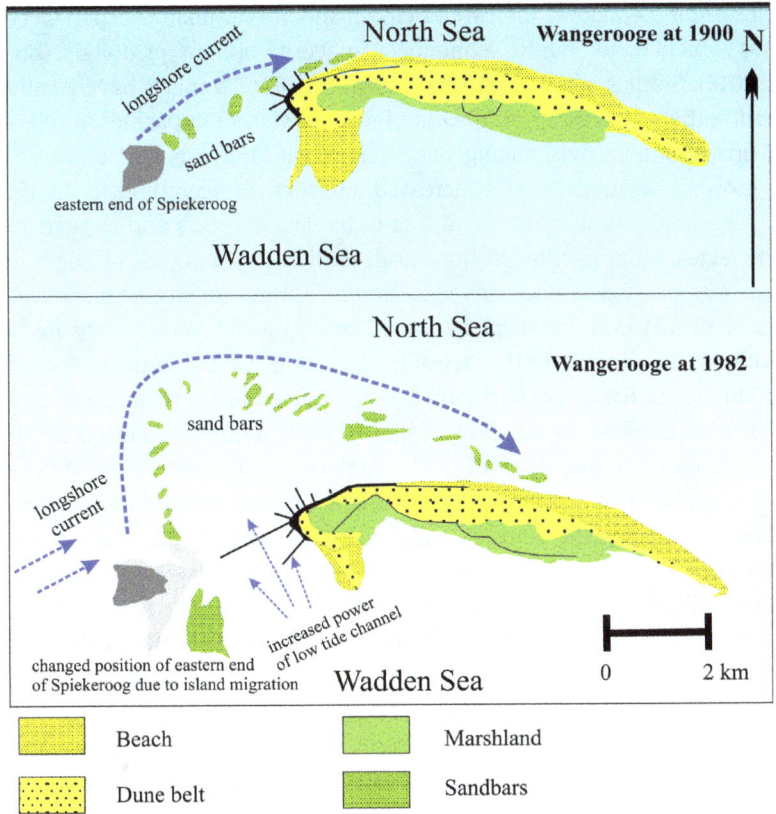

Fig. 5: Simplified map of the East Frisian Barrier Islands Spiekeroog and Wangerooge in along the North sea coast of Germany. (Modified after Hempel, 1983: 92).

The Fig. 5a and 5b show the effect of a narrowing and deepening of the tide channel at the end of the 1970s. Figure 5a shows the relatively undisturbed material transport at AD 1900. The strengthening of low tide current in the low tide channel resulted in a change of the deposition sites, at a larger distance from the islands. In 1982 this resulted in a pertubation of the sediment transport of the longshore current. As a consequence the barrier island Wangerooge experienced more erosion at its eastern part, whilst the longshore current enhances deposition at the beaches at the northwestern parts of island.

The superimposition of the sea-level rise and human interferences into coastal systems has sometimes dramatic effects such as more frequent high tide-inundation and coastal flooding during extreme water level events, groundwater inundation, and beach erosion (Rotzoll and Fletcher 2013; Vitousek, 2017, Goudie 2019).

An extreme example is Jakarta, the capital city of Indonesia. Jakarta experiences regular floods which have caused economic damage of billions of dollars (Budiyono et al. 2016). Studies on flooding have shown that flood impacts have greatly increased during the last decades as a result of too low storage capacities in rivers and canals, unsustainable river management, increased land use, and urbanization for the growing population, and increased subsidence. According to Abidin et al. (2011), Jakarta has sunk up to about 4 m in the last 40 years and appears to be one of the fastest sinking cities in the world. Preliminary analyses of possible tectonic influences on subsidence rates indicate that this factor can be excluded, and subsidence results from overexploitation of ground water, mostly for supply water for drinking and industry, the dewatering of soils for the construction of high-rise buildings and the associated compaction, exploitation of oil and gas, and natural compaction (Andreas et al. 2017). Sea-level rise and human-induced subsidence clearly increase the frequency of tidal inundations and inundations due to severe storms. Jakarta is only one example. Human-induced subsidence is noted for several coastal areas on the globe (Goudie 2019). However, in Bangkok, it was possible to reduce the rate of subsidence by regulations on deep well pumping. According to Phien-Wej et al. (2006), this reduced local subsidence rates from about 12 cm/year during the 1980s to about 2 cm/year. Even without subsidence, the sea-level rise increases the risk of inundation. Firstly, because of the higher water level at the coast and secondly, as the sea water propagates into the lower reaches of the rivers, which is associated with a decrease in river transporting capacity and encourages the deposition of sediments at a new and higher level. This sediment aggradation favors further flooding during high stage water discharges (Chorley et al. 1984).

3.5 Sea-Level Rise and Deltas

Deltas accumulate enormous volumes of sediments, and particularly deltas in formerly unglaciated areas are often zones of an isostatically driven subsidence, which results from the increased weight at the deposition site or the increase of weight due to flooding the continental shelves. Thus, such delta areas are highly prone to inundation and erosion. For the Mississippi delta, the isostatically driven subsidence rates are estimated to range from 0.3 to 3.6 mm/year (Syvitski 2008). A further factor contributing to subsidence is the compaction of sediments. Particularly clay-rich sediments and sediments rich in organic material are prone to compaction by losses of pore-water, whilst in organic-rich materials, volume losses are also induced by oxidation processes (Goudie 2019). These compaction rates are estimated to be less than 3 mm/year (Ericson et al. 2006; Syvitski et al. 2009) though

Zoccarato et al. (2018) documented rates of up to 20 mm/year for the Mekong delta in Vietnam.

Groundwater withdrawal, exploitation for methane, the demand for sand and gravel for building industries and constructions, and aquacultures contribute to the increase of the rate of subsidence of the deltas. Sea-level rise, delta erosion and subsidence, and the increasing use of groundwater are closely associated with the issue of salinity and changes in water quality (Syvitski et al. 2009). As the density of saltwater is higher than that of freshwater, the saltwater can displace the less saline groundwater and any decrease in the amount of freshwater will be associated with a rise of the underlying saltwater. Particularly on delta surfaces with intense irrigation practices, saltwater incursions may threaten agricultural activities. Soils become impermeable which affects the root development of the plants, whilst an excess of sodium ions from saltwater has toxic effects on plants (Goudie 2019).

Besides subsidence deltas are threatened by various human-induced processes. In a study including the 24 largest deltas of the world, Syvitski et al. (2009) concluded that more than 80 % of the investigated deltas are threatened by human impacts, either due to the trapping of sediments in dams or by human-induced compaction. On a global scale, more than 45,000 dams are trapping about 25 to 30 % of the river load (Ericson et al. 2006). Extreme examples are the Indus river and the Rhone river. Giosan et al. (2014) note that about 94 % of the sediments of the Indus river and 85 % of the sediments of the Rhone river are retained in dams and other structures. According to Ericson et al. (2006) and Syvitski et al. (2009), the largest deltas of the world are now undernourished with sediments and the ongoing rise in sea-level tends to exacerbate the losses and the process of delta erosion. This is clearly a harmful interaction into the delta systems as currently, about 300 million people are living on the 24 largest deltas of the world.

4 Conclusions

Global changes result from both human interferences in marine and terrestrial environments and climate change due to the release in greenhouse gases. Human interferences have affected the sensitivity to change in climatic conditions by altering and transforming land surfaces and the magnitude and frequency distribution of extreme events. The response to these changes is commonly not governed by simple cause-effect relationships but is controlled by complex feedbacks resulting from the interaction of the processes at different temporal and local and regional scales. However, there are not always well-defined thresholds in the various process systems. As a result of the coupling of the subsystems, a change in one subsystem can increase the risk that thresholds are crossed in other process system. Abrupt changes in the magnitude and frequency distribution of events result from the crossing of a series of thresholds as the changes propagated into various subsystems and induced a cascade of multiple reactions at different temporal and spatial scales. However, the response to a change often depends also on antecedent environmental conditions and landscape settings inherited from the past. Therefore, it is likely that different process domains (e.g., fluvial processes, gravity-controlled processes, aeolian controlled processes) exhibit different sensitivities to the forcing by ongoing climate change in similar landscape settings (e.g., coasts, mountains, river floors). Similar process- domains, on the other hand, are likely to exhibit different sensitivities to climate change in different landscape settings and different ecozones (Harrison et al. 2019).

The increasing areal extent of landscape transformations and anthropogenic landscapes has influenced not only the global hydrologic, erosion, soil formation and atmospheric processes, vegetation, and faunal types but also influenced processes associated with the global carbon cycle. Particularly in the past seventy years, the ecosystems have often been deprived of their potential to regenerate within a reasonable time (Glaser, 2014). Human-induced climate change provides another driver, affecting firstly the most sensitive components of the Earth's ecosystems and, as a function of the strength of coupling between the different processes, tends to alter the interaction of the subsystems. Climate change results primarily from the release of greenhouse gases. At least in the last 800,000 years, the concentration of CO_2 has never been higher than now, and some authors note that it may be even higher than in the last 3 million years (Glaser 2014, Lowe and Walker 2015).

However, even if the combustion of fossil energy resources and hence, the release of greenhouse gases, was stopped today, the climate system would not recover instantly but only after several decades. The effects of human interference in the environments, on the other hand, will remain and will continue to affect the interplay of the processes as human interference appears set to increase in the future. In the last decades, the human consumption of raw materials and fuels has increased, particularly in the industrial nations. Since 1950, the world population has grown from 2.5 billion to about 7.6 billion in 2018. The threefold increase in the world population is associated with a nearly fourfold increase in the consumption of raw materials until 2010 (Schaffartzik et al. 2014). According to the United Nations Report (2017), the global yearly average consumption of raw materials in 2010 was at about 10.1 metric tons per person year, with richer nations consuming 27.6 metric tons per person and year, whilst low-income countries consume on average only 2 metric tons per person and year. Compared to pre- industrial societies the average energy demand per person has increased by a factor of fifty in the industrial period (Glaser 2014). The increase in raw material and energy consumption and the increase of industrialized forms of agriculture with the use of phosphorus and nitrogen in fertilizers has achieved levels that could damage and undermine the resilience of several ecologic subsystems (Rockström et al. 2009).

Most of the problems result from the increased consumption of resources and go hand in hand with the growing economies in nearly all parts of the world, globalization, and increasing individual demand. The issues of global change are closely associated with the future behavior of societies in terms of changes in lifestyle, consumption patterns, and economic decisions. The intricate pattern of the interaction of societies, economics, and global environmental changes shows that the search for a solution to the problems is clearly an interdisciplinary issue that can only be resolved by the collaboration of various disciplines. Some geo-engineering options and technological advances may support a striving of a more sustainable development. However, besides the problem that technological solutions suffer too often from the risk of unknown side-effects, future challenges appear to be closely related to developments in societies and economics.

The apocalyptic dimension of environmental and climate change may be interpreted as the all-encompassing human interference in natural process-response systems on earth. Apocalyptic texts and images may help raising awareness to environmental changes by reflecting our contemporary reality and human enmeshments, thereby showing how we got into the crisis and how we can learn from our mistakes.

Bibliography

Ahnert, Frank (1998) *Introduction to Geomorphology* (London: Arnold).
Abidin, Hasanuddin Z. et al. (2011) "Land Subsidence of Jakarta (Indonesia) and Its Relation with Urban Development," *Natural Hazards* 59.3, 1753–1771.
Andreas, Heri, Hasanuddin Zainal Abidin and Dina Anggreni Sarsito (2017) "Tidal Inundation ("Rob") Investigation Using Time Series of High Resolution Satellite Image Data and from Institu Measurements along Northern Coast of Java (Pantura)," *IOP Conference Series, Earth and Environmental Science* 71.1, 1–11.
Bamber, Jonathan, E. Steig and D. Dahl-Jensen (2009) "What Is the Tipping Point for the Greenland Ice Sheet?" *IOP Conference Series, Earth and Environmental Science* 6.6, 1.
Bird, Eric (2001) *Coastal Geomorphology* (New York: Wiley & Sons).
Blum, Michael D. (2007) "Large River Systems and Climate Change," in *Large Rivers: Geomorphology and Management*, ed. Avijit Gupta (Chichester: Wiley & Sons), 627–659.

Borrelli, Pasquale et al. (2013) "An Assessment of the Global Impact of 21st Century Land Use Change on Soil Erosion," *Nature Communications* 8.1, 1–13.
Boysen, Margret and Hans Joachim Schellnhuber (2007) *Heaven and Earth. From Pergamon to Potsdam* (Potsdam: Potsdam Institute for Climate Impact Research).
Bring, Arvid et al. (2016) "Arctic Terrestrial Hydrology: A Synthesis of Processes Regional Effects, and Research Challenges," *Journal of Geophysical Research: Biogeosciences* 121.3, 621–649.
Brunsden, Denys (2001) "Back á Long: A Millennial Geomorphology" In: *Geomorphological Processes and Landscape Change*, ed. David L. Higgit and E. Mark Lee (Oxford: Blackwell), 27–60.
Budiyono, Yus et al. (2016) "River Flood Risk in Jakarta under Scenarios of Future Change," *Natural Hazards and Earth System Sciences* 16.3, 757–774.
Calef, Monika P. (2010) "Recent Climate Change Impacts on the Boreal Forests of Alaska," *Geography Compass* 4.2, 67–80.
Chorley, Richard J., Stanley. A. Schumm and David. E. Sugden (1984) *"Geomorphology,"* (London: Methuen).
Church, John A. et al. (2013) "Sea-Level Change," in *Climate Change 2013: The Physical Science Basis*, ed. T. F. Stocker et al. (Cambridge and New York: Cambridge University Press), 1137–1216.
Clague, John J. et al. (2012) "Climate Change and Hazardous Processes in High Mountains," *Revista de la Asociación Geológica Argentina*, 69.3, 328–338.
Classen, Aimée T. et al. (2015) "Direct and Indirect Effects of Climate Change on Soil Microbial and Soil Microbial-Plant Interactions: What Lies Ahead?" *Ecosphere* 6.8, 1–221.
Cooper, Hannah et al. (2013) "Sea-Level Rise Vulnerability Mapping for Adaptation Decisions Using LiDAR DEMs," *Progress in Physical Geography* 37.6, 745–766.
Dlugokencky, Ed J. et al. (2019) "Atmospheric Composition: Long-Lived Greenhouse Gases. State of the Climate in 2018," *American Meteorological Society, 48–50*.
Draper, Frederick C. et al. (2014) "The Distribution and Amount of Carbon in the Largest Peatland Complex in Amazonia," *Environmental Research Letters* 9, 1–12.
Dutton, Andrea et al. (2015) "Sea-Level Rise Due to Polar Ice-Sheet Mass Loss During Past Warm Periods," *Science* 349.6244, 153.
Eldevik, Tor and Jan Even Ø. Nilsen (2013) "The Arctic-Atlantic Thermohaline Circulation," *Journal of Climate* 26.21, 8698–8704.
Elicki, Olaf and Christoph Breitkreuz (2016) *Die Entwicklung des Systems Erde* (Berlin: Springer Spektrum).
Ellis, Erle C. and Navin Ramankutty (2008) "Putting People in the Map: Anthropogenic Biomes of the World," *Frontiers in Ecology and the Environment* 6.8, 439–447.
Ericson, Jason P. et al. (2006) "Effective Sea-Level Rise and Deltas: Causes of Change and Human Dimension Implications," *Global and Planetary Change* 50. 1–2, 63–82.
French, Hugh M. (2007) *The Periglacial Environment* (Chichester: Wiley & Sons).
Giosan, Liviu et al. (2014) "Climate Change. Protect the World's Deltas," *Nature* 516.7529, 31–33.
Glaser, Rüdiger (2001) *Klimageschichte Mitteleuropas* (Darmstadt: Wissenschaftliche Buchgesellschaft).
Glaser, Rüdiger (2014) *Global Change: Das neue Gesicht der Erde* (Darmstadt: Primus Verlag).
Goudie, Andrew (2010) "Geomorphological Hazards and Global Climate Change," in *Geomorphological Hazards and Disaster Prevention*, ed. Irasema Alcantara-Ayala and Andrew Goudie (Cambridge: Cambridge University Press), 245–252.

Goudie, Andrew S. (2019) *Human Impact on the Natural Environment* (Blackwell: Wiley & Sons).
Goudie, Andrew and Heather Viles (2010) *Landscapes and Geomorphology: A Very Short Introduction* (Oxford: Oxford University Press).
Goudie, Andrew, S. and Heather Viles (2016) *Geomorphology in the Anthropocene* (Oxford: Oxford University Press).
Green, Sophie M. and Susan Page (2017) "Tropical Peatlands: Current Plight and the Need for Responsible Management," *Geology Today* 33.5, 174–179.
Hails, John R. (1977) "Applied Geomorphology in Coastal-Zone Planning and Management," in *Applied Geomorphology*, ed. John R. Hails (Amsterdam: Elsevier), 317–362.
Harrison, Stephan et al. (2019) "Uncertainty in Geomorphological Responses to Climate Change," *Climatic Change* 156.1–2, 69–86.
Hempel, Ludwig (1983) "Der Sandhaushalt als Hauptglied in der Geoökodynamik einer Ostfriesischen Insel. Abhängigkeiten von Natürlichen und Anthropogenen Kräften," *Geoökodynamik* 1.2, 87–104.
Hidore, John J. and John E. Oliver (1993) *Climatology: An Atmospheric Science* (New York: MacMillan).
Hoegh-Guldberg, Ove et al. (2018) "Impacts of 1.5 °C Global Warming on Natural and Human Systems," in *Global Warming of 1.5 °C. An IPCC Special Report on the Impacts of Global Warming of 1.5 °C above Pre-Industrial Levels and Related Global Greenhouse Gas Emission Pathways, in the Context of Strengthening the Global Response to the Threat of Climate Change, Sustainable Development, and Efforts to Eradicate Poverty*, ed. Valérie Masson-Delmotte et al. (Helsinki: IPCC Secretariat), 175–311.
Hooke, Roger LeB. (1994) "On the Efficacy of Humans as Geomorphic Agents," *GSA Today* 4.9, 222–224.
Hooke, Roger LeB. (2012) "Land Transformation by Humans: A Review," *GSA Today* 22.12, 4–10.
Huddart, David and Tim A. Stott (2020) *Earth Environments* (Singapore: Wiley & Sons).
Huggel, Christian, John J. Clague and Oliver Korup (2012) "Is Climate Change Responsible for Changing Landslide Activity in High Mountains?" *Earth Surface Processes and Landforms* 37.1, 77–91.
Hughes, Terry et al. (2003) "Climate Change, Human Impacts, and the Resilience of Coral Reefs" *Science* 301, 929–933.
IPCC (2007) *Climate Change 2007: The Physical Science Basis*. Contribution of Working Group I to the Fourth Assessment Report of the Intergovernmental Panel on Climate Change, ed. S. Solomon, D. Qin, M. Manning, Z. Chen, M. Marquis, K. B. Averyt, M. Tignor and H. L. Miller (Cambridge, UK and New York: Cambridge University Press), 996.
Jones, David K. C. (1993) "Global Warming and Geomorphology," *The Geographical Journal* 159.2, 124–130.
Kaplan, Jed O. et al. (2010) "Holocene Carbon Emissions as a Result of Anthropogenic Land Cover Change," *The Holocene* 21.5, 775–791.
Kellerer-Pirklbauer, Andreas, Gerhard K. Lieb, Michael Avian and Jonathan Carrivicks (2012) "Climate Change and Rock Fall Events in High Mountain Areas: Numerous and Extensive Rock Falls in 2007 at Mittlerer Burgstall, Central Austria," *Geografiska Annaler: Series A, Physical Geography* 94, 59–78.
Klein Goldewijk, Kees et al. (2011) "The HYDE 3.1 Spatially Explicit Database of Human-Induced Global Land-Use Change over the Past 12,000 Years," *Global Ecology and Biogeography* 20.1, 73–86.

Lancaster, Nicholas (1999) "Desert Environments," in *The Physical Geography of Africa*, ed. William M. Adams, Andrew S. Goudie and Antony R. Orme (Oxford: Oxford University Press), 211–237.

Lenton, Timothy M. et al. (2008) "Tipping Elements in the Earth's Climate System," *Proceedings of the National Academy of Sciences* 105.6, 1786–1793.

Lenton, Timothy M. et al. (2019) "Climate Tipping Points – too Risky to Bet against," *Nature* 575, 592–595.

Li, Peiyue, Hui Qian and Jianhua Wu (2014) "Accelerate Research on Land Creation," *Nature* 510.7503, 29–31.

Lowe, John and Michael Walker (2015) *Reconstructing Quaternary Environments* (London: Routledge).

Machguth, Horst et al. (2013) "The Future Sea-Level Rise Contribution of Greenland's Glaciers and Ice Caps," *Environmental Research Letters* 8.2, 1–14.

McLennan, Scott M. (1993) "Weathering and Global Denudation" *The Journal of Geology* 101.2, 295–303.

Mensching, Horst G. (1990) *Desertifikation: Ein weltweites Problem der ökologischen Verwüstung in den Trockengebieten der Erde* (Darmstadt: Wissenschaftliche Buchgesellschaft).

Mensching, Horst G. (1984) "Veränderungen des morphodynamischen Prozessgefüges durch Desertifikation in Dafur," in *Beiträge zur Morphodynamik im Relief des Jebel-Marra-Massivs und in seinem Vorland (Dafur/Republik Sudan)*, ed. Horst G. Mensching (Hamburg: Akademische Wissenschaften in Göttingen), 166–177.

Miller, J. Andrew and Nicolas P. Zégre (2014) "Mountaintop Removal Mining and Catchment Hydrology," *Water* 6.3, 472–499.

National Snow & Ice Data Center (2020) *Arctic Sea Ice News & Analysis*. <http://nsidc.org/arcticseaicenews/> (accessed 30 January 2020).

Noel, Brice et al. (2017) "A Tipping Point in Refreezing Accelerates Mass Loss of Greenland's Glaciers and Ice Caps," *Nature Communications* 8.1, 1–8.

Osterkamp, Tom E. and J. C. Jorgenson (2006) "Warming of Permafrost in the Arctic National Wildlife Refuge, Alaska," *Permafrost and Periglacial Processes* 17.1, 65–69.

Parola, Gilberto and Graziano Rossi (2008) "Upward Migration of Vascular Plants Following a Climate Warming Trend in the Alps," *Basic and Applied Ecology* 9.2, 100–107.

Pattyn, Frank et al. (2018) "The Greenland and Antarctic Ice Sheets under 1.5 °C Global Warming," *Nature Climate Change* 8.12, 1053–1061.

Phien-wej, Noppadol, Pham Huy Giao, and Prinya Nutalaya (2006) "Land Subsidence in Bangkok, Thailand," *Engineering Geology* 82.4, 187–201.

Reynard, Emmanuel, Christophe Lambiel and Stuart N. Lane (2012) "Climate Change and Integrated Analysis of Mountain Geomorphological Systems," *Geographica Helvetica* 67.1-2, 5–14.

Ritter, Dale F., R. Craig Kochel and Jerry R. Miller (2011) *Process Geomorphology* (Illinois: Waveland Press).

Robert, Christian and Romain Bousquet (2018) *Geowissenschaften: Die Dynamik des Systems Erde* (Berlin: Springer Spektrum).

Rockström, Johan et al. (2009) "A Safe Operating Space for Humanity," *Nature* 461.7263, 472–475.

Römer, Wolfgang (2012) "Late Quaternary Environmental Change and Human Interference in Africa," in *International Perspectives on Global Environmental Change*, ed. Stephen Young and Steven E. Silvern (Rijeka: IntechOpen), 253–274.

Rotzoll, Kolja and Charles H. Fletcher (2013) "Assessment of Groundwater Inundation as a Consequence of Sea-Level Rise," *Nature Climate Change* 3.5, 477–481.

Ruddiman, William F. (2014) *Earth Transformed* (New York: Freeman and Company).

Schaffartzik, Anke et al. (2014) "The Global Metabolic Transition: Regional Patterns and Trends of Global Material Flows, 1950–2010," *Global Environmental Change* 26, 87–97.

Slaymaker, Olaf (2000) "Global Environmental Change: The Global Agenda" in *Geomorphology, Human Activity and Global Environmental Change*, ed. Olaf Slaymaker (Chichester: Wiley), 3–20.

Schönwiese, Christian D. (1994) *Klimatologie* (Stuttgart: Ulmer).

Schönwiese, Christian D. et al. (2004) "Statistisch-Klimatologische Analyse des Hitzesommers 2003 in Deutschland," in *Klimastatusbericht* (Offenbach: Deutscher Wetterdienst), 123–132.

Schultz, Jürgen (2005) *The Ecozones of the World* (Berlin: Springer).

Seibold, Eugen and Wolfgang Berger (2017) *The Sea Floor: An Introduction to Marine Geology* (Cham: Springer).

Seneviratne, S. I. et al. (2012) "Changes in Climate Extremes and Their Impacts on the Natural Physical Environment," in *Managing the Risks of Extreme Events and Disasters to Advance Climate Change Adaptation in A Special Report of Working Groups I and II of the Intergovernmental Panel on Climate Change (IPCC)*, ed. C.B. Field et al. (Cambridge and New York: Cambridge University Press), 109–230.

Stanley, Steven M. (2005) *Earth System History* (New York: W. H. Freeman and Company).

Stocking, Michael, A. (1987) "Measuring Land Degradation," in *Land Degradation and Society*, ed. Piers Blaikie and Harold Brookfield (London: Routledge), 49–63.

Stocking, Michael, A. (1999) "Soil Erosion," in *The Physical Geography of Africa*, ed. William Mark Adams, Andrew S. Goudie and Antony R. Orme (Oxford: Oxford University Press), 326–341.

Syvitski, James P. M. (2008) "Deltas at Risk," *Sustainability Science* 3.1, 23–32.

Syvitski, James P. M. et al. (2009) "Sinking Deltas Due to Human Activities," *Nature Geoscience* 2.10, 681–686.

Taylor, David (1999) "Mountains," in *The Physical Geography of Africa*, ed. William Mark Adams, Andrew S. Goudie and Antony R. Orme (Oxford: Oxford University Press), 287–306.

Thomas, Michael, F. (2006) "Lessons from the Tropics for a Global Geomorphology," *Singapore Journal of Tropical Geography* 27, 111–127.

UNSD (United Nations, Department of Economic and Social Affairs) (2017) *Statistics Division*. <https://unstats.un.org/sdgs/report/2017/goal-12/> (accessed 10 January 2020).

Vitousek, Peter M. et al. (1997) "Human Domination of Earth's Ecosystems," *Science* 277.5325, 494–499.

Vitousek, Sean (2017) "Doubling of Coastal Flooding Frequency within Decades Due to Sea-Level Rise," *Scientific Reports* 7.1, 1–9.

Völkel, Jörg and Jörg Grunert (1990) "The Problem of Dune Formation and Dune Weathering during the Late Pleistocene and Holocene in the Southern Sahara and Sahel," *Zeitschrift für Geomorphologie* 34.1, 1–17.

Walther, Gian-Reto (2002) "Ecological Responses to Recent Climate Change," *Nature* 416.6879, 389–395.
Watson, Christopher S. et al. (2015) "Unabated Global Mean Sea-Level Rise over the Satellite Altimeter Era," *Nature Climate Change* 5.6, 565–568.
Weischet, Wolfgang and Wilfried Endlicher (2012) *Einführung in die Allgemeine Klimatologie* (Stuttgart: Borntraeger).
White, Ian Dean, Derek N. Mottershead and S. J. Harrison (1984) *Environmental Systems* (London: Wiley & Sons).
Wilkinson, Bruce H. (2005) "Humans as Geologic Agents. A Deep-Time Perspective," *Geological Society America* 33.3, 161–164.
Yang, Xiaoping (2010) "Desertification and Land Degradation" in *Geomorphological Hazards and Disaster Prevention*, ed. Irasema Alcántara-Ayala and Andrew S. Goudie (Cambridge: Cambridge University Press), 189–198.
Yi, Shuang et al. (2015) "An Increase in the Rate of Global Mean Sea-Level Rise since 2010," *Geophysical Research Letters* 42.10, 3998–4006.
Yoshikawa, Kenji and Koichiro Harada (1995) "Observations on Nearshore Pingo Growth, Adventdalen, Spitsbergen," *Permafrost and Periglacial Processes* 6.4, 361–372.
Zoccarato, Claudia, Philip S. J. Minderhoud and Piedro Teatini (2018) "The Role of Sedimentation and Natural Compaction in a Prograding Delta: Insights from the Mega Mekong Delta, Vietnam," *Scientific Reports* 8.1, 1–12.

Gerbern S. Oegema
The Apocalyptic Imagination and Climate Change

1 Introduction

Apocalypticism is *en vogue* again and the connection between apocalypticism and climate change is not only original but also highly relevant.[1] Throughout history and culture apocalyptic literature has many times emerged and re-emerged in times of political and social crises, often marking changes in the mindset of people unnoticed by the official historical records.[2] And indeed, also changes in the climate have always been part of the apocalyptic imagery. When dealing with issues of a global scale, apocalypticism is not used to talk about small things and politically carefully negotiated steps like every-day politics; instead, it tends to put things in a world embracing perspective and likes to envision dramatic changes of a cosmic nature; this is what the apocalypse is made of. Therefore, to see the interest in apocalypticism re-emerge in our times, whether in the Bible, literature, film, popular culture,[3] or theology,[4] could point to possible tectonic shifts in society and to changes in the mindset of people;[5] it is therefore reason enough to take it seriously. But let us begin with the history.

1.1 History and Reception

As most scholars agree,[6] apocalypticism begins in the Hebrew Bible and is related to prophecy. It finds its first climax in the Book of Daniel and the

---

[1] On apocalypticism, see, for example, Siegemund (2018) and Oegema (forthcoming).
[2] See Körtner (1988).
[3] See DiTommaso (2014).
[4] See the Encyclical Letter "Laudato Si'" of the Holy Father Francis on "Care for our Common Home."
[5] Just before traveling to Aachen to attend the conference on November 15–16, 2018, there were several demonstrations in various countries such as Canada, Germany, and Belgium, against climate change. Since then, many more demonstrations have taken place under the leadership and inspiration of Greta Thunberg. Also, David McMillan, Frederic Morin, and Meredith Erickson published a cookbook which is titled Surviving the Apocalypse: Another Cookbook of Sorts (2018).
[6] Examples are Lücke, Reuss, Hilgenfeld, Gunkel, Mowinckel, Collins, Hanson, Rowland, among others. See also the history of research in Schmidt (1976).

https://doi.org/10.1515/9783110730203-003

Maccabean Revolt in 167–164 BCE, and their common resistance against the Syrian oppression. During the Greco-Roman period apocalypticism dominated the sectarian movement associated with the Dead Sea Scrolls, as well as the Jesus movement, influenced the Bar Kockba Revolt, until Rabbinic Judaism began to transform its more radical elements into a more general messianic hope for the future. It is a dominant feature of the New Testament and the Early Church, influenced John the Baptist, Jesus of Nazareth and the Apostle Paul, and especially the Revelation of John and its resistance against the Roman Empire. It continued in the many later Judeo-Christian apocalyptic traditions that found their way in Late Antiquity, in the Qur'an, and the Middle Ages, even until today.[7] However, presently it is mostly used as a rather general term for everything "apocalyptic" with a doomsday scenario, often also combined with huge natural catastrophes, and popularized in movies and on the internet. It is therefore important to define what we are talking about.

1.2 Definition of "Apocalypticism"

Whereas there is no consensus on how to define "apocalypticism," the term "apocalyptic imagination" was coined by John J. Collins, author and editor of many books about apocalypticism (Collins 1979, 1999). Collins has spearheaded research into apocalypticism since the 1970s, originally in response to a booklet by Klaus Koch *Ratlos vor der Apokalyptik* from 1970.[8] Whereas this was a small booklet, it led to a very productive period of research that until today does not seem to have come to an end. It marked the rediscovery of the relevance of apocalypticism and was written in a period in modern history, which also saw a growing interest in social and anti-war protests, student revolts, liberation theology, feminism, and indeed also in climate change. It was a time of industrialization and capitalism that had no mercy for the planet; there was pollution everywhere. And it was the time of the report of the Club of Rome published in 1975 on the state of our planet. I am not saying that there is a direct connection between all of these phenomena, especially between the rediscovery of apocalypticism and climate change. However, I do believe that it was no coincidence that this all happened at the same time. One aspect of apocalypticism, as I will

---

[7] See Oegema (1999; 2001; 2003a; 2003b; 2008; 2012a; 2012b; 2013c).
[8] Whereas the term "apocalypticism" and its German equivalent "Apokalyptik" refer more to a phenomenon, mindset or worldview, the expression "apocalyptic imagination" tries to describe the creative process behind it, and "apocalypse" is the actual literary genre, in which both are mostly found.

explain later, is namely its sensitivity to reflect on or represent the *Zeitgeist* or mindset of an epoch, whether in antiquity or in modern times.

Collins himself focuses both on the genre "apocalypse," as researched and outlined in the thematic Journal *Semeia* 14 of 1979 (Collins 1979), and the question what the characteristics are of the genre. This marks one direction, which research into apocalypticism has taken, namely a more literary one. There are other approaches as well, but for now it is worth quoting his definition of the genre "apocalypse," as it has defined much of later scholarship, albeit mostly of a literary and historical character:

> A genre of revelatory literature with a narrative framework, in which a revelation is mediated by an otherworldly being to a human recipient, disclosing a transcendent reality which is both temporal, insofar as it envisages eschatological salvation, and spatial insofar as it involves another, supernatural world. (Collins 1979: 9)

A definition was nevertheless necessary, as apocalyptic literature as a whole let alone something even more vague like the phenomenon "apocalypticism" is difficult to grasp. For one, it is surely not limited to the Hebrew Bible, but is found in many ancient near Eastern cultures and also beyond. However, as to date there is no consensus on a definition of apocalypticism, there exist different levels or approaches to study it, whether as a genre, as an historical phenomenon, or as a world view, and there is also the question of its social relevance and relation to other worldviews, philosophical, and theological ones. Sometimes it seems best just to identify its key aspects instead of trying to come to a definition (as I will do this at the end of this article).[9]

This is partly due to the inter-cultural and cross-historical nature of it. Apocalypticism is found in Judaism, Christianity and Islam as well as in Greek, Roman and Egyptian ancient cultures, but also, for example in early modern Maya culture, in Hinduism, in popular Hollywood movies and in twentieth-century Japan.[10] In other words, to get a sense of the connections between the study of apocalypticism and worldviews, it is worth to have a brief look at its history of research. Coming from there we can then better define its present-day relevance, especially in light of climate change.

---

9 See on this also the excellent article by Patrick Becker and Steffen Jöris (2016).
10 See some of the other articles in this volume.

2 History of Research

According to the histories of research of Joachim M. Schmidt (1976) and John J. Collins (1979, 1999, 2007) the academic study of apocalypticism found its origin in the investigations of the Book of Daniel and the Revelation of John and reached its first culmination in the concise overviews of Friedrich Lücke, Eduard Reuss and Adolf Hilgenfeld in the early nineteenth century. It developed further into the history of literature as well as in the religion- and tradition-historical approaches or models of explanations of the twentieth century (Gunkel 1895 and Mowinckel; Collins 1979, 1999, 2007; Hanson 1979, Rowland 1982). However, some of the early overviews can still be of importance today, if they are adapted to and incorporated with newer discoveries and methodological innovations from the Dead Sea Scrolls to sociological approaches (see Cook 1995).

2.1 The History of Literature: Approach I

Joachim Schmidt differentiates in his 1967 *Habilitationsschrift* "Die jüdische Apokalyptik" (Schmidt 1976) on the history of research of Jewish apocalypticism between the so-called older and younger phase of the history of literature models of explanation (called phases I and II). What one can learn from this approach is that the definition of the genre "apocalypse" always comes with a description of its religious contents as well as with efforts to date the various stages of the genre. However, in a comparison with prophecy, apocalypticism has often received the less favorable characteristics. As for a modern definition of both prophecy and apocalypticism, it is important to point at the work of Paul Hanson (1979) and the influence it has had on recent scholarship. Hanson defines apocalypticism in terms of visionary movement, eschatological perspective and symbolic universe, rivalry groups and contradictions between hopes and experiences, in order to distinguish it from prophecy. Behind the distinction is the supposition that prophecy has an historical worldview and apocalypticism a mythological one. Even if this distinction recently has been questioned by, for example, Lester Grabbe (see Grabbe and Haak 2003) and even if one would rephrase it differently, there is still much to be said about it. Apocalypticism has a strong mythological contents and appeal.

2.2 The Religion and Tradition: Historical Approach

The religion and tradition-historical model of explanation of apocalypticism as developed since the end of the nineteenth century is summarized by Schmidt as follows:

> With the use of the tradition historical approach Gunkel has sharply opposed prophecy ad apocalypticism. The theological importance, which he gave to the latter, may explain the sharpness of his judgment. But there are several objections to be made against his argumentation, which by no means has lost its actuality. Above all and despite his efforts of a historical understanding of apocalypticism he has not given the aforementioned opposition any differentiation. [. . .] On the other hand Gunkel has been led by the image of the ideal prophet. Because for him prophecy was the summit of Israelite history of religion anyways, compared to prophecy's creative genius apocalypticism had to take upon it a contrasting role [. . .]. (Schmidt 1979: 249)

In the work of Hermann Gunkel, we see that prophecy and apocalypticism are treated as two totally different and contrasting intellectual modes, which mutual opposition is defined foremost on the basis of its theological characterization. As for the tradition- and redaction-history, one should not overlook that many older and newer commentaries on both the prophecies and the apocalypses use these methods as a (or the only) bridge between the actual text, the various stages of its development and their respective historical situations. Partly behind this may be an aversion of and opposition to apocalypticism in Protestant theology since Martin Luther, to which the upheavals of the Reformation and the 30-year war, especially also the Anabaptist and their New Jerusalem in Münster may have contributed not a little. Similar reactions can be observed in the case of Bar Kochba and the Rabbinic aversion against everything radical apocalyptic and militant in the second century CE and the same with Sabbatai Zevi in the seventeenth century.

2.3 The Theological Approach

Whereas as of lately little attention has been given to a more theological approach of prophetic and apocalyptic literature, this approach used to be dominant at least until one or two generations ago. There may, however, still be some advantage in giving a theological classification of both types of literature in the way they reflect on central religious questions, such as on the origin of evil and the time of redemption. As these theological classifications do not necessarily have to be appropriated by denominational interests or by theological biases, they can very well serve to further elucidate common and distinctive features. Theological and religiously relevant reflections remain to be relevant as long as society is developing. This growing awareness of the theological relevance of apocalypticism has been very well observed and phrased by John J. Collins:

> The growth in appreciation of symbolic and mythological literature has generally led to a more positive assessment of the apocalypses. Apocalyptic imagery is less often viewed as idle speculation but is seen to express an interpretation of historical situations (often political crises) and to shape the human response to those situations [. . .]. In this respect, the existential interpretation of apocalypticism offered by Bultmann and Schmithals is noteworthy, even if it has not always done full justice to the allusiveness of the mythological symbolism. Martin Buber's sweeping condemnation of apocalyptic determinism and of the use of pseudonymity as an evasion of responsibility can now be seen as a misunderstanding of the function of apocalypses. Equally, the view that the apocalyptic use of history is directed only to a calculation of the end-time has been discredited [. . .]. Instead, the apocalyptic reviews of history serve to highlight the short period before the end, which is the actual time of the author, as a period of decision. (Collins 1979: 360–361)

2.4 The History of Literature Approach and the Definition of the Genre "Apocalypse" in the Latter Part of the Twentieth Century

Whereas Joachim Schmidt discusses mainly the older German scholarship on apocalypticism, John J. Collins, who has just been quoted, offers an overview of the more recent and especially English- speaking studies. Collins sees in the work of Klaus Koch (1970) and the *Society of Biblical Literature "Genres Project"* two important contributions to the modern study of apocalypticism. In the scholarship of Klaus Koch, a differentiation is made between the "apocalypse" as literary genre and "apocalypticism" as historical movement.

Despite the ongoing critique of, for instance, Lester Grabbe, the stage had now been set for a much more detailed study of apocalypses as individual literary products, both concerning their theological contents and their historical and social setting. Apart from other aspects, like the expression "One like a Man", the use of the Hebrew Bible in the apocalypses, the question of traditional sources and the relation between wisdom and apocalypticism, especially the question of the place of apocalyptic literature in Early Judaism has played an important role. As far as the question of literary genres is concerned, it is important to note that during the past decades also in the study of prophetic literature form criticism has gone through important transitional phases and that the question about the intersection between form and life setting is still an extremely important one.

2.5 The Social Setting Approach

After the literary, history or religion, tradition-historical and the newer literary approach of J.J. Collins et al. from the late eighteenth until the middle of the twentieth century a newer approach to apocalypticism was formulated in the efforts to determine its social origins and settings. In his book on *Prophecy and Apocalypticism: The Postexilic Setting* (Cook 1995), Stephen L. Cook offers us his view on some of the so-called proto-apocalyptic texts Ezekiel 38–39; Zechariah 1–8 and Joel and the groups behind them. Contrary to the previous scholarship of Paul Hanson and Otto Plöger, Cook does not believe that the apocalyptic groups are to be found among the socially and economically deprived classes and the marginal and socially alienated figures. Instead, while turning to sociological and anthropological analyses of apocalyptic groups and typologically characterizing them according to their relationship to their own society and to their own or other cultures, apocalypticism may very well have emerged from a wider variety of social matrices and have been under the leadership of many kinds of figures, and thus be much more than the response of a sext to a political crisis. So, instead of apocalypticism being the response of a small sect to a political crisis, apocalypticism may very well have originated from mainstream groups within a society, and instead represent a more universal mindset than a minority opinion.

2.6 The Reception Historical Approach (1990–2008)

During the past two decades a number of studies on apocalypticism have dealt with the history of its reception in antiquity beyond the Second Temple Period. To begin with, *Apocalypticism in the Mediterranean World and in the Near East*, a collection of essays edited by David Hellholm in 1989, is a milestone in research at the end of the twentieth century and represents the papers presented at a colloquium in Uppsala in 1979. Three thematic fields and approaches have been dealt with in this impressive book: 1) the conceptual world of apocalypticism, 2) the literary genre of the apocalypse and 3) the sociology of apocalypticism and the life setting of the apocalypses. At the end of the collection, K. Rudolph emphasizes the following important problematic fields for future research: 1) Jewish-Christian apocalypticism, 2) apocalypticism of primitive and early Christianity, 3) the relation between apocalypticism and Gnosticism, and 4) the influence of Iranian-Zoroastrian tradition on Biblical apocalypticism. For future research he points at the importance of the literary scientific and sociological methods as well as the need of an intensive study of the reception history of apocalypticism until today. Some of this may be covered in an important follow-up conference in 2021 in Munich.

2.7 The Intellectual History Approach

As for the intellectual history approach and especially for the hypothesis of a common apocalyptic worldview, in a collection of articles edited by Gabriele Boccaccini and John J. Collins, *The Early Enoch Literature* from 2007, we find some very useful methodological arguments and criteria of how to compare two different literary corpora, in this case the Books of *1 Enoch* and the Dead Sea Scrolls. The articles in this collection are useful as an analogy to the problem of a relation between prophecy and apocaylypticism, as the Dead Sea Scrolls offer many actualizing interpretations of the Prophetic writings and *1 Enoch* is an early representative of Jewish apocayticism.

However, I want to end this brief history of research to get to the broader question of the intellectual dimension of apocalypticism and the relevance for today. In his book *Weltangst und Weltende: Eine theologische Interpretation der Apokalyptik* (1988) or in English *The End of the World: A Theological Interpretation of Apocalypticism* (1995) Ulrich Körtner addresses the issue of apocalyptic anxiety by offering a theological and philosophical evaluation of what we call "apocalyptic." In particular, Körtner looks at how theology, responding in pastoral sensitivity, should deal with apocalyptic fears and anxieties. He concludes that real meaning and hope for the world is possible only after the world's inhabitants deal constructively with the stark reality of the world's end.

In order to reach his hypothesis of a relevance of apocalypticism for theology today, Körtner plows deep through much of twentieth century intellectual history and sees various moments, in which the end of the world was thought of as philosophically and theologically relevant. Reviewed are, for example:
- the *Untergang des Abendlandes*, by philosophers like Oswald Spengler (1918);
- theories about the end of the world from a natural science point of view (see the work of Teilhard de Jardin; 1946);
- the limits of economic growth (Club of Rome, 1975); and
- the atomic catastrophe, etc. (1982).

One cannot separate climate change from these broader trends in society. And obviously Körtner would have included climate change in his book, if he had written it in our days, as the discussion continues.

3 The Apocalyptic Worldview

We thus come to the question of the apocalyptic worldview and how to connect ancient apocalypticism with both intellectual history and with modern views about the end of world. When trying to summarize what ancient apocalypticism as a phenomenon (and not so much as a literary genre or a feature of Ancient Jewish literature) is about, the key characteristics of the apocalyptic worldview are according to me as follows.

It consists of a myth of origin with the search for the origin of evil often leading to the concept of "fallen angels" or demons, it often has an ethical and cosmological dualism between good and evil, which can also be personalized in God and Satan, Christ and Antichrist, angels and demons, and it understands time as periodized and eschatological: that it to say unfolding in phases towards a final end. The apocalyptic mindset, which is mostly but not exclusively found in the post-Exilic prophets and apocalyptic authors from Hellenistic and Roman period, sees mankind's time on earth being limited between creation and eschaton (Urzeit and Endzeit). It derives from this also the understanding of the eschaton as a new creation, in addition to concepts like a messianic age, Golden Age, which exact time can be calculated. The expected end or latter-day turn-around is often coming with the help of a messianic savior figure, human or cosmic.

However, before this a humanly and/or divinely induced catastrophic end precedes the new world. Often finds an emphasis on human sin, caused by fallen angels/demons, who are responsible for the evil in the world throughout history, with good and bad times interchanging in a periodized history dependent on whether people repent or improve their behavior. As for the latter, there is the possibility of repentance, which is found more often in prophetic literature than in apocalyptic literature, which sees the end more often as an unavoidable catastrophic. The latter results in the observation that the apocalyptic worldview is much more pessimistic and often has detailed doomsday scenarios than other worldviews.

We derive these characteristics from an analysis of the multiple examples of the genre "apocalypse," mainly from antiquity, as they have influenced the later Judeo-Christian tradition, but at the same time we assume that they also reflect elements of a wider ancient apocalyptic worldview, as we also witness it through other apocalypses, from Greek and Roman to Iranian and Egyptian and beyond.

Having said this about the phenomenon "apocalypticism," we can therefore also open up the possibility of a second dimension to apocalypticism, namely as an intellectual mode of thinking or psychological state of mind. This *Zeitgeist* of a certain epoch or expression thereof, maybe even a mindset, when stripped off its mythological language reveals a deeper and universal mindset, which could and can easily be adapted in other cultures and periods in history. This way of thinking reflects a deeper sense of universal *Weltangst* and a fear for the near end of this world, a trend that can be nurtured by certain social, economic and political circumstances, and depending on the situation can be actualized or become dormant again, even in our own days. In other words, it may be a dormant "Angst" present in all of us, that can be triggered through catastrophic events into a more global and deeper felt anxiety about the end of the world.

4 Relevance for Today

When looking at this universal dimension of apocalypticism as expression of a *Zeitgeist*, one can certainly connect it with the present-day debate about climate change and environmental catastrophes, maybe not as the outcome of what ancient apocalypses had predicted, but as expressions of a broader fear that our planet is nearing its end. This end is obviously scientifically argued for and is not based on mythological concepts, as our worldview is based on scientific facts and arguments.

In particular, we are using a Cartesian and technocratic worldview and methodology instead of apocalyptic and demonological worldview and methodology. We argue on the basis of "cause-effect" and used statistics for all of our claims instead of relying on secret knowledge and magical practices. We have technical, medical, and climate experts instead apocalyptic authors and interpreters of the signs of the times. However, when the mythological worldview is unpacked, a theological approach to "la condition humaine" and postmodernism remains relevant, and it is worth to look at the communalities and shared interests.

5 Lessons for Today

My thesis is that when one takes away the mythological character of the apocalyptic language and goes to the heart of its existential and theological message, knowing that its "theology" has always been criticized and sidelined by the established Christian and Jewish theologies, one can certainly still learn a lot from it. I see the following lessons for today:

1) When connecting evil and sin to its potentially catastrophic outcomes, as the apocalypses do, one can emphasize the human responsibility for and contribution to global warming and its partly already real and potentially future catastrophic outcomes. Once we acknowledge that it has been caused by us as human beings, we also have to see that it may already have developed its own momentum. Like in the ancient apocalypses, the world seems to be heading towards a catastrophic end that is hard to stop.
2) When seeing the opposition of much apocalyptic thinking and apocalyptic movements from the side of the establishment in the history of apocalypticism, one can learn from it how to deal with opposition: we should not therefore give up trying to look for peaceful solutions.
3) When seeing the historical perspective, in which many apocalypses understand evil, sin and catastrophe, one can learn from it to also put climate change and catastrophe in an historical perspective: it didn't happen all of a sudden, but was prepared in the past and is due to human inaction heading towards a catastrophe. One can learn from the apocalypses the importance of how previous generations have dealt with catastrophes.
4) When seeing the interconnectedness of everything in apocalyptic literature, namely that the sin of the individual and that of the group and that of society at large in the end has consequences for the whole earth, both in good and in bad terms, one can learn from it. One cannot hide and say, as long as I have it good here and now, everything is fine, because in one way or another everything one does has consequences for the rest of humanity.
5) This historical perspective also opens up the possibility of real change and the chance for a possibly winning fight against climate change in order to improve the life of future generations on earth. And obviously, here we have to work with statistics and scientific models and not demonology, magic and calculations of the end of days, but see them in historical perspective. And thus, the apocalyptic narrative and discourse teaches us to place things in an historical perspective, see how everything is connected with each other and how expressions of human concerns can function as wake-up calls and signs of hope.
6) And what do we do with the apocalyptic expectation of a new heaven and earth, paradise, a messianic age or a Golden Age? Obviously, already now technology offers many improvements of life and the quality of life, both for the individual and society, compared with just one generation ago. Artificial Intelligence may help us manage a more and more complex world, in which we do not have to fantasize about immigrating to Mars, but already in the here and now can improve our life by improving the climate on our own planet.

7) And finally, we have a pastoral responsibility as those, who understand and have access to this "higher knowledge" to care for those, who are in despair and sink into anxiety and depression because of the end of everything that now seems to be so near. This is a real and growing problem among young people, anxiety and depression, and maybe it has something to do with doomsday thinking about the end of our planet. And so, my final word is that when we see the apocalyptic dimension of climate change, we have no other choice but to take action.

Bibliography

Becker, Patrick and Steffen Jöris (2016) "Towards a Scientific Designation: Apocalypticism in Biblical and Modern Studies," in *Horizons in Biblical Theology* 38.1, 22–44.

Boccaccini, Gabriele and John Joseph Collins (eds) (2007) *The Early Enoch Literature* (Leiden: Brill).

Charles, Robert Henry (1913) *A Critical History of the Doctrine of a Future life, in Israel, in Judaism, and in Christianity, or, Hebrew, Jewish, and Christian Eschatology from Pre-prophetic Times till the Close of the New Testament Canon* (London: A&C Black).

Collins, John Joseph (ed) (1979) *Apocalypse: The Morphology of a Genre* (Semeia 14) (Missoula: Scholars Press).

Collins, John Joseph, Bernard McGinn and Stephen Stein (eds) (1999) *The Encylopedia of Apocalypticism: Vol. I: The Origins of Apocalypticism in Judaism and Christianity* (New York: Continuum).

Cook, Stephen L. (1995) *Prophecy and Apocalypticism: The Postexilic Setting* (Minneapolis: Fortress).

DiTommaso, Lorenzo (2014) "Apocalypticism and Popular Culture," in *The Oxford Handbook of Apocalyptic Literature*, ed. John J. Collins (Oxford: Oxford University Press), 473–509.

Grabbe, Lester and Robert D. Haak (eds) (2003) *Knowing the End from the Beginning: The Prophetic, Apocalyptic and their Relationships* (London: T&T Clark).

Gunkel, Hermann (1895) *Schöpfung und Chaos in Urzeit und Endzeit: eine Religionsgeschichtliche Untersuchung über Gen. 1 und Ap. Joh. 12. Mit Beiträgen von Heinrich Zimmern* (Göttingen: Vandenhoeck & Ruprecht).

Hanson, Paul D. (1979) *The Dawn of Apocalyptic: The Historical and Sociological Roots of Jewish Apocalyptic Eschatology*, revised Edition (Philadelphia: Fortress Press).

Hellholm, David (1989) *Apocalypticism in the Mediterranean World and in the Near East* (Tübingen: Mohr).

Hilgenfeld, Adolf (1869) *Messias Judaeorum, Libris Eorum Paulo ante et Paulo post Christum natum conscriptis illustratus* (Leipzig: Fues 1869).

Koch, Klaus (1970) *Ratlos vor der Apokalyptik: eine Streitschrift über ein Vernachlässigtes Gebiet der Bibelwissenschaft und die Schädlichen Auswirkungen auf Theologie und Philosophie* (Gütersloh: Mohn).

Körtner, Ulrich H.J. (1988) *Weltangst und Weltende. Eine theologische Interpretation der Apokalyptik* (Göttingen: Vandenhoeck & Ruprecht).

Lücke, Friedrich (1852) *Versuch einer Vollständigen Einleitung in die Offenbarung des Johannes oder Allgemeine Untersuchungen über die Apokalyptische Literatur* (Bonn: Weber 1852).

McMillan, David, Frederic Morin and Meredith Erickson (eds) (2018) *Joe Beef Surviving the Apocalypse. Another Cookbook of Sorts* (New York: Alfred A. Knopf).

Mowinckel, Sigmund (2002) *The Spirit and the Word. Prophecy and Tradition in Ancient Israel* (Minneapolis: Augsburg Press 2002).

Oegema, Gerbern S. (1999) *Zwischen Hoffnung und Gericht. Untersuchungen zur Rezeption der Apokalyptik im Frühen Christentum und Judentum* (Wissenschaftliche Monographien zum Alten und Neuen Testament 82) (Neukirchen-Vluyn: Neukirchener Verlag).

Oegema, Gerbern S. (2001) *Apokalypsen* (Jüdische Schriften aus Hellenistisch-Römischer Zeit VI.1.5.) (Gütersloh: Gütersloher Verlagshaus).

Oegema, Gerbern S. (2003a) "Conceptions de l'Âge Messianiques dans le Judaïsme," in *Les Représentations du Temps dans les Religions*, ed. Öhnan Tunca (Liège: Librairie Droz), 75–85.

Oegema, Gerbern S. (2003b) "Die Daniel-Rezeption in der Alten Kirche," in *Europa, Tausendjähriges Reich und Neue Welt. Zwei Jahrtausende Geschichte und Utopie in der Rezeption des Danielbuches*, ed. Mariano Delgano et al. (Freiburg-Stuttgart: Universitätsverlag Kohlhammer), 84–104.

Oegema, Gerbern S. (2008) "Back to the Future in the Early Church: The Use of the Book of Daniel in Early Patristic Eschatology," in *The Function of Ancient Historiography*, ed. Patricia Kirkpatrick et al. (Edinburgh: T. & T. Clark), 186–198.

Oegema, Gerbern S. (2012a) *The Apocalyptic Interpretation of the Bible: Essays on Apocalypticism and Biblical Interpretation in Early Judaism, the Apostle Paul, the Historical Jesus and Their Reception History* (Edinburgh: T. & T. Clark / Continuum).

Oegema, Gerbern S. (2012b) "The Heritage of Jewish Apocalypticism in Late-Antique and Early Medieval Judaism, Christianity and Islam," in *Vehicles of Transmission, Translation, and Transformation in Medieval Cultures*, ed. Robert Wisnovsky et al. (Brepols: Cursor Mundi, UCLA Center for Medieval Studies, Turnhout), 103–129.

Oegema, Gerbern S. (2012c) "Prophecy and Apocalypticism," in *The Apocalyptic Interpretation of the Bible: Essays on Apocalypticism and Biblical Interpretation in Early Judaism, the Apostle Paul, the Historical Jesus and Their Reception History*, ed. Gerbern S. Oegema (Edinburgh: T& T Clark / Continuum Edinburgh), 3–16.

Oegema, Gerbern S. (forthcoming) "Climate Change as Apocalypse," in: *Journal of the Council for Research on Religion* 3.

Reuss, Eduard (1892) *Die Propheten* (Braunschweig: Schwetschke).

Rowland, Christopher (1982) *The Open Heaven: A Study of Apocalyptic in Judaism and Early Christianity* (New York: Crossroad).

Schmidt, Joachim (1976) *Die jüdische Apokalyptik. Die Geschichte ihrer Erforschung von den Anfängen bis zu den Textfunden von Qumran* (Neukirchen-Vluyn: Neukirchen Verlag).

Schmidt, Johann Michael (1976) *Die Jüdische Apokalyptik: Die Geschichte ihrer Erforschung von den Anfängen bis zu den Textfunden von Qumran* (Neukirchen-Vluyn: Neukirchener Verlag).

Siegemund, Axel (2018) "Umwelttechnik. Eine Apokalyptische Praxis?," in *Theologie im Konzert der Wissenschaften: Festschrift für Harry Noormann zum 70. Geburtstag*, ed. Monika Fuchs and Marco Hofheinz (Stuttgart: Kohlhammer), 167–182.

Spengler, Oswald (1918) *Der Untergang des Abendlandes. Umrisse einer Morphologie der Weltgeschichte* (Vienna: Braumüller).

Yoshiko Reed, Annette (2005) *Fallen Angels and the History of Judaism and Christianity: The Reception of Enochic Literature* (New York: Cambridge University Press).

Marco Caracciolo
Narrative and the Texture of Catastrophe

1 Introduction

As I write these words in October 2018, the Internet brims with images of the deadly earthquake and tsunami that recently struck Indonesia, killing more than four thousand people in and around Palu.[1] In a few days or weeks at most, this event will have fused, in the memory of most Westerners, with a long series of natural disasters that hit "too far from home" to leave more than trace amounts of emotion. From news reports to documentary film, visions of disaster can rivet our attention and resonate with apocalyptic anxieties, but their impact tends to be tragically short-lived. The reasons for this forgetfulness are complex and reflect a tangle of psychological, cultural, and technological factors: how human morality developed, over the course of evolutionary history, to cope with situations close at hand and not at a mediatized remove (see Greene 2003: 849); the perceived separation between the "safeness" of the West and precarious living in the developing world; and habituation to the daily visual bombardment of mass media, which in turn depends on the technical facility with which images are constantly being reproduced, spread, and discarded. Underlying all this is a basic fact about visual perception: vision is a "distal" sense in that it allows us to perceive things from what is, in many cases and certainly in the case of depictions of a tsunami half a world away, a safe distance.

This chapter explores how verbal narrative may render the lived experience of catastrophe in ways that reduce the physical distance associated with mediatic representation and visual experience more generally. This power of narrative to recreate the immediacy of experience is what researchers in narrative theory have discussed under the rubric of "what it's like" factor (Herman 2009: chap. 6): storytelling, the argument goes, can immerse readers or audience members in lifelike scenarios rich in emotional significance – scenarios that capture effectively what it is like to be in a particular situation. This immersive potential of story is vital to sensitizing Western audiences to the immense challenges

---

[1] While working on this chapter the author received funding from the European Research Council (ERC) under the European Union's Horizon 2020 research and innovation program (grant agreement no. 714166). Thanks also go to Gry Ulstein for her insightful suggestions and stimulating discussions on weird fiction.

involved in anthropogenic climate change and its catastrophic consequences.[2] I suggest that, for this potential to be realized fully, storytelling has to complement predominantly visual imagery with the other senses, and particularly with the "proximal" sense of touch. Fictional narrative in the genre of the novel, through its formal sophistication, serves as an egregious example of how narrative can develop a defamiliarizing alternative to the profusion of mediatic images of catastrophe, bringing us closer than any purely visual representation can to the affective texture of the experience of disaster.

I use the word "texture" advisedly. Texture is haptic pattern, such as the rugged feel of wood or the smoothness of silk; texture is form for the nonvisual senses. In a 2009 contribution to the field of cognitive poetics, Peter Stockwell also foregrounds texture and its role in literary reading; he defines it as "the experienced quality of textuality" (2009: 1). My approach shares with Stockwell's an interest in the experience of narrative and how it can be modulated by stylistic strategies in the context of prose fiction. However, rather than building on the link between text and texture, I see texture as coupled with the sense of touch. Texture is an experienced haptic quality that can be evoked by verbal language through ad-hoc stylistic choices that reduce the imaginative distance between readers and a storyworld and thus elicit feelings of immersion or physical presence – as if we could touch, rather than merely distally see, the narrated characters and situations.[3]

Moreover, I see the form of texture as fundamentally open to the extratextual realities that underlie the experience and complex causal history of catastrophe. The openness of texture as a formal concept reflects work in an important strand of contemporary literary scholarship known as New Formalism. Caroline Levine (2015) has argued for an expanded understanding of form to include social dynamics – such as networks and hierarchies – as well as literary strategies. The definition of form Levine adopts is deliberately broad: "shapes and configurations, all ordering principles, all patterns of repetition and difference" (2015: 3). Within this general framework, Levine assigns central importance to narrative, a macro-form that – she writes – "affords [. . .] careful attention to the ways in which forms come together, and to what happens when and after they meet"

---

[2] See also Erin James's discussion of the ecocritical relevance of the experience of immersion: "econarratological readings of narrative storyworlds, via their analysis of the textual cues that aid the immersion of readers into subjective spaces, times, and experiences, help us appreciate the fact that aesthetic transformations of the real really do stand to reshape individual and collective environmental imaginations. That reshaping is an essential role that literature can play in protecting the earth" (James 2015: 39).

[3] For discussion of immersion as presence, see Kuzmičová (2012).

(2015: 19). In the context of this chapter, I'll stage the meeting of two forms; one of them exists on an extremely broad, cultural level, the other is a textual form well-known to narratologists – namely, the evocation of characters' consciousness (see Cohn 1978; Herman 2007; Caracciolo 2014). The first form is the general configuration of humanity's relationship with the "nonhuman" realities of geophysical or climatological processes: is that form a linear hierarchy with the human at the top, for instance? Or is it cyclical? Or is it a more intricate shape, like the tangle or mesh favored by nonhuman-oriented theorists (discussed in more detail in the next section)?[4] The second form I want to explore is the lived experience of disaster, as it affects the characters of a catastrophic narrative and as it is rendered by way of consciousness evocation – that is, through stylistic choices (for instance, internal focalization or metaphorical language) that convey the felt qualities of the characters' private experiences. My main claim is that tactile patterns are crucial to the translation of the abstract form of human-nonhuman relations into an experience that can be pinpointed at the level of both textual strategies and reader responses. I will discuss the reasons for this foregrounding of touch in the next two sections. In the section that follows, I turn to a concrete example of catastrophic narrative in fiction that uses tactile experience to move beyond a distal account of disaster, immersing readers in a highly vivid – and unsettling – scenario: namely, Jeff VanderMeer's Southern Reach trilogy (VanderMeer 2014a; 2014b; 2014c).

Throughout this discussion, I prefer the terms "disaster" and "catastrophe" to "apocalypse." There is no doubt that the imagination of climate change taps into an emotional vocabulary and cultural repertoire that are fundamentally apocalyptic in a distinctly religious sense, as this volume as a whole demonstrates. However, it seems to me that there are dangers in foregrounding that parallel between anthropogenic catastrophe and end-of-the-world scenarios such as the Judeo-Christian tradition has handed down to us. For one thing, climate change is the result of a complex causality that is not metaphysical in nature, but material, cultural, and historical through and through. Apocalyptic discourse shifts the emphasis away from political responsibility in a way that, I think, should be resisted. Further, it is crucial to realize that climate change jeopardizes the existence of many species on Earth, including our own. But while many species-specific *Umwelten* or "life worlds" will end tragically, and in fact have already started disappearing at a shocking pace, the world itself will not be ended by climate change. The Earth system has withstood similarly dramatic changes in the eons of its history; what is at stake in anthropogenic climate change is not a divinely mandated end of the world, but humanity's

---

4 For more contextualization of the concept of the nonhuman, see *The Nonhuman Turn*, a landmark collection edited by Richard Grusin (2015).

moral involvement in a dramatic loss of life and biodiversity. That is a material responsibility that we share, where the pronoun "we" refers primarily to individuals living in the developed, industrialized world (which is at the historical root of the crisis) and their governments. Any recourse to a "higher," metaphysical dimension runs the risk of justifying our collective failure to find concrete solutions to a problem of our own creation. The language of touch and texture, which I explore in this chapter, is a means of keeping catastrophic climate change uncomfortably close to the physical, human-scale world, so as to avoid – productively, in my view – distancing ourselves from our responsibilities.

2 Touch and the Form of Human-Nonhuman Relations

In a multi-volume collection titled *Textures of the Anthropocene* (2015), the editors – Katrin Klingan, Ashkan Sepahvand, Christoph Rosol, and Bernd M. Scherer – employ texture as a conceptual lens to explore the current ecological crisis. This fascinating work grows out of the two-year "Anthropocene project" (2013–2014) hosted by the Haus der Kulturen der Welt in Berlin. The Anthropocene (Crutzen and Stoermer 2000) is the era in which humankind becomes a quasi-geological agent capable of dramatically altering the composition of the Earth's soil, water, and atmosphere. For the editors, this era is defined by climate change and by the fluidity of boundaries between human activities (such as industrial production), forms of social organization (such as capitalism), and "natural" things and processes. Thinking about texture yields insight into this fundamental interrelation between the human and the nonhuman; as the editors announce, "our intention is to experiment with and on the specific textures that compose the mud in which we find ourselves. This is meant figuratively, but also in a very material sense: grains, vapors, rays. These three registers, as heuristic tools, represent certain distinctive, yet interrelated qualities of temporal-spatial circulation and exchange" (Sepahvand, Rosol, and Klingan 2015: 40). Thus, *Textures of the Anthropocene* uses the distinctive materiality of the three volumes to suggest different textures, which are evoked by physical qualities of the paper and cover: the first volume is devoted to density and granularity, the second to vapor-like dispersion, the third to dynamic fields of light and energy. Interestingly for my purposes, the discussion of texture in the introduction is linked to a catastrophic event, the 2011 tsunami in Japan, which the editors see as an "emblematic image" of the Anthropocene (2015: 24). The material texture of the devastation inspires an enumeration of human and nonhuman traces caught up in an unruly assemblage: "salty seawater, cultivated soils, chemical residues, fats, oils, livestock cadavers, the dispersed debris of houses, trees, cars, plastics, electronics, metal alloys, textiles, crops, stuff," etc. (2015: 24).

Why is texture such a powerful metaphor for capturing the current Anthropocenic predicament, with its deep interrelation of human and nonhuman realities? As often, etymology provides a clue. The words "textile" and "texture" share the same Latin root, "texere," to weave. In this etymological sense, texture refers to woven patterns and their tactile qualities – a meaning that is then extended to tactile patterns in materials other than fabric. In the terminology of cognitive linguistics (Hampe and Grady 2005), the idea of texture evokes the "image schema" or perceptual Gestalt of "linkage," since fabric is made up by multiple strands *woven together.* This interwovenness resonates strongly with contemporary discussions on the Anthropocene. The editors of *Textures of the Anthropocene* favor fluid metaphors that emphasize the breakdown of barriers between the human and the nonhuman; in fact, their preferred way of talking about the reality of the Anthropocene is as "mud" – a "highly amorphous medium of distribution, a turbidity current [sic] sprawling out, blurring boundaries, defining cartographies" (Sepahvand, Rosol, and Klingan 2015: 25). Timothy Morton's "mesh" metaphor in *The Ecological Thought* comes much closer to the etymological roots of the word "texture." Under this rubric Morton discusses an abstract insight into the ecological "interconnectedness of all living and non-living things" (2010: 28). When he justifies the choice of the term, Morton's language turns concrete and textile: "'Mesh' can mean the holes in a network and threading between them. It suggests both hardness and delicacy. It has uses in biology, mathematics, and engineering and in weaving and computing – think stockings and graphic design, metals and fabrics" (2010: 28). Unlike mud, the mesh metaphor does not completely collapse the difference between human societies and nonhuman realities but expresses the complexity and multilinearity of humankind's capture in a more-than-human world – the intricate fabric of human society's relations with biology, the climate, and the geological history of Earth. Better than mud, mesh encapsulates this insight in terms that speak directly to the tactile experience of "the holes in a network and threading between them."

This mapping between ecological interconnectedness and tactile experience reflects a well-known tendency of metaphorical language to bring abstract concepts down to concrete scenarios of interaction with the physical world – a principle known as "experientialism" in cognitive linguistics (Rohrer 2007). Such experiential reduction via metaphorical language is particularly needed when facing phenomena like climate change or the Anthropocene – phenomena whose scale, as has been noted by many commentators (see, e.g., Clark 2015), eludes everyday experience.⁵ Climate change cannot be observed directly, because – in philosopher Dale Jamieson's words – it "poses threats that are probabilistic, multiple, indirect, often invisible, and unbounded in space and time" (2014: 61). But, of course, certain consequences of climate change *can* be experienced directly. This is where catastrophe enters the picture: a natural disaster is the rending of the fabric of human-nonhuman interconnection, and at the same time it is a singular event that *reveals* such interconnection in human-scale and deeply affective terms.⁶ Attempts to narrativize a natural disaster such as a tsunami tap into the considerable epistemological and emotional potential of catastrophe – its capacity to create awareness of human-nonhuman entanglement. But maximizing this capacity requires adopting language that can do justice to the lived texture of catastrophe – where "texture" is used broadly, as any kind patterning in sensory or affective experience.⁷ It is precisely this kind of experiential texture that narrative can capture by way of consciousness evocation. If what I said in the introduction is correct, for this to happen narrative has to complement perception in the distal, visual mode with tactile experiences that convey, from up close, the full gamut of sensory impressions left by a catastrophic event on characters' consciousness. Awareness of the texture of the mesh, in Morton's sense, converges with, and is reinforced by, heightened attention to the fabric-like patterning of experience.⁸ Before turning to my case study, I will attempt to clarify the idea that narrative can render the felt qualities of experience in ways that resonate with our formal, and particularly haptic, imagination.

3 Beyond the Mind's Eye

The word "imagination" has strong visual connotations. Imagery is, first and foremost, an exercise of the "mind's eye" based on the creation of picture-like inner experiences.⁹ This, at least, is the received understanding of mental imagery, in

---

5 For more on metaphor and the Anthropocene, see Caracciolo et al. (2019).
6 On catastrophe as revelation, see James Berger's (1999) insightful study. Cf. also Kate Rigby's remark that "the imaginary space opened by literary disaster narratives discloses the entanglement – material, but potentially also moral – of human and nonhuman actors and factors in the etiology, unfolding, and aftermath of catastrophes that turn out to straddle the dubious nature-culture divide" (2013: 214).
7 See Dretske (2010) for a philosophical discussion of texture in this extended sense.
8 This idea echoes David Abram's (1997) seminal work on how phenomenological philosophy – with its focus on the lived qualities of experience – can deepen environmentalist thought.
9 See Ellen Esrock's *The Mind's Eye* (1993) for an early, and highly comprehensive, study of the role of visual imagery in literary reading.

both philosophy and everyday language. In the area of "enactivist" approaches to the mind, philosopher Evan Thompson has offered a powerful phenomenological argument against this pictorial conception of the imagination: "we do not experience mental pictures, but instead visualize an object or scene by mentally enacting or entertaining a possible perceptual experience of that object or scene" (2007: 138). As this quotation shows, vision remains central to Thompson's account, and indeed his critique of the pictorialist conception of mental imagery starts from visual perception; for Thompson, the fact that we regard the imagination as involving mental pictures stems from a more general assumption that *vision* involves pictorial representations of the world. But, as Thompson notes – and as other enactivist theorists like Alva Noë (2004) have also argued – "our visual experience of the world at any given moment lacks many of the properties typical of pictures, such as uniformity of detail, qualitative determinateness at every point, and geometrical completeness" (2007: 145). By the same token, the notion that mental imagery is based on pictures does not stand up to phenomenological scrutiny. If I imagine the view from my living room window, for instance, I do not experience a mental picture of the street with the tram stop and cars parked on both sides; rather, I am recreating a sensory experience of the street *in the absence of the relevant perceptual stimuli*, on the basis of my memories of observing the street from that particular window. This mental operation involves the imagination of movement – for instance, moving my gaze from one end of the street to the other, which would be my usual way of visually taking in the street.

In fact, one of the fundamental ideas of enactivist philosophy is that eye and body movements are integral part of perception, and this is true – as scholars have argued extensively (Thomas 1999; Troscianko 2010; Caracciolo 2013) – of imagery as well. The difference is that in mental imagery physical movements are not actually performed but only mentally enacted or simulated. This point about the role of enacted movements in the sensory imagination becomes even more forceful if we go beyond the ocular paradigm within which Thompson's argument operates. Imagine the feel of velvet or corduroy. Intuitively, there is nothing pictorial about such tactile imagery. Imagining the tactile qualities of velvet implies enacting the experience of *touching* velvet by drawing on past experiences; it includes a simulation of the hand movements that would accompany one's tactile experience of velvet, as well as of the resulting sensory feel.

The verbal strategies of literary narrative excel at creating sensory feel by activating past experiences and recombining them in creative, and often unexpected, ways. This is true across sensory modalities – for vision and hearing as well as the more proximal sense of touch. But across this imaginative gamut tactile patterns – texture – are a key factor in producing vividness. In *Dreaming by the Book* (2001), Elaine Scarry makes a compelling case for the importance of touch in literary reading. Scarry's point of departure is that mental imagery is volatile and delicate – "gauzy," as she puts it (2001: 10), with a reference to the tactile experience of fabric. There is, thus, a natural link between the "gauziness" of imagery and translucent substances such as haze or light curtains. The way literature can present the experience of something solid (for example, a wall) is by evoking, in the reader's mind, "the passing of a filmy surface over another (by comparison, dense) surface" (2001: 14). Two ideas emerge from Scarry's discussion. First, visual and tactile imagery are yoked together: for something to be imagined vividly in the visual mode, we need the intervention of texture, via stylistic strategies that build on touch. Thus, visual imagery may be the most commonly reported and discussed form of the sensory imagination, reflecting the well-known primacy of vision in both human cognition and Western culture. But the evocation of tactile experiences makes visual imagery more striking and tangible: Scarry notes that, in literature, "what is solid or substantive is often strangely coupled with what is not – namely, the quality of the imagined image itself, which, filmy and tissuelike, can be physically manipulated, as it were" (2001: 89). Second, what aids this imaginative conflation of touch and vision is the experience of *movement*. In all of Scarry's literary strategies for creating vividness, kinetic patterns play a central role: it is motion that enables the conversion of haptic texture into visual substance. Scarry's intuition goes hand in hand with the enactivist insight into the primacy of movement in perception: the more verbal language is capable of creating a dynamic impression, the more lifelike our imagery will be.

Throughout *Dreaming by the Book*, Scarry focuses on appealing textures that invite physical manipulation. Catastrophe narratives produce vividness through opposite emotional qualities, employing texture to unsettle and sometimes repulse the reader, a strategy that channels the anxious precarity of humankind's position vis-à-vis the nonhuman world. Tactile experiences are crucial to this imaginative project: through the imagined form of touch, narrative can make readers aware of the human-nonhuman mesh far more poignantly than it would be possible through vision (or visual representation) alone. What is thus foregrounded – through narrative form and literary strategies of consciousness evocation – is the materiality the editors of *Textures of the Anthropocene* seek to draw attention to. It is time to put these ideas to the test of a catastrophic narrative that exploits brilliantly the imaginative potential of touch: Jeff VanderMeer's Southern Reach trilogy.

4 Touching the "Living Wall" in the Southern Reach Trilogy

Originally published in 2014, the Southern Reach trilogy – which comprises the novels *Annihilation, Authority,* and *Acceptance* – has been widely hailed as a prime example of contemporary fiction in the "weird" mode. VanderMeer himself and Ann VanderMeer have theorized the weird, as well as the distinction between the old and the new weird, in an anthology that traces the history of the genre from H. P. Lovecraft to China Miéville (see VanderMeer and VanderMeer 2012). According to the VanderMeers' introduction, the new weird "has a visceral, in-the-moment quality that often uses elements of surreal or transgressive horror for its tone, style, and effects" (2012: xvi).[10] It is particularly the visceral dimension of the Southern Reach trilogy that interests me here: this quality of VanderMeer's prose is closely related to the evocation of haptic qualities that bring the reader close – and sometimes too close for comfort – to the characters' catastrophic predicament.

The disaster explored by the novel begins in a coastal area of the United States that the authorities have dubbed "Area X." The ecosystem of Area X has undergone a sudden and radical transformation, which the government's official story explains in terms of "a localized environmental catastrophe stemming from experimental military research" (2014a: 94). But in the course of the trilogy, it becomes increasingly clear that the anomalies of Area X run much deeper, and their origin appears to be extraterrestrial rather than human. The federal government creates an organization, the "Southern Reach," to investigate the causes of the anomaly; its headquarters are located near the heavily militarized border of Area X. Several research expeditions are dispatched, but very few team members return, and even fewer return without major psychological or physical damage. The teams are unable to reach any conclusions as to the exact nature of Area X, but the scale of the environmental transformations that affect the region is certainly more than "localized." Indeed, it transpires at the end of the second novel (*Authority*) that Area X has taken over the headquarters of the Southern Reach, and keeps expanding. The Southern Reach trilogy is thus set apart from most postapocalyptic fiction by the fact that the narrative unfolds *during* a catastrophic event rather than in its aftermath.[11]

---

10 For discussion of the weird as a genre and as a concept, see Ulstein (2017: 81–83) and Luckhurst (2017).
11 I discuss the distinctive temporal profile of postapocalyptic fiction in Caracciolo (2018a).

Instead of imagining the consequences of a disastrous event for the rest of the world, most of the plot unfolds at the heart of the catastrophic anomaly, reconstructing its murky history. In the process, Area X almost takes on the role of a character in the trilogy, an agent of catastrophe whose ways are mysterious but recognizably purposeful.[12] The first novel, *Annihilation*, begins with the twelfth expedition having just crossed the border into Area X; the narrator is the expedition's biologist. The second novel, *Authority*, is largely set at the Southern Reach facility and narrates, in third-person, internally focalized prose, the arrival of a new director, John Rodriguez (but mostly known by his nickname, "Control") and his attempts to dispel the thick fog that surrounds Area X. At the end of *Authority*, Control joins Ghost Bird, a doppelganger of the biologist from the first novel and an apparent "creation" of Area X. Together they travel into Area X; their experiences are narrated in the third installment of the trilogy, *Acceptance*, which weaves together multiple temporal frames and narrating or focalizing characters: Control, Ghost Bird, two characters from the twelfth expedition (the biologist as well as the psychologist who led the team and was also Control's predecessor as director of the Southern Reach), and a lighthouse keeper, the first person to come into contact with the contamination that was later to take over Area X. While the first two novels deploy consistent narrative situations (first-person narrative and internally focalized third-person narration, respectively), the third novel complicates that picture significantly by introducing a plurality of voices and perspectives, including Ghost Bird's nonhuman consciousness. The temporality of *Acceptance* also becomes fragmented, with frequent flashbacks to events that preceded the first instalment of the trilogy. That formal complexity is one way in which narrative can attempt to render the human-nonhuman mesh. Even more saliently, the trilogy brings out that sense of enmeshment by combining the evocation of consciousness with spatializing strategies: the characters' unsettling experience of the space of Area X points to their deep entanglement with nonhuman phenomena and, simultaneously, fosters readerly immersion.

The coastal geography of Area X is defined by two landmarks: the lighthouse and a tunnel with a stairway descending into the depths of the earth. Early on in *Annihilation*, the space of the tunnel presents the first instance of a textural image that will accompany readers throughout the trilogy: I call it the motif of the "living wall." In the following passage, the members of the twelfth expedition begin descending into the tunnel – which the biologist keeps calling, with a mix-up that the novel explicitly thematizes, "tower":

---

[12] For more on Area X as a character, see Caracciolo (2018b: 184–185).

> At about shoulder height, perhaps five feet high, clinging to the inner wall of the tower, I saw what I first took to be dimly sparkling green vines progressing down into the darkness. I had a sudden absurd memory of the floral wallpaper treatment that had lined the bathroom of my house when I had shared it with my husband. Then, as I stared, the "vines" resolved further, and I saw that they were words, in cursive, the letters raised about six inches off the wall. (2014a: 23)

Remember Scarry's observation that imagining solidity – for instance, that of a wall – is more difficult than imagining a gauzy and impalpable substance. Writers can work around this problem and produce vivid imagery by superimposing texture and movement on a solid object. VanderMeer follows the advice to the letter in this first-person account of the biologist's experiences. The "vines" she notices stick out visually and haptically; they form an irregular texture that invites tactile exploration ("Don't touch it, whatever it is," remarks the anthropologist, one of the biologist's companions, on the same page). The biologist's incongruous memory of a "floral wallpaper" continues in the same vein, with the wallpaper being a literal papery texture pasted onto a solid wall. Further, VanderMeer's prose creates a sense of movement, not just because the vines/words seem to "progress down" the wall, but also because their "sparkling" appearance produces a flickering effect in the reader's mental imagery. All this contributes to creating a sense of vividness but also of physical closeness to the wall, as if readers were standing next to the biologist and equally tempted to touch the strange vines. This impression of proximity is reinforced, a few lines below, by a rich description of the smell given off by the words on the wall, which turn out to be made of living matter: "a loamy smell came from the words along with an underlying hint of rotting honey" (2014a: 24). Because smell is, like touch, a proximal sense, this comment further confirms the imaginative closeness of the biologist's surroundings.

The haptic quality of the reader's wall imagery captures the unstable nature of this place, where ontological boundaries are dissolved through touch. The words on the wall seem to be alive, like fungus; the abstract patterning around the words "resembled the sharp branching of hard coral" (2014a: 49). Along with "vines" and "wallpaper," these comparisons keep diffracting the reality of the wall, and thus confounding the reader's imagination through the sheer multiplication of metaphorical sources. Visually, the reader has a hard time imagining the wall's appearance, which enhances the tactility of the wall as an alternative to the impasse of the pictorial imagination. The biologist follows the anthropologist's order and does not touch the wall at first, but the wall manages to touch her: "a tiny spray of golden spores," coming from the words, enters her nose (2014a: 25). This is a turning point in the trilogy's plot, because the biologist's transformation at the hands of Area X begins with this seemingly minor contagion.

When the biologist does touch the wall, a few pages later, a strange thought dawns on her: "the walls when I went to touch them carried the echo of a heartbeat [. . .] and they were not made of stone but of *living tissue*" (2014a: 41). This realization is thus followed by the even more disturbing idea that the wall itself could be alive, as if the biologist and her companions "were descending into an organism" (2014a: 41). It is worth pausing here to remark on the significance of the word "tissue," which derives – like "texture" – from the Latin "texere," to weave. Tissue is a close cognate of texture in the sense of tactile pattern in fabric, but it takes on the added meaning of *organic* material, with a direct conflation of life and haptic form. In short, the wall blurs the basic ontological boundary between animate organisms and inanimate matter, and this blurring is grounded in the organic (and deeply tactile) form that the wall takes in the reader's imagination.

The motif of the living wall emerges again at the end of *Annihilation*, where it is linked to a monster – known as "the Crawler" – whose nature seems fundamentally bound up with the mystery of Area X. When the biologist confronts the monster, her vision breaks down: "It so overwhelmed my ability to comprehend shapes within it that I forced myself to switch from sight, to focus at first on reports from other senses" (2014a: 176). Instead, the biologist's knowledge of the monster becomes first olfactory and gustatory ("a burning smell [. . .]. The taste on my tongue was like brine set ablaze"), and finally haptic: "a wall of flesh that resembled light, with sharp, curving elements within it and textures like ice when it has frozen from flowing water" (2014a: 177). Here light is not the medium of vision but a mere object of resemblance, while the essence of the monster is tactile and thus deeply connected to the visually unstable description of the wall at the beginning of the novel.

The living wall motif becomes even more significant in *Authority*. When Control watches a video from the first expedition into Area X, he is struck by an obscure, monstrous presence that "[conjures] up the idea of a fluid wall of ribbony flesh" (2014b: 198). Later in the novel, Control has a hallucinatory experience – reported in internally focalized language – while trying to open a door in the Southern Reach: "Control reached out for the large double doors. Reached for the handle, missed it, tried again. But there were no doors where there had always been doors before. Only wall. And the wall was soft and breathing under the touch of his hand" (2014b: 290). This is a first but unmistakable sign that Area X is encroaching on the Southern Reach. A new chapter begins, with a flashback to an earlier point in Control's life, when he is being interrogated in a cell. The living wall motif provides the transition: in the cell, "the texture of the wall felt like a manta ray from the aquarium: firm and smooth, with a serrated roughness but with more give, and behind it the sense of something vast, breathing in and out" (2014b: 293). The gesture of touching the wall, which normally serves as guarantee of a stable, dependable reality, has the opposite effect of collapsing ontological domains in both temporal and conceptual terms: the unsettling experience at the Southern Reach merges with the character's past, inanimate space fuses with the feel of a living creature. When Control recovers from the hallucination, he can't shake the texture of the living wall off his hand: "[He kept] trying to get the feel of the wall off his hand, wiping it against the seats, the steering wheel, his pants. Would have plunged it into dog shit to get the feeling off" (2014b: 296); "the texture [of the wall] remained on his hand like an unshakable phantom" (2014b: 301). As readers, we experience Control's disgust vicariously, because we have been familiarized in the course of the two novels with the tactile imagery of the wall and its disturbing connotations. The tactile feel of the wall stands in for the unsettling catastrophe that is about to enfold the Southern Reach and the world at large – a catastrophe that disrupts, like the living wall, the comfortable conceptual coordinates of human society: the stable binaries of human and nonhuman, animate and inanimate, that are at the cultural roots of the current Anthropocenic predicament.

In the last volume of the trilogy, *Acceptance*, it is again touch that serves as a vehicle of the characters' "acceptance" of the precarious position of the human in a deeply more-than-human world. Catastrophe reveals this precarity, but also offers consolation via heightened appreciation of the textural forms of nature. The third novel is particularly rich in tactile language: when the psychologist faces the lighthouse keeper as he is transforming into the Crawler, she observes that "he is as porous as volcanic rock" (2014c: 57); likewise, the biologist of the twelfth expedition has turned into a monster whose skin is marked by "green-and-white stars of barnacles [. . .] in the hundreds of miniature craters, of tidal pools from time spent motionless in deep water" (2014c: 195). Through skin and its tactile qualities, the novel encourages readers to imagine bodies transformed by the nonhuman world – the offshoot of a catastrophe that is as deeply generative as it is destructive. Control and Ghost Bird – the biologist's doppelganger – are central to this realization. Control's aesthetic appreciation of the uncanny beauty of Area X's landscape, while mainly couched in the language of visual pattern, is ultimately linked by the narrator (and, via internal focalization, by the character himself) to Ghost Bird's "touch":

> Yet still the blue heron in the estuary stalked tadpoles and tiny fish, the black vulture soared on the thermals high above. There came a thousand rustlings among the islands of trees. Behind them, on the horizon, the lighthouse could be seen, might always be seen, even through the fog that came with the dawn, here noncommittal and diffuse, there thick, rising like a natural defense where needed, a test and blessing against that landscape. To appreciate any of this was Ghost Bird's gift to him, as if it had seeped into him through her touch. (2014c: 264)

Control's appreciation of the landscape "seeps into" his body, through physical contact, before reshaping his more distal senses. Equally tactile is Ghost Bird's final encounter with the Crawler, now explicitly presented as an emanation of Area X: "She reached out a hand, felt a delicate fluttering against her fingers as though encountering a porous layer, a veil. Was this first contact, or last contact? Her touch triggered a response" (2014c: 286). Porosity is a textural interface between the human and the monstrous, but also between our planet and the cosmic scale: touching the Crawler offers Ghost Bird an insight into "the cataclysm like a rain of comets that had annihilated an entire biosphere remote from Earth" (2014c: 286–287). The contagion of Area X is finally depicted as a cosmic event that remains ambiguously suspended between annihilation and aestheticized grandeur ("a rain of comets").

No matter how we interpret the ending and the overall trajectory of VanderMeer's trilogy, it seems clear that tactile imagery plays a major role in both the novels' stylistic strategies and in their effects on readers. Indeed, the epistemological centrality of touch brings together characters – Control, the biologist, Ghost Bird – whose personalities and responses to Area X are otherwise significantly different, spanning a wide range of emotional registers from the sublime to the pastoral to cosmic horror. Reading the Southern Reach trilogy means becoming attuned to a haptic imagination of catastrophe that challenges the rigid conceptual barriers erected by a culture founded on the dichotomies of vision. The living wall motif, which I traced through this close reading, is key to destabilizing human-nonhuman binaries and calls for an alignment – driven by first-person narration and internal focalization – of readers' mental imagery with the richly tactile qualities of the characters' experiences. But the living wall motif is certainly not the only expression of the novels' haptic imagination. By foregrounding touch and its capacity to reconfigure patterns of perception (including those of vision), the trilogy presents readers with a unique opportunity for sensing the fragile texture of human-nonhuman enmeshment.

5 Conclusion

My goal in this chapter was to show that "texture" is a productive concept in imagining catastrophe through narrative representation. Besides being etymologically related to the word "text" and having been discussed by Stockwell in connection to the experience of literary style, texture resonates with an approach to narrative that explores the intersection of literary strategies, the imaginative experience of engaging with narrative, and broader socio-cultural forms. These are the three intersecting dimensions of texture I have examined. First, I have argued that my case study, VanderMeer's Southern Reach trilogy, uses strategies of consciousness evocation – in both internal focalization and first-person narrative – to recreate the lived quality, the "what it's like" factor, of characters' experiences as they are exposed to the unsettling spatiality of Area X. Put otherwise, the sensory texture of consciousness is evoked through verbal language, and metaphorical language more specifically (see Caracciolo 2014: chap. 4). Second, the impact of these strategies can be described at the level of *readers'* own experiences. Elaine Scarry's work in cognitive literary studies and philosophical discussions on mental imagery (within the so-called "enactivist" movement) have proven useful to describe the ways in which literary narrative can foreground haptic patterns in reading, challenging the cognitive and cultural primacy of vision. The evocation of texture – in the sense of tactile form – increases the vividness of mental imagery, creating an impression of experiential immediacy and immersion and thus deepening readers' affective engagement with characters. Finally, the interwovenness of texture is an emblematic form of human societies' embedding in a more-than-human reality – which Morton captures through the equally textile metaphor of "enmeshment." In this sense, texture stands in opposition to hierarchical or linear ways of understanding human-nonhuman relations, ideological forms that have become bound up (in Western culture) with the idea of human mastery over the natural world.[13] Texture also challenges a religious (apocalyptic) reading of catastrophe, which too easily falls back on a metaphysical view of history, shifting the focus from human to divine responsibility. Instead, texture emphasizes the materiality of catastrophe and how human societies are morally and physically bound up with it.[14]

Not only do catastrophic events reveal, ex posteriori, the deep imbrication of human and nonhuman processes, but they leave an indelible mark on the memory and consciousness of those who experience it. My core claim in this chapter has been that, by adopting haptic ways of imagining catastrophe through narrative representation, stories can offer a highly embodied route into human-nonhuman enmeshment. Readers of fiction like VanderMeer's Southern Reach novels – that is, fiction that captures the etiology and impact of catastrophe by focusing on its haptic texture – are confronted with the ramifications of a catastrophic event in ways

---

13 Manuel De Landa offers an incisive critique of linearity in *A Thousand Years of Nonlinear History* (1997), where he develops an account of Western history that is fully attuned to the materiality of the human-nonhuman mesh.
14 Importantly, while the climate crisis stems from Western practices such as capitalism and large-scale industrialization, its catastrophic effects tend to be more felt by vulnerable communities in other parts of the world.

that question the reassuring distance of vision. These ramifications are conceptual (the breakdown of dualistic binaries, including human vs. nonhuman and animate vs. inanimate, as we have seen) and, at the same time, affective (hence the frequently mentioned "visceral" qualities of VanderMeer's prose). Thus, via the textural mode of the imagination it can foster, literary fiction affords a rich opportunity for rethinking and deepening the representation of catastrophe in other media as well as in nonfictional genres.

Bibliography

Abram, David (1997) *The Spell of the Sensuous: Perception and Language in a More-Than-Human World* (New York: Vintage).
Berger, James (1999) *After the End: Representations of Post-Apocalypse* (Minneapolis: University of Minnesota Press).
Caracciolo, Marco (2013) "Blind Reading: Toward an Enactivist Theory of the Reader's Imagination," in *Stories and Minds: Cognitive Approaches to Literary Narrative*, ed. Lars Bernaerts, Dirk De Geest, Luc Herman and Bart Vervaeck (Lincoln and London: University of Nebraska Press), 81–106.
Caracciolo, Marco (2014) *The Experientiality of Narrative: An Enactivist Approach* (Berlin: de Gruyter).
Caracciolo, Marco (2018a) "Negative Strategies and World Disruption in Postapocalyptic Fiction," *Style* 52.3, 222–241.
Caracciolo, Marco (2018b) "Notes for an Econarratological Theory of Character," *Frontiers of Narrative Studies* 4.1, 172–189.
Caracciolo, Marco, Andrei Ionescu and Ruben Fransoo (2019) "Metaphorical Patterns in Anthropocene Fiction," *Language and Literature* 28.3, 221–240.
Cohn, Dorrit (1978) *Transparent Minds: Narrative Modes for Presenting Consciousness in Fiction* (Princeton: Princeton University Press).
Clark, Timothy (2015) *Ecocriticism on the Edge: The Anthropocene as a Threshold Concept* (London: Bloomsbury).
Crutzen, Paul J. and Eugene F. Stoermer (2000) "The Anthropocene," *Global Change Newsletter* 41, 17–18.
De Landa, Manuel (1997) *A Thousand Years of Nonlinear History* (New York: Zone Books).
Dretske, Fred (2010) "What We See: The Texture of Conscious Experience," in *Perceiving the World*, ed. Bence Nanay (Oxford: Oxford University Press), 54–67.
Esrock, Ellen J. (1993) *The Reader's Eye: Visual Imaging as Reader Response* (Baltimore and London: Johns Hopkins University Press).
Greene, Joshua (2003) "From Neural 'Is' to Moral 'Ought': What Are the Moral Implications of Neuroscientific Moral Psychology?" *Nature Reviews Neuroscience* 4.10, 846–850.
Grusin, Richard (ed) (2015) *The Nonhuman Turn* (Minneapolis: University of Minnesota Press).
Hampe, Beate and Joseph E. Grady (eds) (2005) *From Perception to Meaning: Image Schemas in Cognitive Linguistics* (Berlin: Walter de Gruyter).

Herman, David (2007) "Cognition, Emotion, and Consciousness," in *The Cambridge Companion to Narrative*, ed. David Herman (Cambridge: Cambridge University Press), 245–259.
Herman, David (2009) *Basic Elements of Narrative* (Chichester: Wiley-Blackwell).
James, Erin (2015) *The Storyworld Accord: Econarratology and Postcolonial Narratives* (Lincoln: University of Nebraska Press).
Jamieson, Dale (2014) *Reason in a Dark Time: Why the Struggle against Climate Change Failed – and What It Means for Our Future* (Oxford: Oxford University Press).
Klingan, Katrin, Ashkan Sepahvand, Christoph Rosol and Bernd M. Scherer (eds) (2015) *Textures of the Anthropocene: Grain Vapor Ray* (Cambridge, MA: MIT Press).
Kuzmičová, Anežka (2012) "Presence in the Reading of Literary Narrative: A Case for Motor Enactment," *Semiotica* 189.1/4, 23–48.
Levine, Caroline (2015) *Forms: Whole, Rhythm, Hierarchy, Network* (Princeton: Princeton University Press).
Luckhurst, Roger (2017) "The Weird: A Dis/Orientation," *Textual Practice* 31.6, 1041–1061.
Morton, Timothy (2010) *The Ecological Thought* (Cambridge, MA: Harvard University Press).
Noë, Alva (2004) *Action in Perception* (Cambridge, MA: MIT Press).
Rigby, Kate (2013) "Confronting Catastrophe: Ecocriticism in a Warming World," in *The Cambridge Companion to Literature and the Environment*, ed. Louise Westling (Cambridge: Cambridge University Press), 212–225.
Rohrer, Tim (2007) "Embodiment and Experientialism," in *The Oxford Handbook of Cognitive Linguistics*, ed. Dirk Geeraerts and Hubert Cuyckens (Oxford: Oxford University Press), 25–47.
Scarry, Elaine (2001) *Dreaming by the Book* (Princeton: Princeton University Press).
Sepahvand, Ashkan, Christoph Rosol and Katrin Klingan (2015) "MUD: All Worlds, All Times!" in *Textures of the Anthropocene: Grain Vapor Ray*, ed. Katrin Klingan, Ashkan Sepahvand, Christoph Rosol and Bernd M. Scherer (Cambridge, MA: MIT Press), 7–42.
Stockwell, Peter (2009) *Texture: A Cognitive Aesthetics of Reading* (Edinburgh: Edinburgh University Press).
Thomas, Nigel J. T. (1999) "Are Theories of Imagery Theories of Imagination? An Active Perception Approach to Conscious Mental Content," *Cognitive Science* 23.2, 207–245.
Thompson, Evan (2007) "Look Again: Phenomenology and Mental Imagery," *Phenomenology and the Cognitive Sciences* 6, 137–170.
Troscianko, Emily (2010) "Kafkaesque Worlds in Real Time," *Language and Literature* 19.2, 151–171.
Ulstein, Gry (2017) "Brave New Weird: Anthropocene Monsters in Jeff VanderMeer's 'The Southern Reach,'" *Concentric: Literary and Cultural Studies* 43.1, 71–96.
VanderMeer, Jeff (2014a) *Annihilation* (New York: Farrar, Straus and Giroux).
VanderMeer, Jeff (2014b) *Authority* (New York: Farrar, Straus and Giroux).
VanderMeer, Jeff (2014c) *Acceptance* (New York: Farrar, Straus and Giroux).
VanderMeer, Jeff and Ann VanderMeer (eds) (2012) *The Weird: A Compendium of Strange and Dark Stories* (New York: Tor Books).

Diana Dimitrova
Hindu Apocalyptic Notions, Cultural Discourses, and Climate Change

1 Introduction

The present-day urgent issues of environmental deterioration have occupied Hindus and scholars of Hinduism for several decades now. The *Vedas*, the *Upaniṣads*, the *Mahābhārata* and *Rāmāyaṇa* epics, the *Purāṇas* as well as later yoga manuals, and popular religious movements reveal the richness and complexity of the ways in which Hindu traditions have reflected on the natural world.[1] Similar to other world religions, traditional ancient Hindu texts and practices reveal an intrinsic eco-religious and eco-cultural thinking as a way of life. Hindus referred to Earth as Mother Earth and Mother-Goddess and worshipped her accordingly. Thus, it is not surprising that Hindu texts and practices do not express any modern environmental concerns. Rather, these questions are the result of modern-day preoccupations and modern-day problems, resulting from the desire to "catch up" with developed industrialized nations, oftentimes abandoning eco-religious traditional ways of living and adopting "modern", but unsustainable practices. Nonetheless, by exploring and reflecting on Hindu texts and practices, scholars of Hinduism contribute to the formation of an environmental ethic that gives rise to multiple religiously colored environmental discourses.

Hindu imagination sees time as cyclic, and not linear, and understands the cyclic creation and dissolution of the universe as a repetitive and normal process that is good, desired and necessary. In the Vaiṣṇava tradition, Vishnu and his *avatāras*, or bodily descents, in which he incarnates in various anthropomorphic and non-anthropomorphic forms, comes down to earth in order to save humankind from natural calamities and disasters, such as floods, draughts, etc.

---

[1] The system of transliteration in this work follows a standard system for Sanskrit and Hindi, in which long vowels are marked with a macron, for instance *ā*, and retroflex consonants with a dot beneath the letter, for example *ḍ*. Nasalization is indicated by the sign *ṃ*, which follows the nasalized vocal. No special symbol is used for *anusvāra* (superscript dot denoting homorganic or other nasal consonant) in the transliteration, the appropriate nasal consonant being written to avoid confusion in the pronunciation. All Hindi words and titles of works are spelled according to the transliteration system for Hindi. The names of authors, thinkers, philosophers, gods, rivers, plants, trees and cities have not been marked with diacritics.

In Śaiva and Śākta traditions, Shiva and Devī[2] are the savior gods. All Hindu traditions see Earth als the body of the Goddess, and thus deify rivers and mountains and revere them as goddesses. Similarly, the proliferation of contemporary discourses on climate change, are often immersed in Hindu mythology and religious culture, and cannot be ignored when discussing the issues of apocalyptic imagination and climate change in Hindu traditions.

Thus, my chapter seeks to explore the complex links between Hindu eco-religious and eco-cultural traditions, the mythologizing of nature, and the mythologizing of contemporary cultural and religious discourses on climate change. In the following, I will discuss Hindu apocalyptic notions in the *Vedas*, the *Upaniṣads*, in the epics and in the Vaiṣṇava and Śaiva-Śākta Paurāṇic traditions. At the end of my chapter, I will reflect on modern environmental discourses and activist movements.

2 Hindu Apocalyptic Notions in the *Vedas* and *Upaniṣads*

As Hilary Rodrigues and Lance Nelson have pointed out, Vedic literature abounds in references to earth and nature's phenomena. Indeed, Vedic deities are called *devas* and they embody natural phenomena. Thus, Pṛthvī, is the goddess of Earth, Agni the deity of fire, Uṣas, the goddess of dawn, Indra the god of thunder, Varuṇa the god of water, Vāyu the god of wind, etc. Furthermore, the entire cosmos is envisioned in organic terms, *hiraṇyagarbha*, the golden egg, or as a cosmic person *Puruṣa* (Rodriques 2010: 329).

Additionally, the central myth of the *Ṛgveda*, which depicts the cosmic battle between Indra, highest god in the Vedic pantheon representing thunder, and Vṛtra – the demon who had drunk all the water and who had caused profound suffering, could be considered as one of the first examples of apocalyptic imagination. Similarly, the myth of Daksha's sacrifice to which the god Shiva had not been invited, makes Daksha's daughter Sati sacrifice herself. As devastated Shiva

---

[2] Throughout this chapter, I use the Sanskrit word Devī, and mean by it the Great Goddess (singular), as opposed to Devī (plural), goddesses of India (Spouse Goddess, i.e., female consorts of male Hindu gods, and village goddesses). Tracy Pintchman argues that the concept of "the Great Goddess develops over time as a result of the blending of Brahmanical and non-Brahmanical religious tendencies and divinities. Yet the essential identity of the Great Goddess as 'Great' appears to be constructed at least initially largely in and by the Brahmanical tradition." See Pintchman (1994: 2–16).

carries her dead body, parts of it fall all over earth, creating sacred sites, or *Śākta-pīṭhas*. This Vedic myth conveys a clear message that the entire world is the body of the Goddess and that it should be treated with love and respect.

In the *Upaniṣads*, specifically in the texts, which expound monistic ideas, *ātman* (pure consciousness, inner breadth within, the self) is identical with brahman, with the Absolute, with the ultimate reality. Their union is *mokṣa*, liberation from the cycle of birth and rebirth and the highest goal for every Hindu, which one could achieve by studying with a guru for many years and by mastering techniques of breath control, meditation and concentration, in lines with the philosophy of Yoga, as revealed in Patanjali's *Yogasūtras*.

3 Hindu Apocalyptic Notions in the Epics and in the *Vaiṣṇava Purāṇas*

In the period of classical and epical Hinduism, and with the emergence of theistic thought, the *Upaniṣad*'s view of the union of *ātman* and *brahman* is represented in the union of the devotee with the theistic concept of the divine, *iśvara*, be it Vishnu, Shiva or Devi, the Goddess. There are many instances of panentheism in the epic of *Mahābhārata* and the philosophical poem of *Bhagavadgītā*, in which Krishna (Vishnu-Krishna) is depicted to contain the entire universe in his body. The texts stipulate that meditation on Vishnu-Krishna, and love and devotion to him are the supreme ways to be saved through Vishnu's love and grace.

The *Purāṇas* represent a genre of devotional religious texts, which deal with topics such as the creation and dissolution of the world, the genealogy of the gods, and all the episodes related to the "lives" of the deities. They can be dedicated to Brahma, Vishnu, Shiva or Devī (The Goddess). In the *Viṣṇu Purāṇas*, Vishnu comes down to earth in one of his *avatāras*, or bodily descents, in which he incarnates in various anthropomorphic and non-anthropomorphic forms in order to save humankind from natural calamities and disasters, such as floods, draughts, etc.

Thus, as revealed in the *Purāṇas*, Hindu imagination sees time as cyclic, and not linear, and understands the cyclic creation and dissolution of the universe as a repetitive and normal process that is good, desired and necessary. Hindus believe that the deity Brahma is the creator of the world, the deity Vishnu is the one who maintains and preserves it, and the deity Shiva destroys it. This destruction is necessary and important, as without it the world could not be re-created. It is said that the cycle of the universe would last for one *mahāyuga*, or great *yuga* – the equivalent of 4 320 000 solar years, which would be divided into four *yugas*, or cosmic eras, each of a slightly different duration of thousands and millions of solar years. After the dissolution of one *mahāyuga*, another *mahāyuga* would start and so on.

While it seems that Hindu mythological discourses on the cyclic notion of time would be well at ease with any possible aspect of the apocalyptic imagination, in the *Purāṇas*, climate change and natural disaster remain a concern within the scope of concrete human lives, situated in one specific *yuga*, or cosmic era. This is particularly true for the current cosmic era, Kali *yuga,* which is marked by the prevailing of *adharma* (non-righteousness, evil) over *dharma* (moral/religious duty/righteousness/good). This is why the notion of *bhakti*, or, loving devotion and service to Vishnu and his *avatāras,* remains central to the apocalyptic imagination. Through his power, Vishnu can prevent natural disasters and he can save humans and the earth from calamities. *Bhakti* or loving devotion toward Vishnu, who can assume panentheistic dimensions in some texts, needs to be situated in the context of the limitations of human agency, as well as in the context of the impact of *karma* on free will and predestination in Hindu traditions. Thus, the mythologizing of the divine is a potent trend in Hindu apocalyptic imagination. As discussed earlier, both the *Bhagavadgītā* and the *Mahābhārata* provide abundant textual material on this issue.

4 Hindu Apocalyptic Notions and Goddess-Traditions

Hindu traditions entail the notion of sacred geography where the earth, the mountains and the rivers embody different goddesses. As discussed earlier in my chapter, the myth of Daksha's sacrifice in the *Vedas* and the dismemberment of Sati point to the identification of Earth with the Goddess through her body. To Hindus, Earth is Mother-Earth, Earth is the embodiment of the Goddess. In this way, many Hindus perceive the pollution of rivers, the creation of dams or the construction of mines as the violation of river or mountain goddesses. Thus, it would be unthinkable to discuss the aspect of ecology and the sacred geography of Hinduism without dealing with the Shaktism and the notion of the Goddess, Devī, Śakti[3] in Hinduism whose figure is associated with Mother-Earth, river and mountain Goddesses. It is therefore important to state the importance

---

[3] The concept of Śakti is complex and deserves further clarification. It is understood as the creative energy that generates and continues to activate the universe. It is conceived as female and often personified as the consort of a male deity (the Spouse Goddess) or as the independent Goddess (Devī).

of Goddesses traditions for environmental discourses. Goddesses-traditions provide multiple resources for thinking about the earth, particularly through Bhū Devī, the Goddess-Earth, and to study areas of environmental concern, such as forests, trees, plants, sacred rivers and places; animals, especially sacred animals and vegetarianism, and how they inscribe in modern-day environmental imagination and discourses.

Similarly, Sita in the *Rāmāyaṇa*, whose name literally means furrow and who is the daughter of Mother Earth herself is goddess on earth and Rama's spouse. Thus, they incarnate the Hindu god Vishnu and his consort Lakshmi on earth. The kidnapping of Sita by the demon Ravana represents the violation of Hindu dharma. Rama embarks on a journey across the Indian subcontinent to save Sita and restore Hindu *dharma*. This culminates symbolically with the defeat of evil and the killing of Ravana and the establishment of Ram's ideal perfect rule and kingdom – his *rāmrājya* in Ayodhya. Sadly, the image of Ram's ideal kingdom has been misappropriated and exploited by Hindu nationalists for their own chauvinistic nationalistic *hindutva* (Hinduness) agenda for a Hindu India, in which there is no place for other religious minorities – that is unless they embrace Hindu ideals.

Although the scope of my chapter does not allow me to deal with it here, I would like to mention here that *hindutva* is a very complex notion. It is an invented, imagined, and constructed notion of a collective Hindu-Indian identity. It is supposed to be a unifying notion of "Hinduism" as a cultural, not religious reality. However, it has not remained immune to the conservative and nationalistic agenda of dominant political parties, and it has become increasingly linked to Hindu nationalism. (Dimitrova 2017: 1–11)

While the multiplicity of texts and topics reveal the richness of apocalyptic imagination and environmental discourses, this also points to the limitations of an attempt to study Hindu apocalyptic notions and climate change only within the realm of one single tradition, for instance the Vaiṣṇava tradition. A comprehensive study of the topic would inevitably involve an in-depth discussion of Shaiva and Shakta interpretations. Let's not forget that it is the God Shiva who performs the necessary and good cyclic destruction dissolution of the universe, and it is the Goddess who is worshipped and deified in the sacred geography of India.

5 Hindu Apocalyptic Imagination, Cultural and Environmental Discourses

My chapter has sought to present the complex links between apocalyptic imagination, the mythologizing of the divine, and cultural and religious discourses evoked by human religious feelings towards the violation of Mother Nature. It is important to note that the proliferation of new discourses on climate change, immersed in Hindu mythology and religious culture, are imbued with the religious feelings of pain, devastation and anger, associated with the violation of goddesses and cannot be ignored when discussing current discourses on climate change. Thus, we can talk about religiously motivated and inspired environmentalism.

A prevailing theme among modern environmental and cultural discourses is the view of Hinduism as an eco-environmental and eco-cultural tradition. Scholars, such as Kiran Prasad point to the existence of the figure of Mother Earth, also perceived as Goddess Earth, and a sophisticated differentiation between three kinds of forests, depending on the degree of cultivation and the purpose of habitation. One such example of Hindu eco-religion as a way of life are the Bishnois of Rajasthan, fifteenth century, who follow the 29 tenets or principles of guru Jambeshwar (Prasad 2018: 10–11).

Additionally, Prasad points to a threefold concept of *vana* (forest) in Hinduism: *mahāvana* (forest with natural growth with no human habitation), *tapovana* (penetrable forest with abundant natural flora and fauna and forest, where monks and sages perform *tapas*, or ascetic practice), and *śrīvana* (groves and gardens surrounding a village). Significantly, another term for forest, *araṇya*, refers to a place of no war, thus probably implying harmony between humans and the natural world. Furthermore, traditionally, the ground on which a new building was built was always worshipped by performing *bhūmi pūjā*, the Hindu religious service of worshipping and honoring the ground as a deity. The author also talks about the worship of trees and the sacredness of five groves – banyan tree, peepal tree, ashoka tree, bela and the halada tree, as well as the tulsi plant, which is venerated by all Hindus. Prasad also states that buildings were built in a sustainable way, according to the laws of *vāstuśāstra* (architecture). (Prasad 2018: 4–10)

Even though the author does not make this argument, it is important to clarify here that the ancient Indian discipline of architecture, as well as of many other sciences, have always been seen as part of Hinduism and as part of Hindu auxiliary literature. Thus, we may state that not only religion, but also science has had an eco-environmental and eco-cultural orientation in ancient India. Prasad reflects on the importance of the five *pañcabhūtas* (elements), air, water, fire, earth, and ether as the basis of all human creation, as well as on the importance of *prakṛti* (nature) in Hindu philosophy. (Prasad 2018: 4–10) The author does not elaborate on this point, as his major concern is sustainable development. However, it is important to state here that in the philosophical system of *Sāṃkya-yoga*, matter is not simply "nature," but rather the force or principle according to which the material world is evolving, through the interactions of *prakṛti* (nature, matter, conceived of as a female principle) and *puruṣa* (consciousness, perceived as a male principle). Once again, we see the interconnectedness between environmental, religious and philosophical discourses in Hindu traditions.

However, I must disagree with Prasad's simplistic and idealistic presentation of the *varṇāśrama* system. As I have argued elsewhere, a discussion of *dharma* ("moral, religious duty") *varṇa* ("class," "caste"), *jāti* ("subcaste") and the issues of purity and pollution would show a picture that is far from idealistic and harmonious. The levels of "otherness" are multiple: one can be outside one specific *varṇa* (if one belongs to a different *varṇa*, ouside one *jāti* (if one belongs to a different *jāti*), or completely outside the *varṇa* system, for instance as an untouchable or a non-Hindu.[4] The exclusion can also be gender–specific. Thus, *strīdharma*, the *dharma* ("moral, religious duty") of women is different from that of men. Traditionally women had been excluded from many ritual activities, had not been allowed initiation (*upanayana*) and had been considered impure at numerous occasions. However, it is important to note that Hindu traditions are not uniform, and that the notions of *varṇa*, purity and pollution, can be quite different in *bhakti* (devotional) Hinduism, in the Sikh tradition and in many reform Hindu movements of the nineteenth and twentieth centuries. These traditions reject or reinterpret the caste system and the notions of purity and pollution, inherent in what we may call "mainstream" or traditional Hinduism (Dimitrova 2014b: 3–4).

Importantly, it would be impossible to deal with present-day environmental concerns and discourses in modern India without mentioning Gandhi's legacy. Gandhi has revisited the Hindu notion of *ahiṃsa* or non-violence and has emphasized the problem of pollution, thus inspiring many contemporary environmentalists in India. Partly because of his emphasis on simple living and his critique of global economies and consumerism, his writings and example have helped define the global development of ecological values. Similarly, several modern activist movements, such as the Chipko movement in the 1970s, which had its precedent in the eighteenth-century Bishnoi movement in Rajasthan, and the anti-Tehri Dam movement should be mentioned here.

In the 1970s, Chandni Prasad Bhatt and Sunderlal Bahaguna led the "Chipko *āndolan*" ("hugging") movement in which local villagers began to hug trees in the Himalayan forest to prevent commercial deforestation. Chipko has succeeded in changing government policies and has influenced similar non-violent environmental movements across the globe. More recently, the Chipko movement has been involved in protests against the construction of the Tehri dam on the Bhagirathi river. (Nelson 2008: 108) Indiscriminating hydro-electric projects, which had threatened

---

4 On the concepts of varṇa, jāti, dharma and on purity and pollution, see Klostermaier (1994) and Flood (1996).

to displace and destroy the livelihood of the Adivasi (indigenous tribal population of North-East India) has prompted Adivasi activists to stage neo-Gandhian *satyāgraha* (insistence on truth) fasts in order to protest the construction of Sardar Sarovar dam on the Narmada river. (Rodrigues 2010: 332) These activist movements should be seen in the context of the same intellectual discourse, which has also motivated thinker and activist Vandan Shiva to propagate a new, eco-friendly version of Gandhianism.

Gandhi's insistence on non-violence and vegetarianism, and his attention to meditation and the practice of yoga resonates with Vivekananda's contribution to introducing yoga on the global stage and to reviving yoga in India in the late nineteenth and early twentieth centuries. It is especially important to mention here the philosophy and practice of yogic traditions, which include physical, metaphysical, and ethical speculations and practices for purifying body and mind, and for bringing the microcosm of human being in harmony with the macrocosm of the universe, in pursuit of *mokṣa*, or liberation from *saṃsāra*.

This exploration of environmental and cultural discourses, climate change and Hindu traditions would not be complete without considering the broader humanistic discussions on the Anthropocene, the "Orbis Hypothesis" and the Columbian Exchange (Lee and Beckelheimer 2020: 110–129), or the reflections on "the climate of history" (Chakrabarty 2009: 197–222). We need to emphasize that they all invite us to rethink global life and the present human condition.

Has global life happened by coincidence in what many scientists and scholars believe to be the new geological era of the Anthropocene, in which human beings are not just historical and social agents, but also geological agents? Or, is it rather the result of the colonial project of the empire, which was motivated by power and the desire to dominate people, animals, plants and resources globally? In this sense, the call to decolonize the Anthropocene, and to honor and include the voices of the marginalized, such as of former colonized countries, like India, of indigenous people, of women, of low-castes, of untouchables and, as Greta Thunberg has recently taught us, of children, and of other disadvantaged groups becomes one of the most important humanistic projects of our time.

6 Conclusion

We reflected on some important eco-religious and eco-cultural aspects of Hindu traditions and reviewed several important Hindu texts, which are abundant in apocalyptic images, calamities and salvific notions of deities. While the textual material depicts the victory of good over evil and the Hindu savior gods saving humanity from a calamity, the texts do not offer any critical self-reflection on climate change and humans' actions in this respect. Thus, environmental sensibilities, ethic and discourses are the product of modernity.

Nowadays, modern thinkers and scholars have turned anew to Hindu texts in order to alert to problems of climate change and the catastrophic consequences of irresponsible and destructive profit-oriented consumerism. By revisiting concepts such as non-violence, vegetarianism, by evoking religious feelings of discontent at the violation of Mother Earth, river and mountain goddesses, and by propagating the holistic, wholesome and sustainable body-mind practices of ancient yoga, they engage their contemporaries in religiously inspired environmental discourses and urge awareness about climate change.

We discussed the questions of climate, power and the Anthropocene in relation to Hindu traditions and indigenous ecological consciousness. While this chapter does not want to present an idealized and romanticized picture of Hinduism, turning a blind eye on socio-cultural problems, such as caste and gender inequality, nationalism, pollution and other environmental problems, we would like to point to the complexity of all questions discussed, and to suggest Hindu eco-religious and eco-cultural thought as an inspiration for universal progress.

It seems befitting to conclude this chapter on Hindu apocalyptic imagination and climate change with the ancient Vedic Gāyatrī mantra, which has become nowadays the beloved mantra of yoga universalism and yoga-inspired environmental consciousness throughout the globe. The Vedic Gāyatrī mantra is dedicated to the vivifying Sun deity Savitṛ. Traditionally, only twice-born Hindu men of the upper castes could recite it. Modern Hindu reform movements have spread the practice of making the Gāyatrī mantra accessible also to women and to people of all castes and creeds, and it is in this sense, that I would like to conclude my chapter by "reciting" the Gāyatrī mantra first in Sanskrit, and then in English. There are several possible translations and interpretations of the Gāyatrī Mantra. I have chosen a translation, which conveys a message of faith in the wisdom of humankind to look up to Nature for guidance and answer to the pressing questions of climate change.

ॐ भूर्भुवः स्वः ।

तत् सवितुर्वरेण्यं ।

भर्गो देवस्य धीमहि ।

धियो यो नः प्रचोदयात्

Let us meditate on that excellent glory of Savitṛ, the divine vivifying Sun, May he enlighten our minds. — Ṛgveda 3.62.10

Bibliography

Billimoria, Puroshottama, Joseph Prabhu and Renuka Sharma (2007) *Indian Ethics: Classical Traditions and Contemporary Challenges* (London and New York: Routledge).

Chakrabarty, Dipesh (2009) "The Climate of History: Four Theses," *Critical Inquiry* 35, 197–222.

Chapple, Christopher Key and Mary Evelyn Tucker (2000) *Hinduism and Ecology: The Intersection of Earth, Sky, and Water* (Cambridge, MA: Harvard University Press).

Dimitrova, Diana and Thomas de Bruijn (eds) (2017) *Imagining Indianness: Cultural Identity and Literature* (New York: Palgrave Macmillan).

Dimitrova, Diana (2017) "Introduction: On "Indianness" and Indian Cultural Identity in South Asian Literature," in *Imagining Indianness: Cultural Identity and Literature*, ed. Diana Dimitrova and Thomas de Bruijn (New York: Palgrave Macmillan), 1–11.

Dimitrova, Diana (ed) (2014a) *The Other in South Asian Traditions: Perspectives on Otherism and Otherness* (London and New York: Routledge).

Dimitrova, Diana (2014b) "On Otherism and Othering," in *The Other in South Asian Traditions: Perspectives on Otherism and Otherness*, ed. Diana Dimitrova (London and New York: Routledge), 116.

Dwivedi, O. P. and B. N. Tiwari (1987) *Environmental Crisis and Hindu Religion* (New Delhi: Gitanjali).

Framarin, Christopher (2014) *Hinduism and Environmental Ethics* (London and New York: Routledge).

Glood, Gavin (1996) *An Introduction to Hinduism* (Cambridge: Cambridge University Press).

Gosling, David A (2001) *Religion and Ecology in India and Southeast Asia* (London: Routledge).

Jain, Pankaj (2010) *Dharma and Ecology of Hindu Communities: Sustenance and Sustainability* (Farnham, UK: Ashgate).

James, George (ed) (1999) *Ethical Perspectives on Environmental Issues in India* (New Delhi: A. P. H.).

James, George and Pankaj Jain (2015) "Environmental Ethics: Indian Perspectives," in *Ethics, Science, Technology, and Engineering: A Global Resource*, 2d ed., vol. 2, ed. J. Britt Holbrook and Carl Mitcham (Farmington Hills, MI: Macmillan), 119–121.

Kent, Eliza (2016) "Hinduism and Environmentalism in Modern India," in *Hinduism in the Modern World*, ed. Brian A. Hatcher (New York: Routledge), 290–308.

Klostermaier, Klaus (1994) *A Survey of Hinduism* (Albany, NY: State University of New York Press).

Lee, James Jaehoon and Joshua Beckelhimer (2020) "Anthropocene and Empire: Discourse Networks of the Human Record," *PMLA: Publications of the Modern Language Association of America* 135.1, 110–129.

Narayanan, Vasudha (2001) "Water, Wood, and Wisdom: Ecological Perspectives from the Hindu Traditions," *Daedalus* 130.4, 179–206.

Nelson, Lance (2008) "Ecology," in *Studying Hinduism: Key Concepts and Methods*, ed. Sushil Mittal and Gene Thursby (New York: Routledge), 97–111.

Nelson, Lance E. (1998) *Purifying the Earthly Body of God: Religion and Ecology in Hindu India* (Albany: State University of New York Press).

Pintchman, Tracy (1994) *The Rise of the Goddess in the Hindu Tradition* (Albany: State University of New York Press).

Prasad, Kiran (ed) (2018) *Communication, Culture and Ecology: Rethinking Sustainable Development in Asia* (Singapore: Springer Nature).

Rodrigues, Hillary (2010) "Hinduism and Ecology," in *Introducing Hinduism*, ed. Hillary Rodrigues (New York and London: Routledge), 329–33.

Judith Eckenhoff
The Desert Wasteland and Climate Change in *Mad Max: Fury Road*

1 Introduction

Throughout the first two decades of the twenty-first century, climate change has established a growing presence in literature and popular culture, sometimes taking center stage, especially since climate change fiction, aka cli-fi, has developed as a genre, and sometimes providing a backdrop for its dramatic plots to unfurl against in narratives that span from young adult dystopian fiction to natural disaster films. As general awareness of climate change and activists' demands for political action have as of now become an integral part of public discourse, the massive scale and complexity of climate change continue to pose a challenge to representation. Images of rising sea levels, fire, or an anthropomorphized planet suffering from high temperature constitute attempts to meet this challenge and make the consequences of climate change palpable. Similarly, desert wastelands such as featured in the action film *Mad Max: Fury Road* (2015) provide the popular imagination with a sublime landscape of destruction visualizing the anthropogenic environmental impact that is ultimately impossible to represent comprehensively. Addressing the problem of representation, Maggie Kainulainen argues that, while "many of us are able to comprehend basic climate science and can even imagine the effects of climate change and how they might motivate us to act," climate change, "as a rhetorical object, is hydra-headed, referring as it does to processes, loops, and national and cultural responses, making it possible to interpret and imagine climate change in very different ways" (2013: 110). These different ways of course tend to manifest different courses of action according to not just our understanding of climate change but also of our agency to mitigate its effects.

With roughly one third of the earth's land surface threatened by desertification, which tends to be exacerbated by climate change as billions of tons of fertile soil are lost each year and many regions are facing drought, growing deserts have come to be emblematic of the processes that are endangering millions of human lives and livelihoods as well as non-human nature. With the crucial role that soil and vegetation play in binding carbon, unviable agricultural practices and mismanagement of water resources contribute to the pressure ecosystems in drier areas of the world are facing under changing climate conditions. According to the UN Convention to Combat Desertification, at least two billion people already live in

https://doi.org/10.1515/9783110730203-006

countries that experience high water stress and "about 71 per cent of the world's irrigated area and 47 per cent of major cities experience at least periodic water shortages. If this trend continues, the scarcity and associated water quality problems will lead to competition and conflicts among water users" (unccd. int 2020). Against this background, the desert wastelands of postapocalyptic narratives like *Mad Max: Fury Road* may seem like extreme, albeit not altogether implausible, speculations about the long-term effects of climate change and land degradation, portraying a fictional future that manifests the fears associated with current developments.

The wasteland has a long tradition as a literary trope manifesting the physical destruction of war and environmental exploitation. Landscapes ravaged by disaster allow us to visualize the toll of violent human actions as well as the devastating power of natural phenomena. In the Anthropocene these have become closely entangled and, while the complex interactions of different factors involved in climate change present a problem of representability, drought and land degradation in many regions of the world can be seen as palpable results of a warming planet. Throughout literary history, the post-disaster wasteland has been prominently evoked by authors such as T.S. Eliot, Walter M. Miller Jr., or Cormac McCarthy, whose portrayals of decaying environments also tend to mirror the societal and psychological cost of war and environmental destruction. This chapter examines how the depiction of the desert wasteland in *Mad Max: Fury Road* engages environmental themes and imaginatively explores the consequences of climate change and land degradation. The analysis focuses on three major areas: The ecofeminist politics of the film addressing exploitative power structures and resource scarcity, the centrality of cars and fossil fuels in the context of the film's postapocalyptic death cult, and the representation and aestheticization of the desert environment, which I argue expresses a sense of postapocalyptic sublime as well as solastalgia in its hyperbolic depiction of what a future on a planet changed by climate change and war might look like. Rather than examining the level of accuracy in its depiction of scientific predictions for the future, this chapter is concerned with investigating how cultural imagination in the form of popular action cinema addresses the issues of climate change and environmental destruction and represents a bleak future projection of current problems.

In the postapocalyptic genre and the added context of climate change and currently ongoing land degradation, the desert has come to exemplify the extent to which anthropogenic ecological changes literally lay waste to the world. The wasteland becomes the site where extreme environmental conditions meet themes of extreme exploitation, trauma, and deprivation. Control of resources means social power, usually enforced by violence, and engendering dystopian, often fascist, racist, and patriarchal social structures among survivors of the disaster. The 2015 postapocalyptic film *Mad Max: Fury Road*[1] interweaves its spectacular action with ecofeminist ethics, which – although climate change is never explicitly mentioned – contribute to its overall critique of the capitalist greed, continued reliance on fossil fuels, and increasing resource scarcity that are at the core of the discourse surrounding climate change. Far from any pretense that it depicts a *realistic* future world, it nevertheless presents a critical speculative engagement with the collapse of civilization and the survival of humanity in its hyperbolic postapocalyptic worldbuilding and plot. *Fury Road* is the critically acclaimed fourth instalment in George Miller's series of *Mad Max* films, which from 1979 on have been depicting the deteriorating state of the world, tracing the developments of society from failing, overwhelmed institutions to violent anarchy to re-establishment of tribal social structures under the rule of tyrannical warlords. One of these warlords – Immortan Joe, a self-fashioned redeemer of the wretched – is the main antagonist in *Fury Road*. Max Rockatansky, roaming the wasteland after avenging the brutal murder of his wife and child in the first movie, tends to get caught up in helping other people's causes, which also comprises the plot of *Fury Road*.

The film opens with Max (Tom Hardy) getting captured by the followers of the warlord Immortan Joe (Hugh Keays-Byrne), the War Boys, who suffer from an unnamed disease that requires regular blood transfusions. Max is identified as universal donor and consequently used as a human "blood bag." When a group of young women, who have been enslaved as Immortan Joe's "wives" and "breeders," escape from his Citadel with the help of one of his lieutenants, Imperator Furiosa (Charlize Theron), the War Boys give chase and Max is taken along. Max manages to free himself after a crash and reluctantly forges an alliance with Furiosa and the women. When it becomes clear that their destination of Furiosa's childhood home, the "Green Place," no longer exists and chances of survival in the wasteland are slim, the women decide to turn back, fight, and take the Citadel and with it, stewardship over water and other natural resources. While ending the violent regime of the post-capitalist, patriarchal villain contains a clear environmentalist message, one might say that *Fury Road* complicates its own critique through the delightfully chaotic carnage of the car chases and reveling in the ensuing violence and destruction. The affective thrill of the action, the trademark wasteland aesthetics, and the exuberantly modified cars present a counterweight to the grim devastation of the postapocalyptic world, which results in making the portrayed future "both existentially terrifying and fundamentally exciting," as Hassler-Forest puts it. He states that "no other film series has

---

[1] I shall refer to the film *Fury Road* in the following.

made the post-apocalyptic, warlord-ravaged hellscape that seems like the inevitable end game of global capitalism so much fun" (2017: 301).

Besides the visual artistry of the cinematography and editing, the stunt work, and production design, it has been mostly *Fury Road*'s feminist politics that have dominated the discussion on both popular and academic platforms. Hassler-Forest points out that despite the nightmarish dystopian storyworld, the *Mad Max* series also contains "stubborn and remarkably resilient utopian imaginaries" (2017: 304) and although, as Michelle Yates has shown, the characters' attempted recovery of a nostalgic Edenic nature is impossible, *Fury Road*'s ending leaves a slight possibility for hope. The following analysis will address the ideological stance of the movie in relation to the themes of exploitation and environmental degradation as well as fossil fuel consumption and car culture. It will then extend the existing scholarly criticism on *Fury Road* by presenting a cognitively informed ecocritical reading of the movie's representation of the desert environment. Taking into consideration the dimensions of "both emotional identification and embodied affect" (Ingram 2014: 25), the analysis will show how *Fury Road* portrays the disastrous consequences of anthropogenic environmental destruction and climate change for human and – albeit much less explicitly – nonhuman life, whereas its highly aestheticized depiction of the wasteland landscape and *mise-en-scène* of the desert also evoke a sublime sense of a posthuman world.

2 Who Killed the World and Who Will Redeem It?

The short exposition montage, consisting of Max's monologue over a black screen with the opening titles interspersed with voiceover fragments, sketches out the apocalyptic event as humanity having "gone rogue, terrorizing itself" in "oil wars" and "water wars," the latter presumably exacerbated by climate change. The result of the "thermonuclear skirmish" that followed is that "the earth is sour. Our bones are poisoned. We have become half-life." The words are accompanied by a black and white clip of a forest swayed by the force of a nuclear detonation, establishing that not only has humanity all but self-destructed but also destroyed the natural environment it depends on for survival. This impact is also embodied by a two-headed gecko shown in the first shot of Max, his car, and the wasteland. As monstrously mutated animals with too many heads, eyes, or limbs tend to be a popular symbol for otherwise invisible nuclear fallout, the gecko visually complements the implications of a poisoned planet, moving from the foreground towards Max, who stands surveying the desert and promptly catches and devours the animal.

Scarcity and starvation are also exemplified by the wretched masses gathered around the rock formation that is Immortan Joe's Citadel. Emaciated and impoverished, they are at the mercy of the warlord and his generosity, as he announces "I am your redeemer. It is by my hand you will rise from the ashes of this world," before opening three gigantic valves that pour forth water for a few brief moments, some of which people manage to catch in their waiting vessels while much of it is wasted and seeps into the desert ground. The cynicism of Immortan Joe's speech from atop the Citadel, which in several wide shots is shown to be covered in a lush green oasis and houses hydroponic hanging gardens growing produce, sustained by a "ridiculous amount of clear water" pumped up from the earth, is all the more poignant when he adds the absurd advice "Do not, my friends, become addicted to water. It will take hold of you and you will resent its absence." It becomes clear that the failings of civilization, which brought the world to its current state and humanity to the brink of extinction, find continuance in the postapocalyptic remnants of society, where patriarchal oppression and the capitalist logic of exploiting and objectifying people ensures the power of warlords like Immortan Joe. In their analysis of the economic system of *Fury Road*'s storyworld, Vachris and Mateer argue that the lack of property rights, and indeed most basic human rights, leaves the remainder of humanity in a Hobbesian state of *bellum omnium contra omnes*, which only contributes further to the waste of scarce and precious resources. To maintain its power and defend its resources the Citadel relies on indoctrinated soldiers ready to sacrifice themselves in the hope of "McFeasting in Valhalla" and a barter economy of trading Aqua Cola (water), produce, and Mother's Milk (harvested mechanically from fattened women in the Citadel, turned into cattle robbed of agency and personhood) for guzzoline and ammunition from Gas Town and The Bullet Farm, respectively. Thus, *Fury Road* "exposes and rejects one of capitalism's most brutal and necessary functions: the reduction of certain bodies into commodities" (Boulware 2016: 3).

Ecofeminist approaches to *Fury Road* highlight how "nature is used as a tool of power" (Yates 2017: 354), which also entails the patriarchal control of sexual reproduction that the enslaved women are escaping from. Discovering and very much resenting the absence of his "prize breeders," Immortan Joe is confronted with the graffiti they have left behind, including the assertion "WE ARE NOT THINGS" and the rhetorical question "WHO KILLED THE WORLD?" The young women's teacher and mentor, Miss Giddy (Jennifer Hagan), who stayed behind, tells him "You cannot own a human being. Sooner or later someone pushes back!" Ironically, the pushback seems to have at least been facilitated by the piles of books that the women were locked up with, which disrupts the apparent "(re)produc[tion of] a dichotomy in which men, culture and agency are aligned with human subjectivity, while women are aligned with nature" (Yates 2017: 354).

Although Yates argues that "women and nature become the subordinate ground, the object, upon which dominant male-driven culture acts" (2017: 354), the association of the slave-wives with culture, education, and a refusal to participate in the system of perpetual violence (another graffiti reads "OUR BABIES WILL NOT BE WARLORDS") complicates that notion of a clear nature/culture dichotomy. Throughout the film, the escaped women also demonstrate an understanding of the mechanisms that have produced anthropogenic climate change as well as the subsequent wars and thorough, widespread land degradation.

The women's goal of reaching the Green Place, home of the matriarchal tribe of the Vuvalini, that Furiosa was kidnapped from as a child, in hope of finding personal freedom and a livable, fertile place in the wasteland has drawn criticism of gender essentialism. Belinda DuPloy writes that there is a certain "conflation of presumed innocence, women, maternity and nature," which ought to be seen critically (2019: 14). However, the discovery that the Green Place, like the rest of the world, has gone sour and become poisoned, undercuts such simplified readings, as does the fact that both Max and the War Boy Nux join the women's cause, resisting their own objectification as full-life blood bag and half-life battle fodder within Immortan Joe's system. Thus, *Fury Road*'s environmental themes are enmeshed with its feminist politics, as the "message is clearly about collaboration and cooperation as essential for the redemption of a world in which gendered inequities and abuses of power remain deeply disconcerting obstacles" (Du Plooy 2019: 2).

In light of the environmental destruction wrought by climate change and nuclear war, the movie uses the contrasting symbols of seeds and bullets – "antiseed, plant one and watch something die" – but aligning them less with a nature/culture dichotomy than with a culture of cultivation and stewardship over nature as opposed to the culture of violence perpetuating a system of oppression and exploitation that continues in the same vein as the one that destroyed human civilization. Taylor Boulware writes that *Fury Road*

> is utopian, not in the sense that it presents an ideal world, but that it imagines successful liberatory revolution and the destruction of decrepit systems of oppression, out of which a more perfect, egalitarian world can then emerge. Through the grotesque, parasitic tyranny of Immortan Joe's monstrous necropolitics that reduces subjects to mere bodies for the deathly reproduction of the decaying corpse of capitalism, the film exposes the inextricable links between traditional masculinity, patriarchy, and capitalist exploitation.
>
> (2016: 1)

Nevertheless, no revolution will be able to restore the collapsed ecosystems of the earth and in this regard, *Fury Road* "offers no false hope," as Brogan Morris argues, and "there is no solution offered for the reversal of irreversible climate change, and nor should there be" (2015). This becomes apparent in the scene in which the Keeper of the Seeds (Melissa Jaffer), one of the surviving Many

Mothers of the Green Place, shows the "heirloom" seeds she carries to the Dag (one of the slave-wives, portrayed by Abbey Lee), telling her, "I plant one every chance I get. So far, nothing's took. Earth's too sour." The image of a tiny basil plant growing inside a small animal skull that she carries in her bag of seeds – the green leaves standing out vibrantly in the otherwise darkly lit scene – still does suggest a cycle of decay and revitalization. However, the temporal scale of global ecosystems recovering and evolution producing species of plants and animals adapted to the conditions of a changed climate and nuclear fallout certainly stakes the odds against humanity's survival.

The recurrent question of who killed the world thus implicates the audience in their responsibility for the devastated planet of the fictional future, as it follows the current trajectory of climate change, land degradation, burning rainforests, pollution of the oceans, corporations siphoning water for profit in unchecked and unsustainable amounts, as well as ongoing violent international conflict over finite fossil fuel resources to its extreme conclusion. In a confrontation between the women and Nux, he insists "We are not to blame," like a mantra absolving the War Boys from previous generations' failures – which falls flat, however, as he is still complicit in the Ur-Fascism[2] that is the successor to the ideologies that *are* to blame. While a rejection of accountability for the state of the world is a relatable individual response, a minimally self-aware audience might at least take up the invitation to reflect on the collective responsibility that we bear, which would have us ideally *not* kill the world, if that is still possible.

The realization that the Green Place no longer exists and that there is no safe paradise left to escape to marks a "moment of environmental nostalgia, the cautionary moment in which the audiences are encouraged to consider and conserve the pristine, Edenic nature that still exists in our material reality, even if it no longer exists in the film" (Yates 2017: 359). However, Yates argues that *Fury Road*'s disruption of the traditional Edenic recovery narrative ultimately serves a more viable "environmentalist ethics: the need to seek 'home' where we actually make our living to recover environmental sustainability" (ibid.: 367). Initially, the women, after joining forces with the surviving members of Furiosa's tribe, plan to make their way across a salt desert without any certainty that they will find another livable place beyond. When Max suggests turning back to take the Citadel, now undefended while Immortan Joe has taken up pursuit of them with his entire war party, he tells them: "It'll be a hard day. But I guarantee you

---

2 Marc DiPaolo identifies Immortan Joe's cult as a kind of Ur-Fascism, drawing on Umberto Eco's description of the elements of Ur-Fascist culture, and emphasizes that it represents the "opposite of the socio-political values espoused by environmentalist advocates of ethical stewardship over the planet" (DiPaolo 2018: 186).

that a 160 days' ride that way, there's nothing but salt." The successful revolution that follows gives the four former wives that survive to the end the opportunity to transform their former prison according to their utopian ideals. It also gives Max and Furiosa a chance to find the redemption they seek – Max, for his previous failure to help the people who needed him, and Furiosa, for her actions as one of Immortan Joe's henchmen. As Yates writes, the kind of sustainability that is advocated by *Fury Road* thus "involves taking responsibility for solving problems in the places humans actually inhabit, not seeking solutions in a romanticized elsewhere" (ibid.: 367).

Some critics argue that Furiosa eventually killing Immortan Joe suggests a change in regime, replacing her as "benign ruler" (DiPaolo 2018: 202), and that she "and her female compatriots will (re)claim The Citadel and distribute the resources more equitably, which will permit the reproduction of crops and food more abundantly," as Clavin claims, making "precious liquids like oil, water and milk [. . .] more available" (2016: 60). Besides the disturbing assumption that Furiosa, once in charge, would continue the practice of milking human beings like cattle, these readings of the ending imply that the water resources would not suffice to quench the thirst of the "politically unmotivated, uneducated, weak, and perhaps even quasi-human residents" (Bordun 2016: 77). Such a characterization of the wretched survivors of the apocalypse, many of whom are indeed physically deformed, unsightly, and have been reduced to animal survival instincts, unquestioningly seems to perpetuate their dehumanization. Indeed, Clavin's concerns that a humanistic perspective of environmentalism has made overpopulation a taboo in favor of shifting the debate towards consumption result in an interpretation of *Fury Road* – whose plot, after all, centers on women fighting for personal and reproductive freedom – that seems to bemoan Immortan Joe's vilification, although he and his inner circle are "the transmitters of the only representation of population limits and resource governance" (2016: 59) and "sustainable practices are marginalized through negative connotations" (2016: 60). Considering the low life-expectancy of the half-life War Boys and the destitute and elderly inhabitants of the wasteland, overpopulation seems hardly the primary problem in a postapocalyptic future where most of humanity has perished. Although the Citadel's resources are explicitly stated to be plenty, bartering them for ammunition and guzzoline instead of making them equally available seems hardly sustainable.

3 The Death Throes of the Combustion Engine

With the *Mad Max* series' indebtedness to car culture movies and much of the action of *Fury Road* taking place in, on, under, and around motor vehicles, it is also worthwhile to consider its relationship to fossil fuel and the scavenged and modified remnants of a civilization that run on it. In light of the oil wars that contributed to the apocalypse in this fictional future, not to mention the real climate-changing effects of the carbon emissions that came along with the Great Acceleration, the cars, the War Rig, and motorcycles portrayed in the *Max Mad* films are relics of an unsustainable past. Carter Soles suggests in his analysis of petroleum and gender politics in the series that the fact that the vehicles in *Fury Road* depend on gas – guzzoline – represents a step backward from *Beyond Thunderdome*, in which alternative energy sources play a central role. Soles argues that "if the film carried the premise of the third film to its next logical step, the cars in *Fury Road* would all run on pig shit" (2018: 193). However, with the focus shifted to water and habitable space in the poisoned wasteland, "the acquisition and/or production of refined petroleum is not of any concern" (ibid.). Although people do seem to depend on the vehicles and reinforce and modify them for combat, their carnivalesque exorbitance, excessive use of flamethrowers, and sensational destruction during the car chase scenes are not only the main source of affective thrills and visual spectacle throughout the movie, they are also emblematic of the reproduction of the destructive oil business that caused the catastrophic events of the apocalypse. Significantly, the War Rig, one of the mightiest and most prestigious vehicles in Immortan Joe's fleet, is first appropriated by Furiosa and "becomes a type of womb that carries the slave-wives and births them into freedom, thus, an inversion of the original slave ships" (Du Plooy 2019: 14). However, due to its unsustainable dependence on gas and association with the careless disregard for the finitude of fossil fuel, it must ultimately be turned into a tool that can only be useful in being destroyed when Nux deliberately crashes the Rig in a canyon to block the passage for the pursuing war parties on the way back to the Citadel.

While Soles sees "contradictory impulses at play in *Fury Road*," because the "emphasis on spectacular car stunts and brutal violence, while appropriate for a great piece of action cinema, undermines or at least complicates its bid to be read as an ecofeminist text" (2018, 198), the celebration of mayhem and the destruction of technology that has become all but irreplaceable in the wasteland might also be read as a joyful annihilation of the destructive remains of the old world. Considering how recent car culture films, most notably the *Fast and Furious* franchise, as Murray and Heumann have shown, "reinforce patterns of thought and action that contribute to environmental degradation, and rest on the environmental impact that is inherently a part of car culture" (2010: 154), *Fury Road*'s central focus on cars can certainly be seen critically. In this context, the negative press that the production got for allegedly causing damage to some of its filming locations in the Namibian desert definitively adds a stale note to its environmental themes. According to reports from 2013, there had been no environmental impact assessment prior to filming in "areas meant to be protected, endangering reptiles and rare cacti" (Tay, March 05, 2013). This made evaluating the potential environmental harm done by the production difficult. Since then, Namibia has introduced new environmental legislation that would prohibit filming in many of *Fury Road*'s locations.

Although the movie participates in and to some degree continues to perpetuate the harmful practices of car culture and many action blockbusters, it forgoes a materialist fetishization of the cars in favor of a hyperbolic death cult that has the War Boys dreaming of "[dying] historic on the Fury Road" and an afterlife in which they "ride eternal, shiny and chrome." Consequently, *Fury Road* rather parodies the nostalgic car culture clichés "associated with the freedom of the open road" (Murray and Heumann 2010: 159). These associations, however, are primarily rooted in American culture and *Mad Max* is, after all, an Australian series, often characterized as Australian Gothic. This context remains relevant, even though *Fury Road* features an international cast of actors and was not filmed in Australia like its three predecessors, because "the profound discomfort of colonial dispossession has saturated [Australian] stories," as Ben Wilkie writes, even the ones that are "not ostensibly about colonialism" (2015).

In *Fury Road* the roads have all but disappeared into the wasteland, signaling not only that there are not enough people anymore to use them but also suggesting geographical disorientation and a sense of being lost. Whereas in the first *Mad Max* film, "the road appears as a specific and violently contested site" (Falconer 1997: 249), it has practically vanished by *Beyond Thunderdome*. Falconer argues that this disappearance "represents both the road's liberation from colonial narratives of empire and its absorption into a *deregulated* postcolonial spatiality" (1997: 249, emphasis in original). From an ecocritical perspective this may, on the one hand, be regarded as the nonhuman landscape and its material agency reconquering colonized spaces like roads. On the other hand, that very landscape is inextricably entangled with humanity because the wasteland becomes an emblem of the Anthropocene and the large-scale irreversible changes in the planet's geography wrought by humans.

4 The Apocalyptic Sublime and Solastalgia of the Wasteland

In this final section on *Fury Road*, I will discuss the representation of the desert wasteland itself regarding its affective and aesthetic quality and the cultural significance of the desert. Desertification is a phenomenon easily connected with the human impact on natural environments as drought and land degradation signal mismanagement of water resources and unsustainable agricultural practices. In the context of climate change as an aggravating factor in these developments, the spread of deserts materializes the fears of planet Earth possibly becoming uninhabitable for humans in the future. While the desert, or more precisely, the manmade wasteland, is a kind of landscape that epitomizes large-scale destructive environmental exploitation, it also holds an aesthetic appeal for many people and, in the realm of fictional narrative, it provides an environment for imaginative exploration of what climate change means for our future.

In his study *The Sacred Desert*, David Jasper discusses various cultural representations of the desert, arguing that it is an environment that decenters the human self, dissolving time and space: "Physically the harshest places on earth, deserts also defy our sense of reality, its proportions and the boundaries we set on our lives and experience" (2004: 71). The environmental conditions, most of all the scarcity of water, which make it an inhospitable place for human and much nonhuman life, contribute to its otherness – "an absolute otherness that negates and exposes every construction and defense of human civilization and culture" (Jasper 2004: 73). Yet, precisely these qualities predispose the desert for its role in various mythologies – and religious narratives often render it a space of spiritual significance. To cross the desert and to face its physical and psychological challenges sometimes means facing God, sometimes the incomprehensible scale and sublime power of the natural world.

In the *Mad Max* series, the wasteland has come to comprise the whole world of the characters. *Fury Road*'s *mise-en-scène* highlights the desert's sense of negation and emptiness in numerous wide shots showing the characters and cars dwarfed by the massive scale of the environment, decentering the humans and illustrating the vast dimensions of the anthropogenic destruction. In contrast to various other postapocalyptic films that defamiliarize landscapes of ruin and disaster by emphasizing their dreary and dying characteristics by means of desaturated, grey and grim color schemes, *Fury Road* stands out with its bright and highly saturated orange, red, and yellow colors and deep blue filter laid over the night scenes. Instead of just functioning as a faded background of negative space the desert is thus foregrounded and aestheticized, visually highlighting the extreme environmental conditions.³

The evocation of dry heat and harsh sunlight facilitates affective responses and an embodied sense of the environment of hot sand and rock, which is additionally intensified by the countless explosions. The inhabitants of the wasteland have become visually incorporated into the landscape, as for instance the apparently nomadic mountain tribe is camouflaged in brown tones, vanishing into the terrain. Meanwhile, the people dwelling at the foot of the Citadel are shown to wear faded, sand colored screen contraptions that serve as protection from the glare of the sun but also seem to merge them almost seamlessly with the ground, reminiscent of animals adapted to visually vanish in their surroundings. While especially the latter highlights the dehumanizing effect of existing in the wasteland, making visible what Rob Nixon has described as the slow violence of climate change and environmental degradation that disproportionately affects the poor of the global south (2011), one could argue more optimistically that it also suggests a natural survival instinct realized by adapting to extreme conditions. This kind of adaptation dissolves the dichotomy of human and animal, which is also illustrated in the scene of the characters passing through the former Green Place – now more of a blue and black place – showing the silhouettes of dead trees, crows, and people quietly and slowly passing through the bog on stilts, four-legged and rag-covered, as the War Rig slowly drives past in the background. Significantly, the crows are the only nonhuman inhabitants of the wasteland (besides the two-headed gecko that Max gobbles up in the first scene and a bug that Nux finds and also immediately eats). Their stereotypical association with death and penchant to be shown scavenging battlefields underscores the hopeless sense of post-war decay and with the formerly resilient ecosystem of the Green Place finally collapsed, the film suggests that their days, too, are numbered.

Although the environment produces some of the obstacles of the journey, in the shape of a massive electrical sand storm and the War Rig getting bogged down and stuck, the material conditions also appear to sometimes work in the protagonists' favor as the obstacles never slow them down too much and the wide space allows the pursuers to be always visible on the horizon. A dead tree stump lets them pull the War Rig from the mud, causing a rockslide in the canyon lets them block the pursuers' path, and the storm gives them an opportunity to

---

3 Miller had originally intended for the film to be black and white and released a monochromatic "Black and Chrome Edition" in 2017, which takes the desaturation of many postapocalyptic movies to an extreme and provides an interesting counterpoint to the colorful cinematic version of *Fury Road*.

lose Immortan Joe's war party, at least momentarily. However, the storm also functions as a reminder of the destructive power of nature, in the face of which the mayhem of the car chase looks insignificantly small. With the characters driving towards the immense, towering dust clouds that take the shape of a wall of sand rising hundreds of meters and marking the edge of the storm, the shot slowly zooms out from the War Rig until it and the pursuing vehicles are barely visible against the encroaching storm. As Furiosa keeps driving and whirlwind currents within the storm haul cars and War Boys into the air right next to her and its electrical charges cause their fair share of explosions, it is the sequence that is most reminiscent of other eco- disaster films. Extreme weather phenomena, particularly powerful storms, have come to be one of the frames of reference allowing us to directly see the damage done by climate change and by placing characters in the midst of the chaos, climate change films may evoke what Niklas Salmose describes as an apocalyptic sublime. He distinguishes between action sequences like this, that are "narrative and protagonist driven and work inclusively through embodiment" and a "second variant [with] a more existential and poetic configuration, which emphasizes the more universal dimensions of catastrophe" (2018: 1419). In *Fury Road*, the apocalyptic sublime is also marked by Tom Holkenborg's (aka Junkie XL) score, with orchestral music somewhat distinct from the industrial rock and fast-paced strings and percussions that accompany the car chase and action sequences. The storm is, for instance, musically complemented with a more opulent orchestration of horns and a choir in addition to the strings. While generally the score contributes significantly to the affective thrill of the film in its combination of heavily distorted industrial sound with orchestra and choir,[4] it has a tendency for aligning the industrial sound with the mechanical and industrial visual aesthetics and the predominantly orchestra-heavy music with the vast natural landscape, especially in the less hectic sequences.

The more poetic variant of the apocalyptic sublime that Salmose identifies manifests itself in the eerie quality of the wide shots showing the bog and the crows or the scene of Furiosa walking away from the group after hearing of the destruction of her old home. The scene marks a turning point in the narrative and as Furiosa is framed dropping her bionic arm prosthesis and walking off into the dunes before she falls to her knees and screams in despair, the shots increase the distance to her until she is a tiny, lonely figure in the sand, embodying the utter hopelessness of the postapocalyptic state of the world and the kind of environmental grief that has come to be referred to as solastalgia. The

---

4 Parts of the soundtrack quote *Dies Irae* and incorporate the version from Giuseppe Verdi's *Requiem*, which was prominently utilized in the film's theatrical trailers.

concept was developed by Glenn Albrecht to describe the psychoterratic[5] effects of one's home being subject to environmental devastation and is defined as "the pain or distress caused by the loss of, or ability to derive, solace connected to the negatively perceived state of one's home environment. Solastalgia exists when there is the lived experience of the physical desolation of home" (Albrecht et al. 2007: 96). While Salmose criticizes disaster blockbusters like Emmerich's for the structure of the action-adventure ultimately "negat[ing] any real impact and instead establish[ing] a nostalgic and conservative anthropocentrism" (2018: 1417), *Fury Road*'s postapocalyptic storyworld, even though the narrative as such remains anthropocentric, refuses to promise any kind of restoration of pre- apocalyptic normalcy. Instead, it establishes the wasteland as a posthuman landscape, both in the sense that it is produced by and follows humanity as well as that it will outlast humanity. Despite the utopian impulse of the ending and the prospect of the Citadel becoming a bastion of hope, the fictional quote of the First History Man that closes the film before the credits roll – "Where must we go, we who wander this wasteland, in search of our better selves?" – plays on the mythical trope of a spiritual awakening experienced while crossing the desert but conveys an absence of direction. The sense of divine or spiritual guidance that is often crucial to mythical narratives of ordeals in the desert has been lost in a world where there is no crossing the desert to a better place.

Bibliography

Albrecht, Glenn, Gina-Maree Sartore, Linda Connor, Nick Higginbotham, Sonia Freeman, Brian Kelly, Helen Stain, Anne Tonna, and Georgia Pollard (2007) "Solastalgia: The Distress Caused by Environmental Change," *Australasian Psychiatry* 15.1, S95–98. doi:10.1080/10398560701701288

Bordun, Troy (2016) "What Becomes of Endings on Film? *Elysium, Mad Max: Fury Road, Snowpiercer*," *Science Fiction Film and Television* 9.1, 76–79.

Boulware, Taylor (2016) "'Who Killed the World': Building a Feminist Utopia from the Ashes of Toxic Masculinity in *Mad Max: Fury Road*," *Mise-en-scène: The Journal of Film & Visual Narration* 1.1.

---

5 Albrecht et al. define psychoterratic illness "as earth-related mental illness where people's mental wellbeing (psyche) is threatened by the severing of 'healthy' links between themselves and their home/territory" as opposed to somaterratic illnesses, which "threaten physical wellbeing and are caused mainly by living in ecosystems that have been contaminated by pollutants and toxins" (2007: 65), which manifests, for instance, in the War Boys' illness in *Fury Road*.

Clavin, Keith (2016) "Living, Again: Population and Paradox in Recent Cinema," *Oxford Lit Review* 38.1, 47–65. https://doi.org/10.3366/olr.2016.0179.

DiPaolo, Marc (2018) *Fire and Snow: Climate Fiction from the Inklings to* Game of Thrones (Albany: State University of New York Press).

Du Plooy, Belinda (2019) "'Hope Is a Mistake, If You Can't Fix What's Broken You Go Insane': A Reading of Gender, (S)Heroism and Redemption in *Mad Max: Fury Road*," *Journal of Gender Studies* 28.4. https://doi.org/10.1080/09589236.2018.1491395.

Falconer, Delia (1997) "We Don't Need to Know the Way Home": The Disappearance of the Road in the *Mad Max* Trilogy," in *The Road Movie Book*, ed. Steven Cohan and Ina Rae Hark (London: Routledge), 249–270.

Hassler-Forest, Dan (2017) "*Mad Max*: Between Apocalypse and Utopia," *Science Fiction Film & Television* 10.3, 301–306.

Ingram, David (2014) "Emotion and Affect in Eco-Films: Cognitive and Phenomenological Approaches," in *Moving Environments: Affect, Emotion, Ecology, and Film*, ed. Alexa Weik von Mossner (*Waterloo, ON*: Wilfrid Laurier University Press), 23–40.

Jasper, David (2004) *The Sacred Desert: Religion, Literature, Art, and Culture* (Malden, MA: Blackwell).

Kainulainen, Maggie (2013) "Saying Climate Change: Ethics of the Sublime and the Problem of Representation." *Symplok: A Journal for the Intermingling of Literary, Cultural and Theoretical Scholarship* 21, 109–123.

Mad Max (1979) Dir. George Miller (Kennedy Miller Productions).

Mad Max 2 (1981) Dir. George Miller (Kennedy Miller Productions).

Mad Max Beyond Thunderdome (1985) Dir. George Miller (Kennedy Miller Productions).

Mad Max: Fury Road (2015) Dir. George Miller (Warner Bros.).

Morris, Brogan (2015) "*Mad Max* and the Function of Cinematic Dystopia," *New Humanist*. <https://newhumanist.org.uk/articles/4918/mad-max-and-the-function-of-cinematic-dystopia> (accessed 5 February 2020).

Murray, Robin. L., and Joseph K. Heumann (2010) "Fast, Furious, and Out of Control: The Erasure of Natural Landscapes in Car Culture Films," in *Framing the World: Explorations in Ecocriticism and Film*, ed. P. Willoquet-Maricondi (Charlottesville, VI: University of Virginia Press), 154–169.

Nixon, Rob (2011) *Slow Violence and the Environmentalism of the Poor* (Cambridge, MA: Harvard UP).

Salmose, Niklas (2018) "The Apocalyptic Sublime: Anthropocene Representation and Environmental Agency in Hollywood Action-Adventure Cli-Fi Films," *J Pop Cult* 51.6, 1415–33. <https://doi.org/10.1111/jpcu.12742>

Soles, Carter (2018) "*Mad Max*: Beyond Petroleum?" in *Gender and Environment in Science Fiction*, ed. Christy Tidwell and Bridgitte Barclay (Lanham, MD: Lexington Books), 185–202.

Tay, Nastasya (2013) "*Mad Max: Fury Road* Sparks Real-Life Fury with Claims of Damage to Desert," *The Guardian*, 5 March. <https://www.theguardian.com/world/2013/mar/05/mad-max-fury-road-namibia> (accessed 4 March 2020).

United Nations Convention to Combat Desertification (2020) *Land and Drought*. <https://www.unccd.int/> (accessed 15 March 2020).

Vachris, Michelle A., and G. Dirk Mateer (2018) "Never a Lovely Day: The Wretched Economics of *Mad Max: Fury Road*," in *Dystopia and Economics: A Guide to Surviving Everything from the Apocalypse to Zombies*, ed. Charity-Joy R. Acchiardo and Michelle A. Vachris (Milton: Routledge), 15–27. Routledge Economics and Popular Culture.

Weik von Mossner, Alexa (2014) "Introduction: Ecocritical Film Studies and the Effects of Affect, Emotion, and Cognition," in *Moving Environments: Affect, Emotion, Ecology, and Film*, ed. Alexa Weik von Mossner (Waterloo, ON: Wilfrid Laurier University Press), 1–22.

Wilkie, Ben (2015) "*Mad Max* as Australian Gothic: Don't Leave the Road If You Want to Survive," *The Guardian*, May 21 <https://www.theguardian.com/commentisfree/2015/may/21/mad-max-as-australian-gothic-why-we-love-the-road-and-find-freedom-in-the-car> (accessed 3 March 2020).

Yates, Michelle (2017) "Re-Casting Nature as Feminist Space in *Mad Max: Fury Road*," *Science Fiction Film & Television* 10.3, 353–370. https://doi.org/10.3828/sfftv.2017.24.

Jon Hegglund
Drawing (on) the Future: Narration, Animation, and the Partially Human

1 Introduction

What kind of continued human existence are we capable of imagining within a world that is currently undergoing massive climate-driven transformation? How can we *narrate* the human, at a wider, species-based level, in a climate-altered, Anthropocene future? How do we reconceive the role of humanity somewhere between the extremes of a fully humanist redemption narrative, on the one hand, and the null set of human extinction, on the other? All narratives that represent a human future take place within a broad cultural complex involving science, politics, religion, and popular culture, but here I will focus on fictional narrative for its self-consciousness: when it comes to visions of a future world, such stories activate an entire complex of assumptions about the temporality of the future, about the space of the planet, and about the nature of humanity that will (or will not) continue to exist in the world.

I begin from the premise that we cannot separate these three levels: to talk about climate change is to talk about the future is to talk about humanity. The first of these seems relatively easy to engage on a conceptual (if not a practical) level: the popular terms 'climate change,' or 'global warming,' present a thing, and a temporal process happening to that thing. But it can be easy to view the human orientation toward climate change in a reactive, passive way. Even as the modifier 'anthropogenic' is often tagged onto the beginning of the term 'climate change,' most popular representations of climate transformation figure it as something happening *to* humans, something that should elicit a human response or human reaction but is conceptually, constitutively external to human identity. In *The Great Derangement*, Amitav Ghosh writes that climate disasters have made him aware of the "urgent proximity of nonhuman presences," but he then goes on to argue that "serious fiction" is incapable of registering or notating these presences (2016: 5). Along with other scholars in the burgeoning field of econarratology,[1] I believe that narrative across many genres and modes *can* engage with the massively distributed, complex, unpredictable processes of climate change, but that those narratives will often push the boundaries of

---

[1] This term was coined by Erin James (2015). See also the introduction to and chapters within James and Morel (2020).

fictional convention, involving defamiliarizations of form and/or content. Ghosh is of course aware that climate change, among other things, has brought the recognition that the environment in all its material forms possesses power and agency, but "proximity" is too tame a word to describe this relation. Narrative, across many genres and modes, increasingly expresses entanglement and interconnection more than proximity, a state of being akin to Timothy Morton's notion of the "mesh," a material state in which "[n]othing exists all by itself, and so nothing is fully 'itself'" (2010: loc. 204).

In this chapter, I'll address one mode through which narrative can express the limits and transformations of a human, or at least a 'humanish,' future on the planet. This sense of futurity is based in a view not of the anthropocentric, non-human, or post-human, but of what I'm calling the partially human. The partially human differs from the post-human because it acknowledges that, while we are newly aware of an interconnected enmeshment between humans and world, we are stuck with certain human traits, most notably at the level of a consciousness and cognition that is singularly capable of producing narrative. The partially human has no investment in human exceptionalism or triumphant anthropocentrism; it sees the inherent condition of the human in a compromised, imperfect state. This distinguishes it from the more celebratory versions of post-humanism, which point to human interfaces with the nonhuman world as a source of power or enhanced agency. Where the post-human (in its more optimistic visions, at least) wishes to push through the clouds of anthropocentrism to the shining light of a brave new world, the partially human admits that such wishes amount to a futile attempt to outrun our own shadows.

The notion of the partially human involves an estrangement or defamiliarization from conventional anthropocentric understandings of the human subject, operations which narrative is uniquely suited to perform. Though countless definitions of narrative circulate, I subscribe to David Herman's pragmatic approach, which posits four basic elements: a discursive occasion for telling, a storyworld, experiencing agents within a storyworld, and a sequence of events initiated by or bearing upon these agents (2009: xvi). Narratives thus model relationships between worlds and agents, which is also something that we do as we imagine possible planetary and species futures. Indeed, the future itself is narratively constituted, as any imagined representation of a future prompts a reader, viewer, or listener of such a representation to draw connections in a causal chain from understandings of the world 'as we know it' to an imaginatively transformed version of this world. We can only do so by imagining this in terms of events bearing on human or, at least anthropomorphic agents. The partially-human future will thus entail transformations of both story material and discursive presentation: it is not just a matter of changing contents, but of experimenting with new forms and modes of narrative. Most importantly, the narrative rendering of the partially human will de-emphasize individual character in favor of a more typological, generalized, species-based view of the human. But, as narrative prompts the reader's recognition of the experientiality of storyworld agents, or characters, it needs some sort of anthropomorphic 'hook' to facilitate this empathetic response. The partially human thus involves characterizations that vacillate between, or conceptually blend, conventional individualized character and a more generic, collective version of the human. Operating from the default stance of an "anthropomorphic bias," as Monika Fludernik has termed it (1996: 10), mimetic forms, such as realist narration or photography-based film and visual narratives, must work especially hard to convey the partially human. Forms that tend toward the abstract or anti-mimetic will loosen the bias toward the individuation of characters and, consequently, offer possibilities for the abstraction of human form into something categorical and general. (This is not to say that prose or film narrative cannot accomplish similar goals, but such strategies arguably entail a more conspicuous rejection of representational conventions.)

This chapter considers one such narrative mode, the drawn storyworld, that is particularly suited to expressing a de-individuated human future. This is a mode that appears in multiple media but is a kind of formal building block: it can manifest in comics or graphic fiction in the form of sequential frames, or in animated film as a motion-based narrative form (or in single-frame painting or drawing that strongly implies a narrative context). In either medium, they share the trait of being *representational modes that emphasize a constructed visual channel of narrative*. This is in contrast, most obviously, to text-based narrative, which relies entirely on linguistic cues, and to photography-based film and video narratives, that encode assumptions about the reproduction of an already-existing world. Drawn storyworlds, be they in comic or animated form, tend to foreground a defamiliarization from the cognitive predisposition to sort space into figure- ground distinctions. As Peter Stockwell has shown, we ascribe certain traits to a visual or textual field – including self-containment, spatio-temporal precedence, and focus – that confer "prominence to the figure that differentiates it from the ground" (2002: 15). Where text-based narratives rely on linguistic markers to prompt a default figure-ground organization, and where photography-based film and video reproduces the spatial organization of the eye's visual field, drawn storyworlds only simulate a figure-ground space from the artist's *active construction* of this space. This difference opens up many avenues to a revision of a naturalized figure-ground relationship, and in particular a *defamiliarization of the appearance of human characters within storyworld environments*. Where the cognitive predisposition is to naturalize a distinction between human agents within a nonhuman storyworld, drawn storyworlds, in both sequential and animated form, put an extra burden on the viewer's cognitive activity to understand characters as distinct narrative entities. The uncanny ambiguity of the drawn storyworld mode can, in narratives that feature speculative, future-looking scenarios, help rethink a fundamental relation between human agents and storyworld environments. I will look briefly at two such examples – from Richard McGuire's 2014 graphic novel *Here* and Don Hertzfeldt's animated film from 2015, *World of Tomorrow* – to highlight the ways in which drawn storyworlds can more readily prompt reflections not simply on futures within an altered environment but how such narratives prompt consideration of partially-human futures.

2 Open-Ended Anthropomorphism

One useful way to think about the cognitive reception of drawn storyworld narratives is through the lens of anthropomorphism. As such narratives highlight the cognitive labor in sorting out narrative agents from storyworld environments, it makes sense that the attribution of human traits to ambiguous storyworld entities is at issue – because the figure-ground relation is defamiliarized, we are less inclined to naturalize characters as human. Unfortunately, anthropomorphism has had a bad rap in many circles, especially in animal studies and ecocritical thinking. In these contexts, the term is generally freighted with pejorative associations: to anthropomorphize is to be unable to see outside of human frames of reference or acknowledge any kind of radical difference. In environmental and animal studies it is often grouped with anthropocentrism and as a failure of imagination, ethical judgement, and (so it is often implied) morality. It reflects an unthinking elevation and exceptionalism to the human species while reducing all other creatures – especially nonhuman animals – to categorically inferior beings whose only interest lies in the ways in which they can reflect our own species narcissism back to us: we need know nothing of a beehive, for example, but the humanized roles assigned to the "workers," "drones," and the "queen." This negative view of anthropomorphism swings the pendulum entirely the other way toward what Franz de Waal calls "anthropodenial," or "the a priori rejection of humanlike traits in us" (2016: 25). The negative view of anthropomorphism proceeds from the assumption that the category of the human is self-evident and ontologically stable, and that it becomes an ethical and moral failing to apply this framework to beings whose behaviors and potential consciousnesses are categorically different.

My use of anthropomorphism is actually more interested in the way we anthropomorphize *any* entity, potentially including, somewhat counterintuitively, humans themselves. In contrast to the more negative view I just described, research in the cognitive sciences has posited anthropomorphism as a "cognitive default," something humans do as a matter of perceiving and acting within the world. As cognitive behaviorists Esmerelda Urquiza-Haas and Kurt Kotrschal have shown, anthropomorphism occurs in two broad domains: the *implicit* and the *reflective*. Implicit anthropomorphism has more to do with the capacities that evolved in the human species to determine the source and intentionality of other entities in the world. They posit that when humans recognize elements of animacy – such as biological motion, hand and mouth movement, facial expression, and the visible expression of pain – an implicit, "automatic" anthropomorphism is cued. Note that there is no *a priori* distinction of what sorts of entities will prompt this response; rather, it is the response that determines the categorization of the target entity. Certainly, primary anthropomorphism is most likely to be cued by other humans, but many nonhuman animals – particularly those phylogenetically proximate to humans (other primates, dogs, cats) will also trigger identical mechanisms of anthropomorphism. Likewise, other, non-biological forms of perceived animacy will prompt an implicit response: robotic faces, a film of dancing matchsticks, or other non-biological entities that display the requisite forms of animacy, motion, or visible expression. Speaking of nonhuman animals, Urquiza-Haas and Kotrschal note that there is *no qualitative distinction* between the cognition of a human and nonhuman. "[N]onhuman animal behavior," they claim, "is perceived and interpreted via the same mechanisms that evolved mainly for within-species social communication" (2015: 170). If we put aside the categorical essentialisms that separate "dog" from "dancing molecules" from "human," for example, there is no distinction between the cognitive *processes* that detect intentionality and consciousness among these figures. Even when we encounter representations of figures that do not hew to a strict mimeticism, we will still ascribe anthropomorphic qualities based on even minimal perceptual cues.

Implicit anthropomorphism offers a cognitive hook that allows another level to emerge, particularly in the domain of narrative. Urquiza-Haas and Kotrschal posit another level of anthropomorphism, which they describe as *reflective*. Reflective anthropomorphic attributions "are considered to be domain-general mechanisms that are subject to conscious control, are effortful, are slower than automatic processes, are limited by working memory capacity, and appear late in ontogeny and evolution" (2015: 169). Reflective mechanisms work to refine and modulate initial assessments. As they argue, "implicit cognitive mechanisms are responsible for early evaluations, whereas representations that are more detailed emerge later as a result of the involvement of reflective processes" (2015: 169). Key among reflective processes of anthropomorphism are the attribution of inductive and causal reasoning: these might involve more imaginative operations, such as imputing agency and intentionality to a malfunctioning computer or viewing gods as supernatural versions of human beings. It stands to reason that *representations* of entities will occasion more of these secondary processes, and further, that narrative, as a complex system that relies upon causal and inductive reasoning, will often work in this secondary domain. Reflective anthropomorphism is not dependent upon, nor limited by, an initial assessment. This is especially true in language-based narrative modes where the burden of storyworld construction is higher for the reader: as Marie-Laure Ryan notes, "[l]anguage-based narratives require an extensive filling-in work because language speaks to the mind and not directly to the senses" (2014: 42). The upshot here is that modes that do not privilege realist mimeticism operate more strongly in reflective than implicit domains. Drawn storyworlds, of course, can vary in their degree of mimetic convention, but the mode itself is already open to an abstraction that can similarly downplay or mute such cues to implicit anthropomorphism.

In the remainder of this chapter, I will focus on two narratives that feature drawn storyworlds that veer toward the anti-, or minimally mimetic. In doing so, they suppress the cues of the reader or viewer to attribute implicit anthropomorphic traits to characters. That is, they maintain a level of abstraction – particularly in the visual channel of narrative – that, on the one hand, prompts the reader's construction of a storyworld with human agents, but on the other, does so in a way that orients the reader's cognition away from an investment in individual human character. This narrative tactic opens up a larger space for the reflective domain of anthropomorphism, where the human can be thought of more typologically and symbolically, thus facilitating meditations on a broader, more species-wide scale. These minimally mimetic styles also defy generic conventions – while both narratives are clearly interested in ideas of the future, and human futurity in particular, neither fits into the generic templates of cli-fi, dystopian fiction, or even speculative fiction more broadly (though *World of Tomorrow* plays with ideas of time travel). Each is literally *sui generis*, defamiliarizing conventional narrative templates with which readers might orient themselves. As such, both *Here* and *World of Tomorrow* use the minimal coordinates of narrative to open up more philosophical realms of abstraction and speculation with respect to ideas of humanity, environments, and futurity.

3 The Partially-Human Graphic Novel: *Here*

In Richard McGuire's graphic novel, *Here*, this open, emergent presentation of the human species is an effect both of the discursive arrangement of the narrative and the style in which it is drawn. McGuire's conceit in the novel is that each two-page spread depicts an identical space of a corner of the living room of a house somewhere in the northeastern US, with each spread taking place at a different time, indicated by a caption in the corner indicating a specific year. The spreads are not presented chronologically; instead, they jump around to different points in time. Initially, these points are clustered on dates ranging in the twentieth- and twenty-first centuries, and we are cued to see each spread as a moment in the history of the house, though with different families, different decor, and different circumstances in each era. After several pages, however, the spreads include panels from years prior to the construction of the house, where the space holds an empty forest or a scene of interaction between indigenous people. Eventually, the spreads jump temporal scales, including a primeval scene from 3,000,000 BCE and jumping forward to uncanny landscapes thousands of years in the future. On a temporal level, the novel anchors our interest in a recognizably contemporary era, one characterized by the human habitation of a house. But once the spreads begin to widen the temporal scale to the epochal, deep history of the planet, our concern with the human activity that brought us into the novel is displaced by the thought that all of the spaces that we occupy, and unconsciously fit within a human frame of activity, are part of a much wider non-human history.

McGuire uses the affordances of the graphic novel to take advantage of the reader's cognitive reflex to anthropomorphize narrative actors even as the narrative points toward the primacy of a *non*-human storyworld. The novel contains no overt narratorial presence in the form of character narrator, or even non-diegetic commentary. This narrational level is presented the most attenuated, passive way possible: it is simply a fixed visual perspective, as if a camera had been invisibly placed within a set of geographical coordinates that happened to occupy the living room of a middle-class home. This fixed aspectuality already diminishes any anthropomorphic attribution we might make on the discursive, or 'telling' level. *Here* adopts a narrative positionality that Greg Garrard describes as "disanthropic," though he attributes this trait primarily to films. "[T]he ostensible impersonality of the camera – its mechanical indifference, even – makes it possible to bracket out both humans as objects and, to some degree, the human subject in its most obtrusive forms" (2012: 43–44). Although marked with the hand of human style in its drawn form, *Here* tells its story as if through an impersonal recording, eternally fixed in space, outside of human agency or manipulation. McGuire does populate his novel with recognizably human characters: the cues to implicit anthropomorphism are strong enough to identify them as such. Significantly, though, the perspective keeps any character's face from appearing in close-up, and McGuire's minimalist style tends to de-individualize characters, as they remain on the level of types, or generic human placeholders. Thus, there are very few prompts to a reflective anthropomorphism that might see complex consciousness or minds within any of the characters; any clues to an interiority have to be drawn from the minimal evidence of offhand remarks or everyday actions captured in the frozen moment of graphic representation.

With this minimal foregrounding of the human within his storyworld, McGuire gives ample space to environments. Graphically, with the fixed perspective, even frames that contain human characters are dominated by space, with the stylistic variation of these drawings leading the eye away from the human presences to wander around the entire frame. Moreover, the many spreads that include juxtapositions of different years further elevate the drawn storyworld to primary consideration. One such frame is horizontally divided, with two rectangular insets on the righthand page. The upper part of the main frame depicts a scene from 2005, with one elderly, apparently sick, man in a bed speaking to another. The inset frames on the right show a scene of two couples playing charades in 1964 (perhaps the elderly man is one of the players?) and a small frame from 2006 with a speech bubble indicating a telephone's ring. As is McGuire's style throughout, the characters are presented with little facial detail and uttering dialogue that gives no window onto individual personalities or character distinctions. Underneath these scenes is the bottom panel, stretching across both pages, from 2111, of a turbulent ocean scene. Implicit in this, of course, is the idea that sea-level rise will have taken over this domestic space, further framing the domestic scenes in a much wider context that usurps any human activity within. This spread is representative of how *Here* works on a spectrum between human and environment: the human activity in the narrative prompts a general recognition and hence an anthropomorphic hook, but these processes are kept at a minimal, implicit level, allowing a wider spatial field within the storyworld to take precedence.

McGuire incorporates a wider temporal canvas as well, which has the effect of defamiliarizing the biographical, individual elements of the humans depicted. This expansive sweep is accomplished through a fairly simple narrative device: an achronological, jumbled sequencing that both wanders back and forth between spreads, as well as including insets that show different times *within* one spread. But what is most audacious about the novel's sequencing is not the device of achronology but the way that it moves exponentially backward and forward to encompass time both well before the building of the house and well after its destruction. Robert Markley has identified three registers of time that, among other things, connect narrative to the vast, epochal scales of planetary history. Closest to human consciousness is the experiential, which is the temporality associated with moment-to-moment existence, perhaps best rendered in narratives labelled as stream-of-consciousness, such as *Mrs. Dalloway* or the early chapters of *Ulysses*. This bleeds into a register that Markley names the historical, which places experiential time in a social frame, extending it generationally to larger cultural and political institutions and traditions that outlast individual human lives – the temporality of the history book, or in some cases, the multi-generational historical novel. Finally, Markley identifies the "climatological," which "complicates and disrupts the connections among personal identity, history, and narrative" by opening a window onto "the stochastic processes of the natural world that call attention to the limitations of historical representation as a measure of time" (2012: 49). Narrative, with its bias toward individualized character arcs, is magnetically pulled toward the experiential, though it can easily expand to fit comfortably within the historical. Climatological time, by contrast, "resists representation" (2012: 44). *Here* accomplishes this through its attenuated anthropomorphic attachments to its characters, indifferently showing scenes that range, chronologically, from a primeval Earth in the 3.5 billion BCE, to everyday domestic scenes in the late twentieth century, to uncanny glimpses of a climate-warmed (and apparently post-human) future in the year 22,175. All of these devices – from the de-individualized characters, to the emphasis on environments, to the climatological temporalities – diminish the centrality of the human in the unfolding "geo-story" (to use Bruno Latour's term) of the planet (2014: 3).

4 The Partially-Human Animated Film: *World of Tomorrow*

Like graphic narratives, animated film can take advantage of a recalibrated figure-ground relationship to orient a viewer to partially human storyworld presences. But where comic drawing relies on the dual modal channels of image and text, the channels in animated film that calibrate a sense of anthropomorphism are three-fold: image, motion, and sound. Even as the style of visual representation can vary from the extremely stylized and abstract to the strongly mimetic, animated figures are always visibly different from the photographic basis of live-action films, and thus, in the visual realm we will tend to be drawn away from an implicit anthropomorphism as the representational medium is brought to the fore. Even human characters that are "realistically" drawn will have a layer of abstraction interposed between perception and attribution. At the same time, however, animations can incorporate the movement of characters such that we are more likely to attribute some anthropomorphic intentionality (as in the famous moving triangle experiment by Fritz Heider and Marianne Simmel).[2] And, finally, sound is probably the strongest link to an implicit anthropomorphic attribution, especially when dialogue is voiced by actors in a naturalistic way. Animated figures that represent humans or specific anthropomorphic re- imaginings of nonhuman creatures can veer toward human attributions, and abstractions that give minimal cues except for non-random movement, or the suggestion of eyes and mouth, still prompt an anthropomorphic attribution, if in a minimal way. Virtually all animated representations of sentient or living beings will thus fall on this spectrum between mimesis and defamiliarization, relative to visual style, motion, and sound.

Don Hertzfeldt's 2015 short film, *World of Tomorrow*, uses the drawn-storyworld mode of animated film to similarly reorient the figure-ground relation that viewers typically attribute to humans and environments on film. Hertzfeldt, an independent animator who first came to notice with his 2001 short film, *Rejected*, created *World of Tomorrow* around the conversational talk he recorded of his four-year-old niece, Winona Mae, weaving a narrative around these informal recordings. The story begins with a child, Emily, who is visited from the future by a time-traveling third-generation adult clone of herself. Third-Generation Emily (Emily 3G) takes toddler Emily – to whom she refers as "Emily Prime" – on a time-traveling journey into the future, showing her highlights of the world and her own life in 227 years between the story present and the point from which Emily 3G visits. Emily 3G reveals that Earth, in her timeline, is about to be hit by a meteor, ending all human life, and she wishes to transfer her memories into Emily Prime's unconscious so that the intervening consciousnesses of Emily Prime and Emily 2G will preserve her existence, including the visit she makes back to Emily Prime preceding her death. She then sends Emily Prime back to her present era, but a time-travel glitch briefly deposits the child alone, in a snowy, dark prehistoric location. Hertzfeldt holds this shot for several seconds before returning Emily Prime to her home, in her own present tense, where the film ends. Though Hertzfeldt's storytelling and formal style come off as whimsical and light, *World of Tomorrow* creates a complicated, open- ended tale of a partially human future.

Even more so than McGuire's drawn figures in *Here*, the characters in *World of Tomorrow* offer virtually no more than minimal visual cues to their humanness. Were this a silent film, we could only interpret the two Emilys as the most generic human examples, with virtually no prompts toward individuality. Instead,

---

2 The 1944 film, just over a minute long, shows the interactions between two triangles and a dot, as they move around a box, which opens and closes. The film was developed as an experiment to demonstrate the minimal cues necessary to attribute motivations and consciousness to abstract objects. It can be viewed at https://www.youtube.com/watch?v=VTNmLt7QX8E.

Hertzfeldt uses sound, particularly the human voice, as the anthropomorphic hook of his narrative. As the voice of Emily Prime comes from the unscripted recordings of a child, her dialogue acquires a strong degree of naturalistic spontaneity while still retaining the obvious traits of a young child. Hertzfeldt writes in the film's notes, "I learned very quickly that you cannot direct a four-year-old. You cannot even expect a four-year-old to recite lines back at you [. . .] so I recorded her as we drew pictures and talked about the world" (2015: n.p.). Given the lack of anthropomorphic cues in the visual track, Hertzfeldt uses the audio track to cement the implicit anthropomorphic attribution, even it if it does not extend to a strongly individualized human narrative. In other words, we have a vivid aural sense of an embodied human child, but little corresponding visual sense to anchor this voice in a mimetically-based, individualized "person." If presented in a live-action format, we would too readily invest a specific, personalized identity based on the facial features of an actor portraying the character. A strongly anthropomorphized voice allows us to remain at the level of generalization; Emily Prime is a generic human child, but a vividly rendered one through the texture of the recorded voice. In this, Emily Prime is transformed from a child to what Lee Edelman refers to as the Child; that is, the "emblem of futurity's unquestioned value" (2004: 4). Edelman argues that such a figure carries with it a hegemonic power that envisions the only collective futures as those facilitated through heterosexual biological reproduction. Having vividly evoked the Child in the voice of Emily prime, Hertzfeldt spends the rest of his film exploring futures that resist reproductive futurism – mainly through the technology of cloning. The archetypal Child, in *World of Tomorrow*, is thus ironically uncoupled from a vision of human futurity.

Not only does the film defamiliarize assumptions about reproductive futurism, it also uses the affordances of animation to defamiliarize the represented space of the storyworld itself. *World of Tomorrow* exploits the quality of animated film that Aylish Wood refers to as "reverberating space"; that is, "space not wholly held captive by narrative" (2006: 135–136). The film subordinates its characters to the animated environments in multiple ways. In contrast to the stick figures of the two Emilys, Hertzfeldt's environments are pulsating with color and movement. When 3G takes Prime into the "outernet," a Matrix-like neural network, the frames are all flashing, geometric color and light with few gestures toward a naturalistic storyworld. Hertzfeldt further defamiliarizes the environment of the two characters by overt references to the hand-drawn basis of animation. One long sequence takes place in a museum but there are no contextual references to this setting, as the only background is what appears to be a pulsating sheet of parchment. When the scene shifts, the paper background is wiped with the sound of a page turning. Scenes that do take place on the future Earth only contain the faintest of references to a mimetic storyworld, but stylization still rules the day: a hill is pink with red grass and red snow falling, a nighttime scene features an iridescent green sky with lattice shapes floating in it. The dialogue between the two Emilys anchors the visual display in a recognizable narrative, but the represented space comes across as a kind of excess, fulfilling the possibility that animation, to quote Wood, can be "an evocation of space that captivates us as it makes meaning, giving locations for movements and gestures, but which also allows the surprise of space emerging in a process of change" (2006: 135–136).

These dynamic visual elements support a narrative whose time-travel conceit prompts a more thoroughgoing exploration of the partially human. Perhaps the most resonant sequence in the film involves the story of a clone who is placed as a child, without a brain, in a museum exhibit, to live its whole life there as a "work of art." Emily 3G initially refers to the clone as a "body," and refers to "it" rather than using a gendered pronoun, but nonetheless the brainless body becomes a talismanic figure for the community. Illustrating the power of implicit anthropomorphism, the clone acquires a name ("David") and, as 3G narrates David's story, the clone slowly morphs into human significance: "Regular visitors ate lunch in his wing. Classrooms of children came to learn about anatomy. People who'd speak quietly to him in the night. People who'd pay him a visit when they found themselves back in the city and remembered he was there." Given 3G's status as a clone herself, and the lack of any visible difference between clone David and any of the other figures in the narrative, there is, at best, a blurry categorical distinction between a "human" and an "inhuman" clone, as the humans of the future world grow farther and farther from their source parents.

Hertzfeldt undoes human exceptionalism at an even more fundamental, reproductive level, foreclosing any notions of a generationally-based species future. The film never considers that cloning is an exceptional means of reproduction – indeed it seems to be a normative method – and hence it offers a critique of reproductive futurism, Edelman's notion that the future can only be understood through the institutions and frameworks of the heterosexual reproduction of the human species. This queerness extends romantic love beyond species boundaries as well, as Emily 3G notes that she has at times been in love with a moon rock, a fuel pump, and an unidentifiable non-human creature named Simon. The lack of an optimistic "out" through reproductive futurism is compounded by the cul-de-sac temporality of the narrative. We know that the human race, such as it is, is about to end because of the imminent meteor strike, but Emily 3G's visit back to Emily Prime forms a kind of recursion that keeps the "world" of tomorrow in a suspended state, incapable of being projected onto a progressive linear timeline. Emily 3G expresses this sensibility in a declaration that reorients the temporality of human life away from either an indefinite continuation of the present or the sharp cut of extinction: "This is your future, Emily Prime. It is sometimes a sad life, and it is a long life." In this view, human life neither overcomes nor succumbs to a changing world. It merely persists, in transformed, enmeshed, attenuated ways. It functions, but it becomes lossy, glitchy, and diminished like the minds and bodies of the clones several generations removed from their originals.

5 Conclusion

Both *Here* and *World of Tomorrow* avoid the trappings of 'cli-fi' but nonetheless address questions raised by a future that threatens to further unseat the human from its unsteady philosophical perch. Each proposes the idea that the human species has *some* future but also that such a future may involve a radical reconfiguration of the presumed Cartesian superiority over the world and its environments. The more narratives that open up ontological questions about the entities contained within them, the more a new theory of character is needed to account for these partially, or ambiguously, anthropomorphic constructions. Rather than thinking of humans as the normative framing concept that is naturally applied to each and every narrative, we can advance a more contextual model. What counts as human is not based upon transcendental categories, which themselves replicate the worldview of human exceptionalism, but is instead derived from contextual cues within a given discursive presentation and storyworld rendering. In other words, the understanding of the human shifts from a Platonic, exteriorized mode as a one-size-fits-all category to something *open* and *emergent* within individual narratives. Moreover, this emergence gives priority to the storyworlds that cue the construction of human agents within narrative. Herman has defined storyworlds as "mentally and emotionally projected environments in which interpreters are called upon to live out complex blends of cognitive and imaginative response" (2005: 570). This definition, by giving priority to the imaginative world-making of the reader, implies that characters arise within, rather than exterior to, such projections. Anthropomorphism, then, is the cognitive process by which we place emergent storyworld entities on a spectrum between human and not-human.

Narratives that feature drawn storyworlds are a particularly effective mode in modeling this changing relationship between humans and their environments. As such, they discourage an implied temporality by which the future is simply an empty space to be filled with human-centered actions and events. Even narratives of climate change, which give agency to planetary environmental forces, still tend to be understood through this anthropocentric temporal frame: how will it affect *us*? What can *we* do to change it? The future, in these formulations, is external; it is phrased as being a different order or realm of time than the present, or the past for that matter. The default understanding is that future is a kind of content-free container into which we will move, according to the social and material arrangements that we have known in the past: biologically, generationally, serially. Narratives such as those I've discussed tend to defamiliarize our sense of the future and instead invite us to contemplate futurity. In contrast to thinking of 'the future,' futurity implies a metacognitive approach to the future, challenging the givenness of open, empty time and instead understanding *versions* of the future as culturally and historically variable. Futurity denies the comfort of an expansive space into which we can project versions of our present selves, ad infinitum, into a planet that we either survive or don't, or into other worlds in which we either survive, or don't. Any consideration of futurity demands a defamiliarization of conventional narrative mediums and modes. This can happen in any number of ways, but as I hope I have shown, the particularly uncanny blending of space and character models a larger relation between a dynamic, agential, human-indifferent environment and we more-or-less human characters that live within it.

Bibliography

DeWaal, Frans (2016) *Are We Smart Enough to Know how Smart Animals Are?* (New York: W.W. Norton).
Edelman, Lee (2004) *No Future: Queer Theory and the Death Drive* (Durham, NC and London: Duke University Press).
Fludernik, Monika (1996) *Towards a 'Natural' Narratology* (New York and London: Routledge).
Garrard, Greg (2012) "Worlds Without Us: Some Types of Disanthropy," *SubStance* 127, 40–60.
Ghosh, Amitav (2016) *The Great Derangement: Climate Change and the Unthinkable* (Chicago and London: University of Chicago Press).
Herman, David (2005) "Storyworld," in *The Routledge Encyclopedia of Narrative Theory*, ed. David Herman, Manfred Jahn, and Marie-Laure Ryan (New York: Routledge), 569–570.
Herman, David (2009) *Basic Elements of Narrative*. (Chichester, UK: Wiley-Blackwell).
James, Erin (2015) *The Storyworld Accord: Econarratology and Postcolonial Narratives* (Lincoln, NE: University of Nebraska Press).
James, Erin, and Eric Morel, eds. (2020) *Environment and Narrative: New Directions in Econarratology* (Columbus: The Ohio State University Press).
Latour, Bruno (2014) "Agency at the Time of the Anthropocene," *New Literary History* 45.1, 1–18.
Markley, Robert (2012) "Time, History, and Sustainability," in *Telemorphosis: Theory in the Era of Climate Change, Vol. 1*, ed. Tom Cohen (Ann Arbor: Open Humanities Press), 43–64.
McGuire, Richard (2014) *Here* (New York: Pantheon).
Morton, Timothy (2010) *The Ecological Thought* (Cambridge, MA and London: Harvard University Press). Kindle edition.

Ryan, Marie-Laure (2014) "Story/Worlds/Media: Tuning the Instruments of a Media- Conscious Narratology," in *Storyworlds across Media: Toward a Media-Conscious Narratology*, ed. Marie-Laure Ryan and Jan-Noël Thon (Lincoln, NE and London: University of Nebraska Press), 25–49.
Stockwell, Peter (2002) *Cognitive Poetics: An Introduction*. (London: Routledge).
Urquiza-Haas, Esmerelda, and Kurt Kotrschal (2015) "The Mind behind Anthropomorphic Thinking: Attribution of Mental States to Other Species," *Animal Behaviour* 109, 167–176.
Wood, Aylish (2006) "Re-Animating Space," *Animation: An Interdisciplinary Journal* 1.2, 133–152.
World of Tomorrow (2015) Dir. Don Hertzfeldt. Vimeo. <https://vimeo.com/ondemand/worldoftomorrow/155036442> (accessed 12 February 2020).

Axel Siegemund
Environmental Sciences, Apocalyptic Thought, and the Proxy of God

1 Introduction

The deep link between ecological awareness and the apocalyptic thought of the beginning of the twenty-first century is self-evident. Ecology and apocalypticism are mirror-imaged twins because ecological consciousness is equated to the awareness of the disappearance of nature in time. First, I shall describe the interrelationship between our understanding of "time" and "nature" (section 2). I propose to understand both as ideas of mind, which influence the power-structure of ecologically relevant revelations of science (section 3). If the speech of a dead end of the world is an outcome of our particular perspective, then we have to consider the transformative power of today's apocalyptic thought. What is the meaning of apocalypticism in the face of the paradigm of feasibility (section 4)? Finally, I will suggest to search for relations between our religious and technology-based expectations (section 5) while understanding both as creative approaches to the world.

2 Time Consciousness and Ecological Thought

The less "natural" we live, the more "ecological" we want to become. However, the way of human life is cultivation. Thus, the decline of naturalness is an inevitable result of humaneness. At the same time, there is a longing for a natural lifestyle, contradicting the cultural essence of humanity. In this situation we have two main options. One option is to accept culture in general and – in particular – technology to be the "nature of humans". An alternative way is to promote nature as the unquestionable basis of life and simultaneously observing its disappearance. As a result, the loss of nature increases with every further step we take to counter it. This is why the twentieth century described and lamented the end of nature in many ways. Ulrich Beck assumes a perfect socialization of nature:

> Nature is society, society is (also) 'nature'. Those who still speak of nature as a non- social society today speak in the categories of another century that no longer grasp our reality. Everywhere today we are dealing with a high-grade artificial product of nature, an

> artificial 'nature'. There is no hair, no crumb 'natural' about it anymore, when 'natural' means nature's self-sufficiency. (Beck 1986: 109, transl. A.S.)

Around the turn of the millennium, Paul Crutzen proclaimed the "anthropocene", meaning that human action no longer only changes the biosphere, but also the atmosphere and geology of the earth as a whole. He agreed with Bill McKibben, who already proclaimed an "end of nature" in 1989 (McKibben 1989).

Following the idea that the end of nature means the end of human life, there is no other option than ecological apocalypticism. Apocalyptic thought is the very outcome of the idea that "naturalness" was the human way of life instead of cultivation. This apocalypticism is indeed unquestionable as long as ecology means preserving nature from socialization. The most convincing argument of this matter is that there is less and less time for a reversal, as "nature" becomes less day by day. Since the disappearance of nature goes along with the disappearance of time, ecological thought influences our understanding of time and time structures.

In particular, the idea of a disappearing nature changes the awareness of our personal time, because from this perspective there is no difference between nature and our historiography of natural events. The unlimited future as such changes into a limited future for us. In this understanding the ecological thought follows the idea of a linearly-limited time, which we can find in the Judeo-Christian and Islamic tradition. Nature becomes the heir of the predicates of God. On the one hand, nature is the basis of life, which implies that it is unlimited and unconditionally existing. On the other hand, we try to influence nature to preserve our life. While making nature a part of ourselves, we change the character of its development. The widespread discussion of the global catastrophe, mainly expressed by the metaphor "five to twelve!," suggests the complete demise of all life on earth. The metaphor of the end of the world has its origin in the Judeo-Christian idea of the Apocalypse. In part four I will show that there is an important difference between Christian and ecological apocalypticism. What both ideas have in common is the model of a linear-limited time *for us*. The limitations of our time are also evident. Any disaster model divides the future into a near future and a future far away. It says that we will be able to influence the near future, but there will be a distant future which is the outcome of the near future. We influence the distant future indirectly through our present actions only.

The conclusion is that our actions of today and of the near future will decide what happens in the long run. The rhetorical meaning of this is to bring changes in environmental action today and tomorrow, because the day after tomorrow depends on the present mobilization. Anyone who speaks of a global catastrophe or doomsday suggests that we are creating an earth without life and nature instead of an unpredictable change. The future is predictable and the prediction is disaster. However, we have to understand that time consciousness itself is an outcome of our perception of the world. As environmental awareness influences this perception, we have to assume that our idea of time is influenced by ecology itself. Ecological awareness is built on the foundations of the religious understanding of time, but it also influences this understanding. Augustine (354–430) declared that neither past nor future are at hand. We cannot say that past and future exist (Augustinus, Confessiones XI, Ch. 14). Instead of this, we have to say that they just exist as ideas in our mind.

What does this mean for our understanding of the five-to-twelve-metaphor? We cannot capture the future of nature. Whatever we have in mind concerning the status of nature only shows, yet again, what has already happened. Once we construct natural time with a beginning and an end, this can only represent a limited part of our space-time reality. If we create a relationship between the past, the present and the future of the earth, then we are comparing our pictures of the past and of the future with the respective perception of the present. But these representations do not relate to facts and the respective value of our images of nature is the value *for us* today. Thus, the five-to-twelve-metaphor says nothing about the future, but is rather a statement about our today's sense of time and consciousness of nature in the present.

There is a suspicion against our technological perspective here: At least in the context of a metaphor that follows the idea of a clock, we are captured by a picture. What is meant here is not the image of nature of environmentalists or the image of time that Augustine had in mind, but the image of an instrument for time-measurement. Our idea of time-structure follows the idea of measurement just as our concept of nature follows the ability to count, weigh and measure. Feasibility is the precondition of the idea of an end of the world caused by man.

To summarize, we can say that only the technical perspective of a measurable time-scale, which is deeply rooted in the Judeo-Christian tradition, allows us to think about our own situation as one point between the genesis of the world and the apocalypse. In pre-christian antiquity and, even more clearly during the era of Mayan civilization, the idea of the end of the world has been developed from a cyclic imagination. One simply takes a huge cyclic image of the world, that from the perspective of society will come to an end. Yet, from the perspective of God the cycle continues with a new world birth. Both time structures can be found in today's ecology (Schummer 2001: Ch. II.).

2.1 Linear Time and the End of the World

Western ecological thought is led by the dictum "follow the Sciences." This means natural sciences would have to give us information about the best way to act, individually and as a society. We believe that for all our problems there is a scientifically rendered way to find a (technical) solution. We are aware of unintended and undesirable side effects, but all in all we believe that even for new problems sciences will come up with new solutions. The idea behind this is one of a linear development. It includes the conviction that the problem-solving capacity of science is faster than the growing-capacity of our problems. We cannot prove this vision of feasibility, but we can say that the whole scientific description of the world follows the idea of a linear development in terms of time. Even the assumption of an unlimited growth process falls under this scheme. Think about the expansion of the universe according to the Big Bang theory (at least according to one variant) or about the decline in carbon dioxide and increase in ozone over billions of years in our Earth's atmosphere: astronomic and geological time scales follow the same principle, since they both describe a continuous development. Finally, one could also consider the evolutionary differentiation of biological species: there is no repetition of the same, but a development from one state into the other.

However, this idea of linearity is logically linked to the questions "where from" and "where to". It might not be by accident that the Big Bang theory was developed by a catholic priest, George Lemaître, while physicians felt the idea of a "starting point" of the world to be very Christian (Lambert 2015). Today we have accepted the idea as a physical one, but in actual fact it has translated the religious idea of a starting point into a scientific model. The other fixpoint – the end of the world – is taken up by the environmental movement. In this way, we are able to synthesize the past, the future and our own present into one scientifically paraphrased story that is easily accessible to the modern mindset. One has to bear in mind, that this story is very similar to the Christian one which we assume to be premodern.

2.2 The Circular Time Structure

Nature itself is not bound to any time model, but today we perceive natural processes as a cycle that is disturbed by human interventions. Following this, we propagate that the "natural cycles" are models for human action. We should react to what nature is showing us. In fact, the question whether we treat nature as a model for linear or circular development depends on the frame. When looking at a single living object or a species, one can find a starting point and an end. Taking the regeneration into account, we can see nature in the mode of the cycle.

In the 2nd main theorem of thermodynamics, evolution is associated with the entropy of a system. From this perspective, life is perceived as a form of energy consumption. Living beings are entropy generators. This "destruction of energy" – the conversion of usable energy into useless heat energy – led Ilya Prigogine to speak about "dissipative structures". Natural life was no longer the expression of a (thermodynamic) equilibrium. Any natural balance is now linked to the opposite: death. The increasing complexity of organic life, which marks the course of evolutionary processes, as well as the physical conditions, speak against the view that living organisms and ecological systems follow a search for equilibrium.

The romantic admiration of natural regeneration processes again follows cultural ideas instead of scientific ones. In ancient Egypt as well as in the Indian tradition we find the idea of ash rising to the divine harmony of the circular motion of the sky. Going and coming interchange permanently. In our days, the transformation of ecological relationships into norms and objectives is always determined by the addition of intentions and objectives. We speak of the "ecological equilibrium" to underline the fact that it is a good thing to live in a balance with nature. But this saying is not rooted in a given state of nature, but in our striving for harmony with an environment that has long since ceased to be natural. The normative function of the circular model is only possible because in our everyday language we understand "balance" as something what we desire and wish for.

Nature does not give us clear clues about the real time structure. However, we can find all time-structures in natural systems, depending on the perspective. If one only takes the observation period into account, one always finds a limited life span, regardless of whether one examines individuals, species, entire ecological systems or even mere elementary particles. We find cyclical processes at the level of the generation sequence, such as seasonal variations, sky movements, atomic oscillations, etc.

We can see that the perception of the environment and the experience of the loss of nature is strongly linked to our understanding of time. "Time" and "nature" depend on each other, but we cannot say what they really are. Our present understanding mainly is rooted in the ability to measure. We measure time and we measure natural events. Furthermore, we have the willingness to describe a continuous development from the beginning of the world to its end, making today's life a part of this continuum of time and nature.

As our scientific world-view inherits the Christian understanding of the beginning and the end of the world, ecological apocalypticism is part of a story following the traditional setting. It pressures us to act for the betterment of a limited future in the same way as a religious story is able to make people work in a limited world in light of the unlimited. Since pressure means power, we have to ask for the consciousness of power as the second characteristic of today's apocalyptic thought.

3 Technology-Driven Revelation and Power Consciousness

Visions of global disasters and natural cycles change our consciousness of time. Because our consciousness of time is fundamental to our perceptions, evaluations, and actions, this has consequences for our environmental perceptions and -actions. Our memories influence our expectations much more than the other way around. This means whoever wants us to act in a specific way, needs to revive our memories. Either we act for a comeback of a glorified past or we work for a future that is better than all that we already know. But there is a third way to make people act: One can show that only a specific way to deal with the present will save us from an external power that is already waiting for us in the future. Especially the expectation of a threat will transform fear into energy.

Translating the Greek word *apokalypsis* precisely, it doesn't mean "end of the world," but "revelation." The apocalypse is the revelation of a hidden characteristic of the world, especially its temporary nature, which needs to be fulfilled. In today's perspective the hidden characteristic of the world is revealed through the sciences. Past generations were unaware of the massive impact of human activities. Our ancestors did not think about the possibility of an "Anthropocene." Even the description of the green-house-effect by Svante Arrhenius did not cause any significant activity realizing the revelation (Arrhenius 1896: 237–276). This is why we feel that the real revelation came at the end of twentieth century and this was a scientific one. Sciences show us that the earth is structured through features which have been hidden before. Only today's generation got the chance to become aware of the truth. Our present mind – in contradiction to the mind of our ancestors – is enlightened with knowledge about the real interdependence between humans and their environment. This view leads to one important assumption: First of all, we have the duty to accept the revelation. If it is right that the generations before the twentieth century were living in the dark, then we must not ignore the apocalyptic reality of the world we live in. The existence of the earth depends on us – this knowledge calls us to responsibility. The message is that any ignorance would be irrational, because those who ignore the environmental issue would live as people who refuse to live in the light of the revelation.

But what does the revelation say exactly? It does not only shed light upon the hidden character of the world, it mainly tells us that this world seems to have reached a dead end. In this respect apocalypticism is exactly a means of power. If the environmental sciences reveal the hidden feature of the world which is the dead end of our future, then they pressurize us to do something against this dystopia.

The fulfillment of apocalyptic thought is destruction. However, the mood of anxiety is only one side, the other side is the trial to proclaim hope. However, the hope for salvation implies the fulfillment of the provisional period. Above that the hopelessness and the permanence of powerlessness do not mark a finite barrier. Apocalyptic thought means turning powerlessness into a search for another option. It transforms powerlessness into power. Thus, the revelation of the proclaimed end of the world changes the pictorial epitome of fear into a symbol of hope. The world might come to an end, but then again it might not – both is included in apocalyptic thought in general. In particular, environmental sciences offer themselves as the healing power of this transformation. On the one hand, we are able to produce a forecast through meteorology, the study of bio- and atmosphere as well as other ecological methods. But the success of the scientific methods is not only reflected in the procurement of explanations for the future, but in their influence. Sciences give us the power to influence the future of the world in such a way that the revelation becomes relative. Apocalyptic thought does not mean the proclamation of an absolute and definite end, but the promise of a change. However, this change depends on our willingness to follow the revelation.

Again, the power of environmentalism is linked to our understanding of time. The ability to learn from the past and to draw on conclusions on the future, makes us capable of learning and foresighted. It is precisely in this sense that we generalize structures of the past into general time structures. Nevertheless, in comparison to our past, the future will remain relatively indefinite. This indeterminacy of the future leads to expectations. These expectations are prone to emotions such as the hope for improvement or the fear of deterioration. Also, our longing for security and our sense of orientation is a part of it. The relative uncertainty of the future leaves room for intellectual speculations.

While our memories reach back to a limited extent, our expectations are unlimited in principle. The experience of human impotence and the superiority of external power is the basis of apocalyptic understanding. Therefore, apocalypticism is always the quest for power. In today's world we negotiate power politically and technologically. Technology once was the primary instrument of social progress. Today we are aware of its ambivalence. This is why technology is part of our impotence and it is also an external power.

Side effects show that we cannot fully restrain its power. This does not mean that technology was inhuman. Rather it shows that technology is human, that is ambiguous and ambivalent. In particular we experience its power to cause environmental crises. We know that the hole in the ozone layer and many of the natural disasters that are currently erupting again and again, such as floods and cyclones, are not natural phenomena, but consequences of our technology. At the same time, great progress has been made in recent decades in the fields of air pollution control, waste, water treatment and waste disposal. It is precisely in the face of the environmental crisis that we ask for technology, especially environmental technologies. Technology remains our culture, the crisis even reinforces the paradigm. In this way technology objectifies our power consciousness in the light of the ecological revelation. The environment might be destroyed, but then again it might be rescued – both is included in our technological thought. Next, after having considered the meaning of time and power, we now have to ask for the meaning of crises.

4 Crisis Consciousness and the Transformative Power of Apocalyptic Thought

How can we achieve a realistic handling of the environmental irritations caused by global ecological problems? On the one hand, it seems important not to respond to the pressure of the problem in such a way that the future becomes the all-dominant time mode. We need to keep past and present independent from a future-oriented awareness. Our expectations and our memories influence our current perception, this we need to bring to mind. On the other hand, we have to see that our personal time, the time of our culture and natural time follow completely different time structures (Schummer 2001: 188). It is a question of our willingness to take up the plurality of time structures. Does the apocalyptic discourse allow this plurality? Does the pressure of apocalypticism contradict any other perspective? Can we really allow ourselves to discuss the crises, which would mean being ready for compromises in general? Or does the crises situation contradict any democratic idea through the pressure of the five-to-twelve- metaphor? These are the questions we have to answer and the best way to do so will be via a "political theology of climate change" (Northcott 2013).

If we forget that time is a transcendent idea of human mind, then we will create a linear progressive time structure for the future. And we will not be able to think in alternatives. While environmental movements criticize the irresponsible fixation on the present as a cause of ecological problems, they produce a future-cult, saying that all our duty is about the upcoming days. From a historical point of view, we have to say that the future-oriented progress has occurred increasingly since the eighteenth century only. It is an optimistic faith and therefore a secularized form of Christian salvation history. The idea was that one can optimize the living conditions for now and forever. The climax of this idea is that "our children shall live better than we do," which was the creed of twentieth century. Only the overestimation of one's own knowledge and assessment skills has led to consequences that we now regard as ecological problems.

We can describe apocalypticism and technology as expressions of a crisis consciousness that react to social, environmental and political upheavals. We experience the present as an ecological crisis, which should be interpreted and mastered with the help of apocalyptic thought patterns. This leads us to concentrate on the upcoming future. At the same time, we experience our time as a crisis of modern thought, which should be mastered with the help of new technological patterns. Hence, technological and apocalyptic thought join together. However, the environmental technology we use permeates us as a state of mind that precedes all ethically motivated actions. It is more than just a means of making our lives eco-friendly and sustainable. It is an expression of an epochal state of mind. Environmental technology touches on the possibility of the dissolution of boundaries, especially in light of the limits that the ecological crisis presents. Thus, technology transforms the fear of our apocalyptic thought into a will to escape the dead end. It takes up our images of time, power and crises and gives us engineering options to deal with them. How are these options related to the religious meaning of the apocalypse?

5 Technology as the Proxy of God

Christian apocalyptic thought does not commit the revealed world to come to an end. Skrimshire shows that the terms 'apocalyptic,' 'eschatological,' 'millenarian,' and 'millennial' are often and incorrectly used interchangeably (Skrimshire 2014). The only reason of revelation is to transform fear into a "courage to be." This word of Paul Tillich (Tillich 1952) marks the transformation of the fear of senselessness into an existential Yes to exist. This goes back to an anthropological analysis of man in the modern world. The modern world distinguishes between nature and sense and finally decides to concentrate on nature. This is why natural sciences do not include meaning. As an outcome of this, even the environment is silent to us, a senseless being. But to the extent that the environmental crisis marks a borderline situation, it reformulates fundamental questions of modern thought. What sources do we live from, what do we fear and what can we hope for? Technology, which is very different from science, partially fulfills what the secular world believes in and hopes for. The apocalyptic expectation is not a renaissance of religion, but a sense-making program for the technical civilization. Technology is not a substitute for religion. From a religious perspective it is rather a deputy or proxy, waiting for the return of God.

Today, however, we are confronted with the question of what expressiveness the Christian message has in the face of environmental threats on a global scale. If Christian theology stands in relation to that reality which the sciences describe and if statements of the faith are sentences in the dispute over this reality, then we have to say that theology does not add a guarantee of survival to the debate. Religion is not authorized to proclaim safety. Christian faith is not synonymous with hope for the survival of the world. Of course, it is also something other than an apocalyptic hope for another world beyond the catastrophe. Rather, faith affirms the world in the light of the threat of today's actual negation and annihilation.

The Christian mood in this sense is not a mood of hope, but a mood of courage. The Protestant Theologian Paul Tillich and the Catholic Karl Rahner both have emphasized the importance of courage (Körtner 2002: 83). Faith proves itself in protest against the catastrophic view, i.e., in protest against an apocalyptic world-view. The action of faith is action in the face of the absurd and the active proclamation of sense against the senselessness of an abstract dead end. As faith proclaims sense and environmental technology produces sense, we have to ask for the common horizon of both of them. Traditionally, sense can only come from God and even in the face of the possible self-destruction of mankind, it still remains relevant. But the ability to change fear into hope through technology is also a gift of God's creative power. The main task will be to interlink both, our courage to produce sense in a crisis situation and our ability to receive the unavailable meaning of life. The environmental crisis reminds us that we cannot produce everything. The knowledge that not everything concerning the environment will depend on us, provides a relief that turns fear into courage. Precisely this is the meaning of revelation and this is why we negotiate the range of technology in front of the crisis. We do not know its power exactly, but we count on it. This is why we ask for something else than feasibility: creation, that means an untouchable being.

Bibliography

Arrhenius, Svante (1896) "On the Influence of Carbonic Acid in the Air upon the Temperature of the Ground," *Philosophical Magazine and Journal of Science Series* 5.41, 237–276.
Beck, Ulrich (1986) *Risikogesellschaft: Auf dem Weg in eine andere Moderne* (Frankfurt: Suhrkamp).
Körtner, Ulrich (2002) "Glaube, Angst und Hoffnung," *Gegenworte* 10, 79–83.
Lambert, Dominique (2015) *The Atom of the Universe: The Life and Work of Georges Lemaître*, preface by J. Peebles (Cracow: Copernicus Center Press).
McKibben, Bill (1989) *The End of Nature* (New York: Random House).
Northcott, Michael S. (2013) *A Political Theology of Climate Change* (Grand Rapids, MI and Cambridge, UK: Wm. B. Eerdmans Publishing).
Prigogine, Ilya (1977) "Time, Structure and Fluctuations," Nobel Lecture, 8. Dec 1977, URL: http://www.nobelprize.org/nobel_prizes/chemistry/laureates/1977/prigogine-lecture.pdf (accessed 26 Nov 2019).
Schummer, Joachim (2001) "Zeitbewußtsein, Ökologie und Ethik," *Antemnae: Periodico mensile a carrattere scientifico* 3, 172–190.
Skrimshire, Stefan (2014) "Climate Change and Apocalyptic Faith," *Wiley Interdisciplinary Reviews: Climate Change* 5.2, 233–246.
Tillich, Paul (1952) *The Courage to Be* (New Haven, CT: Yale University Press).

Carlos A. Segovia
Four Cosmopolitical Ideas for an Unworlded World

As Félix Guattari anticipated in 1989,

> [t]he Earth is undergoing a period of intense techno-scientific transformations. If no remedy is found, the ecological disequilibrium this has generated will ultimately threaten the continuation of life on the planet's surface. Alongside these upheavals, human modes of life, both individual and collective, are progressively deteriorating. (2000: 27–28)

Therefore, this is the *first* idea I would like to stress: (a) we are living in times of both ecological and social collapse.[1] According to Jörg Friedrichs (2013), one could now claim that the future is not what it used to be, and for within merely a few decades, the world will no longer be what it is now. It is, of course, possible to gradate our fears, yet, the deepest one is obvious: "From a geological point of view," writes Elizabeth A. Povinelli "the planet began without Life, with Nonlife, out of which, somehow, came sorts of Life. These sorts evolved until one sort threatened to extinguish not only its own sort but all sorts, returning the planet to an original lifelessness" (2016: 11). But until that happens – if it happens – we will likely experience the fatal irruption of the unexpected in an ironic reversal of the (enlightened) Kantian sublime: earthquakes, tsunamis, droughts, famines, wars, etc. In short, a gradual un-worlding, a slow, yet perpetual, end of times. And in this sense "we soon will be all Amerindians" (Viveiros de Castro 2014b: 4) – or indigenous peoples of Africa or Australian aboriginals – since our condition will quite probably be the same as theirs: we will be worldless survivals in an un- worlded world.

My *second* idea is that (b) contemporary thought seems to be more or less aware of this troubling circumstance – or, at the very least, aware of the fact that we no longer live in the world as we fancied it to be. In fact, it can be said that this awareness has by now provoked not only diverse cultural narratives but also a multidimensional re-constellation of thought, both within and beyond the traditional boundaries of almost all academic disciplines. A single diagnosis and, thereby, a coherent portrayal of what we are experiencing is lacking. Yet, this is quite normal given the numerous issues that merge on the soil of today's critical

---

1 See the Stockholm Resilience Centre's updated "planetary-boundaries" diagram, available at <http://www.stockholmresilience.org/research/planetary-boundaries.html> (accessed 24 March 2020) and the "Slum Almanac 2015–2016" of the UN Habitat Program, available at <https://unhabitat.org/slum-almanac-2015-2016/> (accessed 24 March 2020).

thinking, as well as the latter's multiform, if not exactly prismatic, quality. Consequently, there are innumerable questions that haunt us. To mention a few (less with the purpose of answering to them, which would exceed the limits of this chapter than to bring the reader's attention to their interrelatedness and disquieting nature):[2] Can the aforementioned ecological *cum* social collapse serve as the barometer of our times or is it that today's biggest challenge comes from cybernetics instead? How should we read, for example, developments in the production of artificial intelligence that are blurring the boundary between the biological and the technological? Which must be our attitude before them? Fascination? Horror? The combination of both in a new form of existential vertigo? Lastly, how does all this affect the earth? Is it still – with all its inhabitants – instrumentally at our disposal, or has it evaporated with our dreams? Alternatively, is it possible to say that the earth is back, and that it demands from us renewed attention and care?

It is this latter question that I intend to respond in this chapter. Three random images may serve to illustrate the three options I have briefly mentioned: the image of Malian women and children with their hands full of the traditional seeds they are beginning to grow back again to counter both the effects of climate change and the biopiracy practiced by industrial-agriculture giants like Monsanto with its patents; the image of coal extraction in Rhineland in Germany; and the image of the almost-total and hardly describable disaster caused by typhoon Haiyan when it seized the Philippines in 2013.

Third idea: (c) in addition to pointing out the ontological fluctuance of our "natural" and "social" environments, the latter question may be said to condense the fluctuance of the "conceptual" environment(s) brought forth to tackle them, and thereby to summon the major primary axes of early-21st-century ontological thought – for, strangely enough, in an age in which almost everything is often taken for granted, thought still seems capable of engaging in the questioning of the real as such. My proposal is to distribute such major axes alongside three concentric circles, one per axis, as shown in the diagram below (Fig. 1). Here, Roman numbers indicate the position of each axis (core-mainstream, semi-peripheral, and peripheral), whereas Latin letters show the different trends of thought linked to each position. The continuous rectilinear lines delimit each trend's distinctive area or micro-region, while the discontinuous rectilinear lines delimit the possible subdivisions of these. The thick lines separate macro-regions

---

[2] On the importance of evoking the major questions of an epoch – provided their interconnectedness – before addressing the specific ones to be dealt with in an investigation that attempts to shed light on what may be called their shared surface of inscription, see Heidegger (1984: 300–301).

III and II and, even more strongly, II and I with decreasing degrees of "ontological" challenge and fluctuance: high in III, low in II, inappreciable in I. Also, their distribution should be read in connection to the three aforementioned questions and the *"pictorial" fluctuance of reality* that they evoke. *Thus, in Region I, the earth is still perceived to be at our disposal; in Region II, it has dramatically vanished; whereas in Region III it announces its transfigured return.*

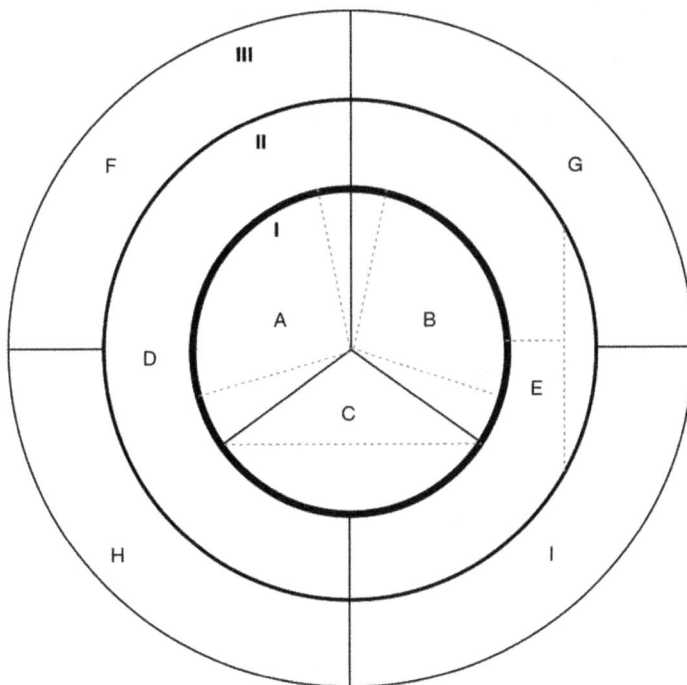

Fig. 1: The primary axes of early twenty-first-century ontological thought.

Let's now consider them separately. In addition to describing their corresponding subregions (i.e., their content), I would like to suggest a premise, a key notion, and a visual metaphor for each of them in order to draw the reader's attention to the possible reversibility of the central and peripheral regions in the future.

(1) The core of the diagram (i.e., Region I) represents today's mainstream thought world, within which three major trends of thought can be distinguished: (A) liberal, (B) socialist, and (C) environmentalist. Here, liberal means in accordance with the ideals of Enlightenment and political economy. Conversely, socialist refers to the endorsement of the former and the questing of the unrestrained character of

the latter. In both cases, adjoining areas (A→B and A←B) are contemplated, signaling either moderate tendencies within each trend and/or their respective accelerationist variants. In turn, in the environmentalist area, I am willing to include all types of environmentalism (e.g., resource conservationism and preservationism)[3] compatible with A and B (inside C's triangular area, but notice too A's and B's adjacent areas to C); these shallow forms of environmentalism differ from more radical variants, which, in turn, tend to reproduce the nature and culture divide characteristic of modernity (Braidotti 2013: 85). I, therefore, take the addition of C to A and B in the late twentieth century to be a stable trait of today's mainstream thought world, which explains why I have placed C inside Region I. There is an additional reason for it: since even the less-reformist variants of C have succeeded to find their place in today's thought world in their quality of adversaries of modernization, they can be said to constitute the outside of an intellectual universe to which they positionally belong – for, as Louis Althusser observed long ago:

> It is impossible to leave a closed space simply by taking up a position merely outside it, either in its exterior or its profundity: so long as this outside or profundity remain its outside or profundity, they still belong to that circle, to that closed space, as its 'repetition' in its other-than-itself.
> (1970: 53)

One also has to consider how the two dimensions of the current cosmo-political crisis are split up into two entirely independent areas (B and C), rather than folding into a single one. It can be assumed that discourses focusing simultaneously on both dimensions belong elsewhere and not in the A, B, or C boxes, which do not present any ontological challenge to contemporary thought. Bluntly: from any of such boxes the present is differently viewed as an "unfinished project", whose modern substrate does not need to be problematized. Such is indeed their common premise, whereas their common concept is that of a virtually endless escalation of what we already have. In turn, an apt visual metaphor among others could be in this case that of the rationally well-planned gardens of Versailles.

(2) The semi-periphery of the diagram (i.e., Region II) includes, on its part, two different areas whose connections tend to be more fluid than those between A, B, and C (their eventual intersections notwithstanding) in Region I.

First, we have Quentin Meillassoux's anti-correlationism and Ray Brassier's transcendental nihilism. Apparently, what Pascal diagnosed in the mid-seventeenth century as the eternal and frightening silence of infinite spaces, i.e., "the discovery that the world possesses a power of persistence and permanence that

---

[3] See the classification proposed by Cramer (1998: 10–13).

is completely unaffected by our existence or inexistence"[4] (Meillassoux 2008: 116), has gathered new momentum in the opening decades of our century. This also involves the view that "[t]here is no nature worth revering or rejoining; [. . .] no self to be re-enthroned as captain of its own fate; [. . .] no future worth working towards or hoping for"; in short, that life is "malignantly useless" (Brassier 2010: 9). In other terms, Meillassoux views the pretension to confer meaning to the world according to what it means to us as the correlationist delusion from which modern science cures us by opening our eyes to a "*glacial* world" (his own metaphor). In this world, "there is no longer any up or down, center or periphery, nor anything else that might make of it a world designed for humans" (2008: 115). Hence, for Meillassoux, the world has become pure contingency.[5] In turn, Brassier extols the pointlessness of the world thus disenchanted: philosophers, he claims, "would do well to desist from issuing any further injunctions about the need to re-establish the meaningfulness of existence, the purposefulness of life, or mend the shattered concord between man and nature" (2007: xi); and he does so *contra* Nietzsche's playfulness:

> Nietzsche conflated truth with meaning, and concluded that since the latter is always a result of human artifice, the former is nothing but a matter of convention. However, once the truth is dismissed, all that remains is the difference between empowering and disempowering fictions, where 'life' is the fundamental source of empowerment and the ultimate arbiter of the difference between life-enhancing and life-depreciating fictions. [. . .] I consider myself a nihilist precisely to the extent that I refuse this Nietzschean solution.
> (Brassier and Rychter 2011: n.p.)

It could be argued, therefore, that Meillassoux and Brassier view the earth as a sort of black nothingness that has taken over what we once naively fancied to be a meaningful world. From this eliminative perspective the present appears as much tainted with contingency as the future reveals itself opaque. Metaphorically speaking, it could be said that their ontological fluctuance presents irrational numbers, unlike the round, natural numbers characteristic of Region I. The earth is here viewed as a sort of black nothingness that has taken over what we once naively fancied to be a meaningful world.

---

4 Thus, against Kant's philosophy, Meillassoux's notion of "non-correlationism" (2007: 5). See for a critique Segovia (2021).

5 It is not totally clear to me how it is possible to endorse the radical contingency of the real and find support for this in modern science given the latter's interest in studying regularities and subsequently coming out with laws, however hypothetical these may be said to be. Cf. Brassier's (2007: 82–83, 87–88) similar argument. Notice too Meillassoux's (2008: 128) attempt to "reconcile [in this way] thought and [the] absolute." For a critique of the notion of contingency, see Gevorkyan and Segovia (2020a).

Secondly, we have Graham Harman's, Ian Bogost's, Levi Bryant's, and Timothy Morton's object-oriented ontologies (henceforth OOO). It is Harman who first moved in an OOO direction.[6] Viewed from a number of scientific and philosophical reductive angles, Harman complains that an object can be several things. It can be "*nothing more than* either final microphysical facts, or [. . .] an empty figment reducible to such facts" (2011:24), as per the teachings of scientific naturalism. It can be "*nothing more than* its accessibility to humans" (24), as idealism holds. It can be "*nothing more than* a byproduct of a deeper primordial reality" or "a derivative actualization of a deeper reality" (24), from a monist perspective. It can be "the fleeting crystallization of some impulse or trajectory that can never be confined to a single moment" (24), an option that Harman identifies with Bergson. It can be "*nothing more than* its effects on other things" (24), as relationism claims. It can be "*nothing more than* its history" (24) for a genealogical approach. It can be "*nothing more than* a nickname for our habitual linking of red, sweet, cold, hard, and juicy under the single term 'apple'" (24), as Hume had it. Or it can be "*nothing more than* the grammatical superstition of traditionalist dupes, drugged by the opiate of noun/verb Western grammar" (24), as the philosophies of difference claim in turn. Who said that all these approaches have enormously complicated the objectuality of objects, making them *something more* than (simple) objects? In Harman's opinion, what they have done is exactly the opposite; due to them we have lost sight of the objects *qua* objects:

> There are other possible ways of discrediting objects in philosophy, some of them not yet invented. My purpose [. . .] is to emphasize that a counter-movement is both possible and necessary [. . .]. [A]ll of these anti-object standpoints try to reduce reality to a single *radix* [...] [since] all say that a full half of reality is *nothing more than* an illusion generated by the other half. (2011: 24)

By "a full half of reality" Harman means, one may infer, the half corresponding to Object within the modern Subject/Object philosophical divide (= Subject/*Object*): if an object is nothing but a modality of some deeper reality, or the name we give to a set of converging sensory qualities, or a cumulation of effects and stories, this means that we take it to be nothing more than a subjective delusion. Therefore, by choosing any of those options, he fears that we re-enter the correlationist room, which we were supposedly in need to leave (= *Subject*/Object). In a nutshell: if an object is any of the aforementioned things, it ceases to be an object in the sense that we are no longer able to think it *qua* object. This, argues Harman, amounts to saying that we are unable to represent it as an

---

[6] See, for a general picture, Bryant, Srnicek, and Harman (2011); Gratton (2014); Shaviro (2014); Harman (2018).

individual substance, as Aristotle would have done, and one must view Aristotle, he adds, as "the permanent ally of all brands of realism; [for] whatever the flaws of Aristotelian substance may be, lack of reality outside the human mind is not one of them" (2011: 27). Hence, Harman concludes that what seemed to be *more than* becomes *less than*, if we take Aristotle's categorical logic as a reference. One of two things: this is either a joke or a philosophical naivety of such proportions that any further comment is unnecessary. Furthermore, Kant's *noumenon/phenomenon* distinction joins Harman's OOO through the backdoor:

> We can neither be downward scientific reducers, nor can we be upward humanistic reducers. We can only be hunters of objects, and must even be non-lethal hunters, since objects can never be caught. The world is not primarily filled with electrons or human praxis but with ghostly objects withdrawing from all human and inhuman access, accessible only by allusion and seducing us by means of allure. Whatever we capture, whatever table we sit at or destroy, is not the real table. (Harman 2012: 12)

Neither science nor politics, but art, can therefore supply a valid model for philosophy (Harman 2012: 14–15). Thus, Harman does not only re-instantiate a subtle form of idealism but also the postmodern shift from ethics (whose primacy already meant the death of politics) to aesthetics, adding to it the feeling that before reality we are lost in translation. As for the objects surrounding us, they are isolated from one another: "[w]hen the things withdraw from presence," writes Harman, "they distance themselves not only from human beings, but *from each other* as well" (2002: 2). Thereby Harman pushes Heidegger's horizon of Being's withdrawal to move along an altogether different – and ultimately non-Heideggerian – axis: if objects are more-than-their-being-present-to-us, Harman suggests, they must also be more-than-their-being-present-to-one-another.

Accordingly, the overall ontological view inherent in any OOO variant is summarized by Bogost in the formula: "The alien [. . .] [is] everywhere" (2012: 133). It is everywhere since we are surrounded by objects – and only by objects: objects we do not control anymore, objects we cannot exactly know anymore, and objects that place us in the uncomfortable position of being at their mercy, although they simultaneously invite us, by being there, to relate to them at the same time. The primacy of the Subject is reversed here, too. However, instead of a meaningless nothingness, like in Brassier (2007), and instead of contingency, like in Meillassoux (2008), we get the Object, now in a position of complete privilege. But then, has philosophy really moved from the aporia established by Schelling in the fourth of his 1795–1796 *Philosophische Briefe über Dogmatismus und Kritizismus* (1914: 23): either no Subject but an absolute Object, or else no Object but an absolute Subject? In other words: does not all of this fall into the "apparatus of capture" (Deleuze and Guattari 1987: 424–474) of a too-simple-

and-stereotypical ontological frame once more? For if modern philosophy turns around the Subject and its production of meaning, we merely seem to be confronted here with the black hole caused by its removal. I am tempted at this point to evoke Bataille:

> Nothing is more foreign to our way of thinking than the earth in the middle of the silent universe and having neither the meaning that man [sic.] gives things, nor the meaninglessness of things as soon as we try to imagine them without a consciousness that reflects them.
> (1989: 20)

Seen from this perspective, the present does not only appear to be irretrievably post-ecological, but also legitimately post-political – one could say that it amounts to a collection of photographs in lack of film; and in last analysis to an aesthetic playground at best.

This impression is reinforced when reading Morton (whose thought I would place in the upper half of section E, i.e., in continuity with OOO but as something different from it due to its idiosyncratic evolution, on which one can find more below). For clarity's sake, I shall distinguish between three periods in the development of Morton's zigzagging contribution to contemporary philosophy. (*a*) In 2007, Morton makes the point that there is nothing like a unified milieu within which – unlike humans, who must be placed outside of it – non-human beings dwell, nothing therefore like Nature. Thus, the title of his 2007 book is *Ecology Without Nature* (or dark ecology). Its subtitle was likewise eloquent: *Rethinking Environmentalist Aesthetics*. "Coming up with a new worldview," he wrote in its opening lines, "means dealing with how humans experience their place in the world. Aesthetics, thus, performs a crucial role for Morton, establishing ways of feeling and perceiving this place" (2007: 2); feeling and perceiving rather than thought – as if politics were interdicted, or impossible, or unnecessary, or old-fashioned. (*b*) In his next book, however, Morton (2013) takes another path. Morton claims that "Hyperobjects", like "the sum total of all the nuclear materials on Earth; or just the plutonium, or the uranium," as well as "long-lasting product[s] of direct human manufacture," like, for example, "Styrofoam or plastic bags, or the sum of all the whirring machinery of capitalism are directly responsible for what I call *the end of the world*" (2013: 4). And this, he goes on to say, has provoked three attitudes in us: hypocrisy, weakness, and lameness.

> *Hypocrisy* results from the conditions of the impossibility of a metalanguage ([. . .] [of which] we are now [. . .] aware [. . .] because of the ecological emergency); *weakness* from the gap between phenomenon and thing, which the hyperobject makes disturbingly visible; and *lameness* from the fact that all entities are fragile (as a condition of possibility for their existence), and hyperobjects make this fragility conspicuous. (Morton 2007: 4)

Yet, Morton subsequently remarks, "[t]his does not mean that there is no hope for ecological politics and ethics. Far from it" (2007: 8); for this lameness must be viewed, he says, as Hölderlin's "'saving power' that grows alongside the dangerous power," as well as Heidegger's "last god" (2007: 20), capable of saving us in a sense that it distills and encourages in us the humble "acceptance" (2007: 153) of our condition. What we therefore need is a kind of political quietism – and a dose of self-complacency to keep it in place. Nevertheless, (c) in his latest book, Morton (2017) has replaced Heidegger by Marx, minus Marx's (modern) anthropocentrism, and discovered that what we really need is – as the subtitle reads – "solidarity with nonhuman people," or, in other words, a communism that includes nonhumans against the capitalist appropriation of indigenous lands, women's bodies, and nonhuman beings.

However, references to the abundant and multidisciplinary scholarship on these matters are scarce. Furthermore, there cannot be found a single sign of true engagement with political activism of any kind against neocolonialism in Morton's work, beyond a brief-but-strategically placed allusion in its opening lines to the Native Americans, who opposed the construction of the Dakota Access Pipeline in the US in 2016. One cannot but wonder, if this is the kind of cosmopolitics we need. For despite the premise being in this case – I would suggest – the belief that we live in times of apocalyptic perplexity, the concept that links all OOO proposals can be said to be that of a self-absorbed lameness, whose visual metaphor could be that of a typical Victorian study room, in which the only thing one can do is to sit by the fire and light up a pipe (Gevorkyan and Segovia 2020b).

On the other hand, Peter Sloterdijk (2011, 2013) develops a twofold proposal, which holds the function of a new ontological constitution to help us better relocate ourselves in the world against the prerogatives of modern anthropocentrism together with the elaboration/re- activation of collective. Moreover, it is put into service as an individual training-techniques that may help us to better adapt to such new environment and remain human. However, it is clearly not enough in this context; for if its relational ontology cannot be said to be exactly flat, it can be described, though, as being exclusively programmatic: something like a minor sequel to the Heideggerean assumption of the *Mitsein*-ness of the *Dasein* (the "being-with"- or "togetherness" of "man" in his quality of situated [*da-*] "existent" [*sein*]). In this sense, Bertrand Stiegler's (2018) attempt to rethink the Heideggerian *Sorge* as an economy of care against the planetary entropy brought about by industrial capitalism, and his proposal to counter the latter with an organicist *cum* processual cosmology *à la* Whitehead,[7] looks more interesting to me; yet it obviates that we

---

7 On the contemporary recovery of Whitehead, see Stengers (2011).

may also need, among many other things, to rethink the correlation of life and death in tragic terms (Segovia and Gevorkyan 2021). Thus, I would also place Sloterdijk and Stiegler's philosophical elaborations inside semicircle E, within the small vertical fringe on its right, whence the world represents a chance to re-situate ourselves and eventually something more.

(3) Lastly, Region III works like a cocktail container with four main components: (F) new ecologies (including general ecologies, meta-ecologies, and trans-species ecologies), (G) new philosophical materialisms (whose vitalism makes them run against the flat ontologies and dark ontologies so far examined), (H) postcolonial (or, better, de-colonial) studies (with their epistemic disobedience to, and delinking from, colonial thought, plus their focus on the uncommon and the need to produce new designs for a pluriverse), and (I) new ontological developments in anthropology (which cannot be said to merely provide a new ethnographic method). I am convinced that these four intersecting fronts form a fourfold surface and that, put together, provide the keys to the ontology we need, and to the new politics of the earth!

By the expression "new ecologies," I am thinking of Erich Hörl's (2013, 2015, 1017) "general ecology" with its stress on the ecologization of all modes of existence, attainable through the interaction of human and nonhuman actors and, more exactly, through the countercultural interplay of art, philosophy, and technology against cyber-capitalism and hyper- industrialization. Hörl also speaks of a "thousand ecologies" – a wink to Deleuze and Guattari's *A Thousand Plateaus* (1987) – and traces his inspiration back to Guattari's latest works (in particular *The Three Ecologies* and *Chaosmosis*). Here, room must be created for Bruno Latour's recent meta-ecological drift (2013a, 2013b, 2015). Through a critical, oblique re-reading of James Lovelock *contra* Galileo, Latour proposes to re-assume the earth's acting capacity and *dynamics*, while avoiding transforming it into a single-acting subject, given its inherent multiplicity. Also, he proposes to explore other ways of understanding and being in the world – in continuity with Isabelle Stengers's *Cosmopolitiques* (1997). Stengers's own work moves a step further in the direction of anti-capitalist politics (cf. her collaboration with Philippe Pignarre [2011]). In turn, Donna J. Haraway's (2008) trans-species ontology re-defines humanity as a "spatial and temporal web of interspecies dependencies" and puts emphasis on "becoming with" as a practice of "becoming worldly" – in a way that differs from, even opposes to, the axiomatic one-world world of modern globalization. Therefore, it deserves to be mentioned at this point as well. Perceptibly, it contains something more than Derrida's (2008) human-animal alter-cogito exchange. From these intercrossing points of view, which I propose to group within a single trend (F), we are then at the crossroads of the world's newly-redefined components, in a sort of active awakening to new explorable ways of being and thinking (onto- logy). These stress the *unity and immanence* of life against the transcendent narrative of logocentric/phallocratic extractivism as represented in Jan van der Straet's famous engraving *America Uncovered*. Here, an unclothed woman (America) welcomes her male European conqueror, who are not only carrying swords but also the symbols of faith and science. This scene is reminiscent of Francis Bacon's verbal depiction of nature as a-woman-to-be-interrogated-and-conquered-by-the-new-science in order to propitiate Man's redemption from his fallen condition and full recovery of his primordial place in the world (cf. Merchant 2003: 69–72).

Another step forward in the production of the type of thought we somehow need today in consists in conceiving of a "monistic universe of intersecting affective relations that [. . .] make the world go round" (Braidotti 2013:55). This view is based on "Spinoza's central concept that matter, the world and humans are not dualistic entities structured according to principles of internal or external opposition" (Braidotti 2013: 56), and that matter itself (= reality's core) is "autopoietic" (Braidotti 2013: 60). This is a type of thought explored, among others, by Brian Massumi (2002) and Jane Bennett (2010), that fits well into the rubric "new (vital) materialism(s)" – vital against the glacial materialism of Meillassoux and Brassier, the perplexed materialism of any OOO, and Iain Hamilton Grant's (2006) and Ben Woodard's (2013) abyssal materialism.

Let's now turn to (H) post-colonial/de-colonial studies, and their current parallel emphasis on the making of *differences*. As Mario Blaser writes, the modern story – the modern worldview – has become "increasingly located in a position of 'dominance without hegemony,'" (2013: 557) and this has rendered "visible" (2013: 554) crucial ontological differences, as well as ongoing ontological conflicts, otherwise unperceived, that is to say, silenced, repressed, denied, and suppressed. "The modern story," he explains, "hinges upon a specific arrangement of three elements: an ontologically stark distinction between nature and culture, a dominant tendency to conceive difference (including the difference between nature and culture) in hierarchical terms, and a linear conception of time" (Blaser 2013: 554). Thus, between the sixteenth and eighteenth centuries – whose cosmopolitical shift has been merely expanded and eulogized in the nineteenth and twentieth centuries – the domain of culture was "subdivided into several 'cultures' as the key diacritic to establish differences among humans," (Blaser 2013: 554) and the position of "modern culture" in relation to its "others" (i.e., in relation to "nature" and other "cultures") was "linked to a hierarchical system mapped out against the background of linear time," (Blaser 2013: 554) so that the two great resulting divides (between nature and culture and between moderns and nonmoderns) "were increasingly understood by moderns in terms of a story that makes modernity not only different but also the spearhead of the evolving [univocal] history of [a single] humanity" (Blaser 2013: 554). Thereby, Blaser regards the aforementioned "two great divides" as being not only "co-emergent," but also "cosustaining" (2013: 554). It is, however, the second one, i.e., the divide between moderns and nonmoderns, that interests me here. Pointing to the European (read: Spanish, Portuguese, French, Dutch, and later British, German, Russian, Scandinavian, and Italian) colonization/exploitation of the "New World" as the earliest conquest-adventure that contributed to the making of the modern story, Blaser comments on this as follows:

> As long as the horizon of alterity in the encounter with the New World was Christianity, the radical Otherness of the natives' worlding was recognized as potentially threatening and the site of an open antagonism (i.e., the Indians were minions to the devil either willingly or because they had fallen prey to his lies), but as reason displaced faith in the constitution of the modern regime of truth, this antagonism was progressively muted: Indians were just ignorant, they were at an earlier stage of evolution, or, as of late, they just had another culture (which, critically, lacked the concept of culture; de la Cadena 2010). (2013: 555)

It is therefore possible to say that "[i]n its latest modality, modernity exorcizes the threatening difference of other worldings by taming them and allowing them to exist just as cultural perspectives on a singular reality" (Blaser 2013: 555). In short, as I have written elsewhere (Segovia 2018), from killing/enslaving the Others, we have moved on to suppress their too- primitive Otherness so as to make them fully human, and then we have moved on to selectively eradicate some essential aspects of their Otherness, while keeping others as culture and folklore, so as to make of them another (exotic) type of global citizen. The strategy has changed, but the logic remains the same;[8] and it remains essentially the same, as there is no modernity without coloniality: modern/colonial form a single composite term.[9]

Countering such strategy could thus be the first move in an attempt to achieve some degree of epistemic disobedience (Mignolo 2009) and conceptual de-linking (Mignolo 2007) of the modern/neocolonial regime of truth. First, through the vindication of (local) "subaltern" knowledges, practices, and ways of being and living. Second, by the delineation of what Walter D. Mignolo (2000: 91–126) calls a "post-Occidental reason," although I would prefer to use the term "thought"

---

8 A logic, by the way, performed in the name of humanism, redressed today as humanitarianism: indigenous populations should not be "left behind," they also must be provided with "education and/or health care," "nation- states" must veil for "all their citizens alike," "human rights should be extensive to all," etc. With Pierre Clastres (1994:45), one could then affirm that the ethics of humanism are the spirituality of ethnocide.
9 See Mignolo's (2000) expression "modern/colonial world system."

instead, and more precisely "thoughts" in the plural. Thirdly, through the subsequent multiplication of ontologies and their respective worldings – or the making of a pluriverse (Escobar 2018) against the "one-world world" (Law 2011) we have been trapped in.

But there is a domain (I) where the ontological differences that frame a pluriverse are, if anything, particularly evident and thereby observable: contemporary anthropology. I am especially thinking of something that was first labeled by Amiria Henare, Martin Holbraad, and Sari Wastell (2007) as an "ontological turn" in current anthropology, associated, among others, with the names of Philippe Descola and Eduardo Viveiros de Castro (Pedersen and Martin Holbraad 2017).

In a groundbreaking and elegantly-written monograph titled *Beyond Nature and Culture* (Descola 2013), which Lévi-Strauss himself welcomed in the promotional blurb of the original French edition (Descola 2005) as "giv[ing] to anthropological reflection a new starting point," and Marshall Sahlins as a "paradigm shift" in the "current anthropological trajectory," (Descola 2013: xii), Descola (2013) distinguishes between four different manners there are to map, namely "nature" and "culture." Let's provisionally keep both terms – be it by delimiting their supposed boundaries as being external to one another or by complicating instead any attempt to trace a clear-cut divide between them. These different world-views – or rather, ontologies *au sens fort* – he calls: (*a*) "animism" – moving beyond Edward Burnett Tylor's recurrent use of such term throughout the 2 vols. of his ambitious 1871 essay on *Primitive Culture* (Tylor 2016) to denote the belief in souls or spirits proper of "lower races" due to their incapability of telling "man [sic!] [. . .] [from] beast [. . .] and plants or even objects" (Harvey 2017: 8); (*b*) "totemism" – a term Descola takes from Lévi-Strauss (1964) by classifying it as a "classificatory" tendency to articulate the social, the natural, and the individual along reciprocal principles, albeit simultaneously conferring it a more straightforwardly ontological quality (Descola 2013: 144); (*c*) "analogism" – which roughly coincides with Foucault's (1970) concept of analogy as the pre-modern *episteme* of western culture, yet, expanding it beyond such rather-narrow temporal and geographical boundaries; and (*d*) "naturalism" – which Descola equates with the very type of mechanicist take on the world distinctive of modern (i.e., Galilean, Cartesian, and Newtonian) science.

In the first case (*a*) all or most "things" are endowed with a living principle of their own (which is the reason why, e.g., many native American languages have "animated" and "unanimated" genres accompanying their nouns and verbs). This authorizes to say that what most of them share in common (their specific living principles notwithstanding) is an "interiority" or "personhood," whereas they totally differ as to their radically different "embodiments," to which different lived, experienced worlds correspond in turn – cf. the parallel concepts of "perspectivism" and "multinaturalism" in Viveiros de Castro (1998; 2014a: 49–75); all of which goes far beyond the timid recovering of the term "animism" by Nurit Bird- David (1999) and Graham Harvey (2017) after A. Irving Hallowell (1960). An example of this alter-ontology is the widespread Amazonian belief that before the "ethnographic present" all differences chaotically communicated with one another so that most animals, plants, geographical features, meteorological phenomena, and celestial bodies were in their appearance as "human" as humans still are, but that they lost their human physicality due to their many ontological becomings, through which they morphed into the biological species and other beings and realities that form the present world (Danowski and Viveiros de Castro 2017: 63–64). According to this view, "what we call 'environment' is [. . .] a society of societies, an international arena, a *cosmopoliteia*" (Danowski and Viveiros de Castro 2017: 69; cf. Segovia 2019). Conversely, in the fourth case (*d*) what all living things have in common is their equal belonging to "nature," with humankind representing the only (partial) exception to this rule insofar as humans have managed to develop something else: apart from nature, and in opposition to it, they also have "culture," which makes them different and justifies their privileged position in a cosmos they attempt to conquer against all possible natural constraints and their own biological limitations. "Totemism" (*c*) differs from these two opposing ontologies (although its connections to animism are actually many) in that it establishes a full, i.e., a twofold continuity: natural and cultural. For in this case, the different human groups share their interiority, i.e., their personhood as well as their embodiment or physicality with the different animal species (one per human group), whose respective pre-cosmological archetypes are ontologically responsible for the production of the different observable ecosystems in nature. Lastly, in the fourth case (*d*) nature and culture differ from one species to another and from one reality to another, so that in rigor one can only speak of an irreducible multiplicity: the world as an infinite collection of singularities. Yet it is simultaneously possible to associate some things to others due to their similar qualities or states of being, i.e., by applying to them the principle of analogy, which thereby allows to ideally portray the world as a web of more-or-less evident or secret relations.

This is no place to complicate the virtual intersecting articulations of such ontological models (on which see Viveiros de Castro [2012] and Segovia [forthcoming b]). I would simply wish to highlight that through this multi-ontological lens anthropology proves to be about nothing shorter from "sticking one's neck out through the looking-glass of ontological difference," as Viveiros de Castro aptly puts it (2014b: n.p.). What Descola (2013) offers as a structural classification,

Viveiros de Castro explores by focusing on Amazonian ontology and its corresponding concept of embodiment: bodies as inscribed "perspectives" rather than self- identical and self-contained substances, and the world as a collection of perspectival embodiments among which there is recurrent transitivity, which confers to the present – to any present – a rather thin stability against a multiplicity of virtual metamorphoses and "other- becomings" – otherness thereby becoming the issue life has permanently to deal with. Thus, thanks to the ontological turn, anthropology proves to be "ready to fully assume its new mission of being the theory/practice of the permanent decolonization of thought" (Viveiros de Castro 2014a: 40); in the sense that its role is "not that of *explaining the world of the other*, but rather of *multiplying our world*, 'filling it with all of those things expressed that do not exist beyond their expression' (Deleuze)" (Viveiros de Castro 2014b: n.p.). These virtual connections between anthropology, postcoloniality, philosophy, and ecology substantiate the view of a creative circulation and reciprocation of ideas among the various areas of this third peripheral region of our map.

In this third region of our diagram – whose purpose is, like with any diagram, both to reflect thought and to generate it – the premise is therefore that we must reimagine worlds to escape the unworld we have all been enclosed in by the modern/colonial/capitalist project. The concept, neither escalation nor lameness, but transition to a pluriverse. A possible visual metaphor would be Wittgenstein's (2009: 204) rabbit-duck drawing turned into an image of ontological univocality and equivocity at the same time – like a Möbius strip.

Fourth concluding idea: as Arturo Escobar writes, "[t]he project of 'reworlding' is thus necessary ontological in that it involves eliminating or redesigning not just structures, technologies, and institutions but our very ways of thinking and being." (2018: 118). Therefore, an option cosmopolitically engaged with those (humans and non-humans alike) whose worlds have been virtually whipped off by the capitalist mega-machine (ourselves included, despite the fact that we no longer seem to remember it), would consist in reimagining the world – or, better, as many worlds as possible – otherwise, this is to say, neither in continuity with modernity (whatever its kind) nor in light of its dialectical negation(s). This latter option points to the cosmopolitics we are in need of in order to escape – even if locally, temporarily, and fragmentarily – the un-world in which we are all trapped. Everything else amounts to de- politicization – a cosmos, or its shadow, without politics. Only that, in the end, even cosmopolitics may not be enough: a poetics of dwelling may be both necessary and urgent. But mentioning it amounts to point *beyond* the diagram into the thinkable if still largely unthought (Gevorkyan and Segovia 2020c).

Bibliography

Althusser, Louis (1970) "From Capital to Marx's Philosophy," in *Reading Capital*, ed. Louis Althusser and Étienne Balibar (London: New Left Books), 11–69.
Bataille, Georges (1989) *Theory of Religion* (New York: Zone Books).
Bataille, Georges (2015) *On Nietzsche* (Albany, NY: SUNY Press).
Bennett, Jane (2010) *Vibrant Matter: A Political Ecology of Things* (Durham, NC & London: Duke University Press).
Bird-David, Nurit (1999) "'Animism' Revisited: Personhood, Environment, and Relational Epistemology," *Current Anthropology* 40.1, 67–91.
Blaser, Mario (2013) "Ontological Conflicts and the Stories of Peoples in Spite of Europe: Toward a Conversation on Political Ontology," *Current Anthropology* 54.5, 547–568.
Bogost, Ian (2012) *Alien Phenomenology, or What It's like to Be a Thing* (Minneapolis and London: University of Minnesota Press).
Braidotti, Rosi (2013) *The Posthuman* (Cambridge, UK & Malden, MA: Polity Press).
Brassier, Ray (2007) *Nihil Unbound: Enlightenment and Extinction* (London and New York: Palgrave MacMillan).
Brassier, Ray (2010) "Foreword" to Thomas Ligotti, *The Conspiracy against the Human Race: A Contrivance of Horror* (New York: Hippocampus Press), 9–10.
Brassier, Ray and Marcin Rychter (2011) "I am a Nihilist because I still Believe in Truth," *Kronos* 16.1. <https://kronos.org.pl/numery/kronos-1-162011/kronos-1162011/> (accessed 8 March 2018).
Bryant, Levi R. (2011) *The Democracy of Objects*. <http://www.openhumanitiespress.org/books/titles/the-democracy-of-objects/> (London: Open Humanities Press) (accessed 24 March 2020).
Bryant, Levi et al. (eds) (2011) *The Speculative Turn: Continental Materialism and Realism* (Melbourne: re.press).
Clastres, Pierre (1994) *Archeology of Violence* (New York: Semiotex(e)).
Cramer, Phillip F. (1998) *Deep Environmental Politics: The Role of Radical Environmentalism in Crafting American Environmental Policy* (Westport, CT: Greenwood).
Danowski, Déborah and Eduardo Viveiros de Castro (2017) *The Ends of the World* (Cambridge, UK and Malden, MA: Polity Press).
Deleuze, Gilles (1994) *Difference and Repetition* (London and New York: The Athlone Press and Columbia University Press).
Deleuze, Gilles and Félix Guattari (1987) *A Thousand Plateaus: Capitalism and Schizophrenia* (Minneapolis and London: University of Minnesota Press).
Derrida, Jacques (2008) *The Animal that therefore I Am* (New York: Fordham University Press).
Descola, Philippe (2005) *Par-delà Nature et Culture* (Paris: Éditions Gallimard).
Descola, Philippe (2013) *Beyond Nature and Culture* (Chicago and London: University of Chicago Press).
Escobar, Arturo (2018) *Designs for the Pluriverse: Radical Interdependence, Autonomy, and The Making of Worlds* (Durham, NC & London: Duke University Press).
Foucault, Michel (1970) *The Order of Things: An Archaeology of the Human Sciences* (New York: Pantheon Books).
Friedrichs, Jörg (2013) *The Future Is Not What It Used to Be: Climate Change and Energy Scarcity* (Cambridge, MA & London: The MIT Press).

Gevorkyan, Sofya, and Carlos A. Segovia (2020a) "Paul and the Plea for Contingency in Contemporary Philosophy – A Philosophical and Anthropological Critique," *Open Philosophy* 3, 625–656.

Gevorkyan, Sofya, and Carlos A. Segovia (2020b) "Post-Heideggerian Drifts: From Object-Oriented-Ontology Worldlessness to Post-Nihilist Worldings," in *Heidegger, Levinas, Derrida e o Nihilismo*, ed. Hilan Bensusan = *Das Questões* 9.1, 3–18.

Gevorkyan, Sofya, and Carlos A. Segovia (2020c) "Tres paradigmas cosmopolíticos: eco-tecnológico, perspectivista y meta-poético," in *Primaveras cosmopolíticas*, ed. Andrea Vidal and Hilan Bensusan = *Das Questões* 8.2, 30–35.

Gevorkyan, Sofya, and Carlos A. Segovia (2021) "Earth and World(s): From Heidegger to Contemporary Anthropology," *Open Philosophy* 4, 58–82.

Gevorkyan, Sofya, and Carlos A. Segovia (forthcoming) "Dionysus and Apollo after Nihilism," in *From Worlds of Possibles to Possible Worlds: On Post-nihilism and Dwelling*, ed. Sofya Gevorkyan and Carlos A. Segovia = *Das Questões* 12.1.

Grant, Iain Hamilton (2006) *Philosophies of Nature after Schelling* (London and New York: Continuum).

Gratton, Paul (2014) *Speculative Realism: Problems and Prospects* (London and New York: Bloomsbury).

Guattari, Félix (2000) *The Three Ecologies* (London et al.: The Athlone Press).

Hallowell, A. Irving (1960) "Ojibwa Ontology, Behaviour, and Worldview," in *Culture in History: Essays in Honor of Paul Radin*, ed. Stanley Diamond (New York: Columbia University Press), 19–52.

Haraway, Donna J. (2008) *When Species Meet* (Minneapolis & London: University of Minnesota Press).

Harman, Graham (2002) *Tool-Being: Heidegger and the Metaphysics of Objects* (Chicago: Open Court).

Harman, Graham (2011) "On the Undermining of Objects: Grant, Bruno, and Radical Philosophy," in *The Speculative Turn: Continental Materialism and Realism*, ed. Levi Bryant et al. (Melbourne: re.press), 21–40.

Harman, Graham (2012) *The Third Table / Der Dritte Tisch* (Ostfildern: Hatje Cantz Verlag).

Harman, Graham (2018) *Speculative Realism: An Introduction* (Cambridge, UK and Malden, MA: Polity Press).

Harvey, Graham (2017) *Animism: Respecting the Living World* (2nd edn; London: Hurst & Co).

Heidegger, Martin (1984) *Gesamtausgabe. Band 5: Holzwege* (Frankfurt: Klosterman).

Henare, Amiria, Martin Holbraad, and Sari Wastell (eds) (2007) *Thinking through Things: Theorising Artifacts Ethnographically* (London and New York: Routledge).

Holbraad, Martin and Morten Axel Pedersen (2017) *The Ontological Turn: An Anthropological Exposition* (Cambridge and New York: Cambridge University Press).

Hörl, Erich (2013) "A Thousand Ecologies: The Process of Cyberneticization and General Ecology," in *The Whole Earth. California and the Disappearance of the Outside*, ed. Diedrich Diederichsen and Anselm Franke (Berlin: Sternberg Press), 121–130.

Hörl, Erich (2015), in exchange with Paul Feigelfeld and Cornelia Castelan, "The Anthropocenic Illusion: Sustainability and the Fascination of Control," in *Art in the Periphery of the Center*, ed. Christoph Behnke et al. (Berlin: Sternberg), 352–368.

Hörl, Erich (2017) "Introduction to General Ecology: The Ecologization of Thinking," in *General Ecology: The New Ecological Paradigm*, ed. Erich Hörl with James Burton (London and New York: Bloomsbury), 1–73.

Latour, Bruno (2013a) "Facing Gaia: Six Lectures on the Political Theology of Nature," Edinburgh University Gifford Lectures on Natural Religion, Edinburgh, February 8–28. <https://www.giffordlectures.org/lectures/facing-gaia-new-enquiry-natural-religion> (accessed 24 March 2020).

Latour, Bruno (2013b) *An Inquiry into Modes of Existence: An Anthropology of the Moderns* (Cambridge, MA: Harvard University Press).

Latour, Bruno (2015) *Face à Gaïa: Huit conférences sur le Nouveau Régime Climatique* (Paris: Éditions La Découverte).

Law, John (2011) "What's Wrong with a One-World World," paper presented to the Center for the Humanities, Wesleyan University, Middletown, CT, September 19. <http://www.heterogeneities.net/publications/Law2011WhatsWrongWithAOneWorldWorld.pdf> (accessed 24 March 2020).

Lévi-Strauss, Claude (1964) *Totemism* (London: Merlin Press).

Massumi, Brian (2002) *Parables for the Virtual: Movement, Affect, Sensation* (Durham, NC and London: Duke University Press).

Meillassoux, Quentin (2008) *After Finitude: An Essay on the Necessity of Contingency* (London and New York: Continuum).

Merchant, Carolyn (2003) *Reinventing Eden: The Fate of Nature in Western Culture*. (London and New York: Routledge).

Mignolo, Walter D. (2000) *Local Histories/Global Designs: Coloniality, Subaltern Knowledge, and Border Thinking* (Princeton NJ: Princeton University Press).

Mignolo, Walter D. (2007) "Delinking: The Rhetoric of Modernity, the Logic of Coloniality and the Grammar of De-Coloniality," *Cultural Studies* 21.2–3, 449–514.

Mignolo, Walter D. (2009) "Epistemic Disobedience, Independent Thought and De-Colonial Freedom," *Theory, Culture & Society* 26.7–8, 1–23.

Morton, Timothy (2007) *Ecology without Nature: Rethinking Environmental Aesthetics* (Cambridge, MA and London: Harvard University Press).

Morton, Timothy (2010) *The Ecological Thought* (Cambridge, MA and London: Harvard University Press).

Morton, Timothy (2013) *Hyperobjects: Philosophy and Ecology After the End of the World* (Minneapolis and London: University of Minnesota Press).

Morton, Timothy (2017) *Humankind: Solidarity with Nonhuman People* (London: Verso).

Pignarre, Philippe and Isabelle Stengers (2011) *Capitalist Sorcery: Breaking the Spell* (London and New York: Palgrave Macmillan).

Sahlins, Marshall (2013) "Foreword" to Ph. Descola, *Beyond Nature and Culture* (Chicago and London: University of Chicago Press), xi–xiv.

Schelling, F. W. J. (1914) *Philosophische Briefe über Dogmatismus und Kritizismus*. Leipzig: Weiner.

Segovia, Carlos A. (2018) "On Humanism and the Spirituality of Ethnocide," paper presented to the symposium *L'Humanisme en questions*, held at the Royal Academy of Brussels (ARB) and the Free University of Brussels (ULB) and organized by the Multi- Disciplinary Centre for Religious Studies of the ULB, the Association of French- Speaking Societies of Philosophy (ASPLF) and the National Fund for Scientific Research (FNRS), Brussels, 26–28 April. <https://www.academia.edu/35935353/On_Humanism_and_the_Spirituality_of_Ethnocide_2018_Conference_Paper_Upcoming_Book_Chapter> (accessed 24 March 2020).

Segovia, Carlos A. (2019) "El nuevo animismo: experimental, isomérico, liminal y caósmico," *THÉMATA* 60, 35–48.

Segovia, Carlos A. (forthcoming a) "The Alien – Heraclitus Cut," *Alienocene: The Journal of the First Outernational*, Stratum 10.

Segovia, Carlos A. (forthcoming b) "Metaphoric Recursiveness and Ternary Ontology: Another Look at the Language and Worldview of the Yaminahua," forthcoming in *Tipití: Journal of the Society for the Anthropology of Lowland South America*, 17.1.

Shaviro, Steven (2014) *The Universe of Things: On Speculative Realism* (Minneapolis: University of Minnesota Press).

Sloterdijk, Peter (2011) *Bubbles: Spheres Volume I: Microspherology* (Los Angeles: Semiotext(e)).

Sloterdijk, Peter (2013) *You Must Change Your Life* (Cambridge, UK and Malden, MA: Polity Press).

Stengers, Isabelle (1997) *Cosmopolitiques* (7 vols; Paris: La Découverte/Empêcheurs de penser en rond).

Stengers, Isabelle (2011) *Thinking with Whitehead: A Free and Wild Creation of Concepts* (Harvard, MA: Harvard University Press).

Stiegler, Bertrand (2018) *The Neganthropocene*. http://www.openhumanitiespress.org/books/titles/the-neganthropocene/> (London: Open Humanities Press and Meson Press) (accessed 24 March 2020).

Tylor, Edward Burnett (2016) *Primitive Culture: Researches into the Development of Mythology, Philosophy, Religion, Language, Art, and Costume*. 2 vols. (Mineola, NY: Dover.)

Viveiros de Castro, Eduardo (1998) "Cosmological Deixis and Amerindian Perspectivism," *The Journal of the Royal Anthropological Institute* 4.3, 469–488.

Viveiros de Castro, Eduardo (2012) *Cosmological Perspectivism in Amazonia and Elsewhere. Four Lectures Given in the Department of Social Anthropology, University of Cambridge, February–March 1998*. <https://haubooks.org/cosmological-perspectivism-in-amazonia/> (Manchester: Hau Books) (accessed 24 March 2020).

Viveiros de Castro, Eduardo (2014a) *Cannibal Metaphysics* (Minneapolis: Univocal).

Viveiros de Castro, Eduardo (2014b) "Who Is Afraid of the Ontological Wolf? Some Comments on an Ongoing Anthropological Debate." Cambridge University Social Anthropology Society (CUSAS) Annual Marilyn Strathern Lecture, Cambridge, May 30. <https://sisu.ut.ee/sites/default/files/biosemio/files/cusas_strathern_lecture_2014.pdf> (accessed 24 March 2020).

Viveiros de Castro, Eduardo(2017) "Landed Natives against State and Capital," <http://autonomies.org/2017/05/eduardo-viveiros-de-castro-landed-natives-against-state-and-capital/> (accessed 24 March 2020).

Wittgenstein, Ludwig (2009) Philosophical Investigations (Chichester, UK, and Malden, MA: Wiley-Blackwell).

Woodard, Ben (2013) *On an Ungrounded Earth: Towards a New Geophilosophy*. New York: Punctum Books. <https://punctumbooks.com/titles/ungrounded-earth/> (accessed 2 April 2020).

Jan Alber and Zoë Takvorian
Climate Change, the Apocalypse, and Other Ideologies in *The Day after Tomorrow*

1 Introduction

Climate change is a topic that has apocalyptic ramifications in today's world. It has often been dealt with within the medium of film, which is capable of triggering intense emotional responses through cinematic devices that have to do with the *mise-en-scène*, cinematography, editing techniques, or the use of sound effects. And yet, are climate change movies capable of shedding light on the harsh realities of the climate crisis or do they merely provide special-effect overloaded (post-)apocalyptic extravaganzas that exploit rather than educate? Since Hollywood cinema reaches a mass audience, it can – on a level above and beyond pure entertainment – be seen as a means of promoting reflection on climate change. In the words of Niklas Salmose, "popular cinema could be an efficient way to warn people about the climate situation and encourage them to act individually and collectively" (2018: 1424).

In this context, we will examine the potential of Roland Emmerich's *The Day After Tomorrow* (2004), the most commercially successful feature film about climate change, including its underlying ideologies and allusions to environmental destruction. We will address the question of whether this film conveys a sense of the devastating consequences of global warming or rather exploits and instrumentalizes the explosive subject matter for other reasons. Climate change movies could indeed play a central role in informing, raising awareness, and clearing the existent conflicts surrounding the issue of global warming, since they have the capability of building a bridge between scientific discourse and mainstream audiences. We will first define the new genre of climate fiction (or 'cli-fi'), and then distinguish between different types of cli-fi-films. Our next step will be to address the question of how the ideological underpinnings of movies can be determined, and, finally, we will turn to our analysis of *The Day after Tomorrow* as well as a short summary of our findings.

2 Theoretical Considerations

2.1 What is Climate Fiction (Cli-Fi)?

In what follows, we will give an overview of the genre of climate fiction, or 'cli-fi.' It is noticeable that narratives focused on climate change have become a major trend in English- language publishing over the last decade. As Ursula Heise points out, "given the steadily increasing urgency of environmental problems for ever more closely interconnected societies around the globe, the explosion of articles and books in the field may not strike one as particularly surprising" (2006: 505). Matthew Schneider-Mayerson argues that while part of the explanation for the great artistic and scholarly attention lies in the increasingly obvious manifestations of climate change, "an additional stimulus is the hope that these plays, novels, short stories, poems, and children's stories might lead to a wider and deeper climate consciousness and thereby contribute to more progressive environmental policies and politics" (2018: 474).

Furthermore, "the ecopolitical value of environmental literature has been a key subtext for the growing interest in climate fiction in (liberal) popular discourse and the academic fields of ecocriticism and environmental humanities" (Schneider-Mayerson 2018: 474). In this respect, cli-fi is often assumed to have a positive ecopolitical influence by enabling readers to imagine potential climate futures and persuading them of the gravity and urgency of climate change. Taking into consideration the potential of narratives to introduce certain topics to the consciousness of readers, one can thus deem the specific medium of cli-fi as a form of environmental persuasion. In this context, Schneider-Mayerson argues that "while ecocritics and other scholars are interested in climate fiction for various reasons, implicit in much of the attention to this category is a belief (and perhaps a desire) that it is particularly important due to its 'instrumental value'" (Schneider-Mayerson 2018: 457).

Moreover, climate fiction can be considered significant for a number of reasons. As Antonia Mehnert notes, literature explicitly focused on climate change "gives insight into the ethical and social ramifications of this unparalleled environmental crisis, reflects on current political conditions that impede action on climate change, explores how risk materializes and affects society, and finally plays an active part in shaping our conception of climate change" (2016: 4). Above that, in all of these ways, it "serves as a cultural-political attempt and innovative alternative of communicating climate change" (Mehnert 2016: 4) The qualitative survey of American cli-fi readers conducted by Schneider-Mayerson has led to several interesting results, such as the fact that by placing cli-fi stories in the distant future, "authors are able to illuminate what is otherwise invisible: the gradual socioecological changes that occur too slowly for human perception" (2018: 484).

Furthermore, a central notion mentioned by Schneider-Mayerson is the "structure of feeling": since emotional response is a fundamental part of the reading experience, it is not surprising that many readers of climate fiction have experienced dramatic, negative emotions during the reception process. Most of these appear to have been elicited through identification with likable and resilient characters, particularly for readers of *Back to the Garden* (Hume, 2013), *The Carbon Diaries: 2015* (Lloyd, 2009), and *Flight Behavior* (Kingsolver, 2012) (Schneider-Mayerson 2018: 489). The author explains that "a newfound awareness of our reliance on and embeddedness in fragile ecosystems led many readers to consider the likely impact of climate change on human societies and the fragility of global civilization itself" (Schneider-Mayerson 2018: 489). Interestingly enough, some readers pointed out that they were surprised by the social, cultural, and political repercussions of climate change and thus not by the scientific facts of drought, sea level rise, and species extinction but by "their potential impacts on everyday life and the 'structure of feeling' of a near future in which climate change is an undeniable, palpable presence" (Schneider-Mayerson 2018: 489). Schneider-Mayerson draws the conclusion that climate fiction might therefore be an effective vehicle for creating an empathetic awareness of climate injustice by means of diminishing the social distance between privileged readers on the one hand and victims of climate change in the Global South and elsewhere on the other (Schneider-Mayerson 2018: 489).

Another aspect that needs to be taken into consideration is that the vast majority of climate fiction employs the "disaster frame," which is problematic according to the psychologist Per Espen Stoknes: "when climate change is framed as an encroaching disaster that can only be addressed by loss, cost, and sacrifice, it creates a wish to avoid the topic" (2015: 82). As Schneider-Mayerson points out, this type of cli-fi leads to a feeling of helplessness and fear, affective emotions which are not simply negative but demobilizing (2018: 490). It is thus crucial to keep in mind that while some negative emotions, such as anger, can create the urge for personal or political action, others, such as guilt, helplessness, shame, and sadness are much less likely to lead to active responses (Schneider-Mayerson 2018: 490). Psychologists thus suggest that climate communications should be framed positively, through frames such as "insurance against risk," "health and well-being," "preparedness and resilience," "values and a common cause," and "opportunities for innovation and job growth" (Stoknes 2015: 122).

All in all, it can be said that climate fiction can be used as an effective tool to enable readers to imagine potential climate futures, to urge them to consider the fragility of human societies and vulnerable ecosystems and also to persuade them of the gravity and urgency of climate change. In addition, the qualitative survey by Schneider-Mayerson has shown that while cli-fi may not play a significant role in convincing sceptics and deniers to reconsider their positions – which can partially be attributed to the fact that they are simply less likely to read these works of fiction – it might effectively urge moderates and remind concerned liberals and leftists of the severity and urgency of anthropogenic climate change, which "in itself is ecopolitically significant" (2018: 495).

2.2 Types of Cli-Fi Films

In this section, we will focus on the different types of cli-fi films based on the 2016 study by Michael Svoboda. This overview will serve as a foundation for our analysis of *The Day After Tomorrow*. Svoboda foregrounds the central role of film with regard to the communication of ideas about global warming as follows: "over the past 30 years, more films have addressed climate change than has previously been acknowledged" (2016: 59). Notably, of the many possible impacts of climate change predicted by scientists, this study finds that filmmakers tend to focus on extreme weather events as well as the possibility of the earth slipping into a new ice age (Svoboda 2016: 43). As Svoboda stresses, these choices "reflect filmmakers' predispositions more than any scientific consensus and thus demonstrate the challenge that cli- fi films pose to climate change communicators" (2016: 43). Following Svoboda's classification, one can place films into seven groups, focusing on either (1) flooding / sea-level rise, (2) extreme weather events, (3) the possibility of an ice age, (4) melting poles, (5) famine / drought, preclima(c)tic stress disorder, or (7) the portraying of a willful antagonist who intends to harm the earth or humanity (2016: 45).

The first group, which deals with the topic of flooding / sea-level rise, is concerned with films that address local, regional, or global inundations. Svoboda distinguishes between films in which these inundations are total and long-term, as in the case of *Waterworld* (1995), *Lost City Raiders* (2008), and *Noah* (2013), and temporary floods, as in *The Flood* (2007) and *Beasts of the Southern Wild* (2013). Furthermore, it is worth noting that films on extreme weather events such as *Twister* (1996) and *Into the Storm* (2014) comprise the largest subset of cli-fi films, namely roughly 40 % (Svoboda 2016: 46). Svoboda points out that all but two of these films follow one of three basic plots:

> (1) scientists or storm-chasers test their knowledge of extreme weather as they compete to gather more data; (2) a scientist with a problematic reputation warns a community about an impending extreme weather event but is ignored or even mocked until a devastating storm strikes the community; or (3) with little warning an everyman faces the challenge of safely

guiding his family and friends through an extreme weather event. Threaded through all three of these plots are one or more romantic or family subplots. (2016: 46)

Third, cli-fi films from the group "into / in ice age" depict the Earth, or at least a portion of it, falling into ice age conditions, as in *The Day After Tomorrow*, in which continent-spanning superstorms result in ice age landscapes. As Svoboda highlights, due to its success, *The Day After Tomorrow* has elevated a low probability scenario into an iconic image for climate change while also influencing on-screen depictions of storms, including meteorological chimeras like flash-freezing superstorms, which still appear in cli-fi films (2016: 59). He also explains that "what distinguishes these films from each other is the cause or event that triggers the ice age conditions and the places where that change is depicted" (Svoboda 2016: 48). The fourth group deals with films that address the melting arctic. Svoboda points out that movies from this category represent several different genres – *Ice Age: The Meltdown* (2006) and *Happy Feet* (2006), for instance, confront us with children's films that feature anthropomorphized creatures, while *The Last Winter* (2007) and *The Thaw* (2011) are horror films that zoom in on the grave consequences of the melting tundra (Svoboda 2016: 49). Furthermore, there are movies that address or incorporate climate change under the theme of famine and / or drought. The most well-known film from this category is *Interstellar* (2014), the movie with the fourth highest international box office hit for a cli-fi film. In this movie, which is set in the near future, a new blight is slowly withering the earth's food crops (Svoboda 2016: 50). What connects the remaining films in this group is that they address the collapse of ecosystems and of the human social systems that depend on them.

Moreover, films in the sixth group – "preclima(c)tic stress disorder" – focus on psychology, specifically on how the environment figures in the stresses of modern life, particularly for those whose lives are already troubled (Svoboda 2016: 50). The final type of cli-fi films mentioned by Svoboda belongs to the group that deals with "antagonists." Svoboda argues that "the films in this final group are united by the fact that each includes a willful opponent, someone or something intent on doing harm to Earth and/or humanity – or intent on obstructing efforts to protect Earth and/or humanity" (Svoboda 2016: 51). For example, the antagonists might be aliens, as is the case in *The Arrival* (1996) and in the environmental remake of the Cold-War-era *The Day the Earth Stood Still* (2008), or political figures, as in *The American President* (1996) (Svoboda 2016: 51–52). The action film *Geostorm* (2017) also belongs into this category. In this movie, a climate-controlling satellite system has been developed to offset the effects of global climate change. When the satellites ostensibly malfunction, they cause catastrophic extreme weather, which is ultimately revealed to have been a villainous weaponization of the technology by a power-hungry Secretary of State.

To summarize: Svoboda's study shows that "successful examples of efforts to mitigate the causes of climate change are almost entirely missing from these films, and only a few address ways to adapt to its consequences" (Svoboda 2016: 59). Geoengineering solutions as in the form of *Geostorm*'s satellites poignantly also do not mitigate any of the causes of climate change but present a convenient science-fictional band-aid to cover its effects. Apart from this, Svoboda points out that modes of production for filmmakers producing lower-budget, made-for-TV movies place a premium on permutation (systematic variation), escalation, and intensification. These cinematic norms can systematically distort depictions of climate science. The author stresses, however, that cli-fi films have made progress in getting beyond traditional cultural and social stereotypes, especially regarding gender (Svoboda 2016: 59). As a closing remark one can say that were "filmmakers to incorporate climate change into the broader context of their plots – rather than making it the focus of the story – they might deliver more consistent, forward-looking messages on climate change" (Svoboda 2016: 59).

2.3 The Ideological Underpinnings of Films

This section will deal with the question of how the ideological underpinnings of movies can be determined. To begin with, we would like to define the term 'ideology.' For Louis Althusser, ideologies are distorting world views: in his usage, the term denotes "imaginary [. . .] world outlooks," that is, world views that do not "correspond to reality" (2001: 1498). Furthermore, it is important to note that everything we do has an ideological orientation because our actions are always influenced by certain belief systems or world views. Althusser also argues that human subjects are interpellated by several ideologies at the same time and that these ideologies do not necessarily aim at reproducing the status quo (as in the case of Marx, for instance). Similarly, Thomas Holt, defines the term 'ideology' as a systematic conjuncture of ideas, assumptions, and sentiments that mediates between our objective experience and our subjective interpretation of that experience. It is the mental framework that lends order and vests meaning in experience (1992: 25).

Since movies are always influenced by underlying world views, they communicate ideologies as well. Furthermore, films make use of specific cinematic techniques in order to establish a certain idea and to convey a particular message. It is important to address these choices, i.e., the question of why a film deploys the strategies it does, since these uses always involve conscious decisions. According to Susan Lanser, narrative techniques may be used to express an "ideological stance" (1992: 73), but there is no intrinsic relationship between the two. Brian Richardson expresses this aspect in more general terms as follows: "no form has any inherent essence or tendencies [. . .]. Ideological stances are frequently enmeshed with practices of narration, but never in a way that can be reduced to an easy equation" (1994: 321). One thus has to take a close look at the specific context within which narrative strategies are used.

For Wolf Schmid, the ideological perspective of a narrative encompasses factors such as "knowledge, way of thinking, evaluative position and intellectual horizon" (2010: 101). Indeed, when we process a narrative, we treat it as "a rational agent who governed its 'choice' of 'action' by a 'consideration' of its 'beliefs' and 'desires'" (Dennett 1996: 27). Importantly, we do not merely engage in processes of mind reading to understand the minds of the characters; rather, we also construct a mind or consciousness behind the narrative as a whole (Alber 2019: 12). In a second step, we then form hypotheses about this mind's intentions or what one might call the narrative's potential 'point' – and this 'point' is motivated by certain belief systems or ideologies. It is also important to note that "narratives do not usually express one ideology only; rather, they tend to merge different world views in often complex manners, and we are invited to disentangle these ideological complications" (Alber 2019: 12).

When considering the ideological ramifications of films, we have to look at the following narrative strategies because these techniques "may carry ideological weight (depending on the specific ways in which they are deployed in a certain context)" (Alber 2019: 8). First of all, there is the feature of the paratext (Genette 1997) which concerns the framing material. In the case of films, this includes the opening and final credits as well as the title and information provided on the production of the film. It is of primary importance to address the colors and the typographical presentation of the letters we see. Several other factors need to be taken into account as well. The most important meaning-making elements in film concern the *mise-en-scène*, cinematographic elements, the process of editing, and the use of sound (Grodal 2005: 169). The term '*mise-en-scène*' denotes everything that gets placed before the camera before the filming begins (such as the setting or film set, the lighting, the costumes, actors and actresses, the performances, and so forth). Cinematography, on the other hand, encompasses those elements that relate to the work of the camera – including the distance between the camera and the filmed identity as well as camera movements (such as pans along the horizontal axis or tilts along the vertical axis) (Grodal 2005: 170). The basic shot distance is the medium shot, which provides a view of the head and upper part of the body; shots that significantly exceed this distance are called long shots, whereas shots that are taken from a shorter distance are called close-ups (Grodal 2005: 170). The term 'editing' refers to the process of connecting the individual takes after the film has been shot: potential options include straight cuts or dissolves. In addition, one has to look at the functions of the used sound patterns, which may be diegetic (i.e., part of the fictional world) or non-diegetic (i.e., not part of the fictional world). Torben Grodal argues that music, the most important non-diegetic sound-type, usually "enhances the mood of a given scene and supports the narrative tempo" (2005: 170).

In terms of the analysis of ideologies, it is crucial to think about the effects of the use of certain images, sounds, language, lighting, the *mise-en-scène*, camera perspectives, camera movements, editing techniques, and so forth. Moreover, it might be important to consider side plots: Hollywood films frequently include a love or family plot, even if we are confronted with disaster films from the cli-fi genre. In this case the question arises of how these (minor) events are related to the main plot. Also, one can take a closer look at the time management that is implemented in the film (e.g., techniques such as flashbacks, etc.) as well as the setting of a film: "when and where is the story set, and what are the associations of these places?" (Alber 2019: 9). In addition, the features of the characters need to be taken into account: do we as viewers encounter flat, round, static, or dynamic figures and why is this so? What are the hierarchies or power imbalances among the characters? (Alber 2019: 9). Finally, analyses that focus on ideological underpinnings should take cinematic metaphors into consideration (see Whittock 1990 and Alber 2011). Film metaphors urge us as viewers to see one entity (X) in terms of a different one (Y) so that the film communicates the idea that X is Y. Fritz Lang's film *Metropolis* (1921), for instance, deals with the inhumanity of factory work. At one point, we see a machine (= X) that explodes and kills various workers. Furthermore, a man-eating monster (= Y) is superimposed on the engine, so that we are invited to see the machine as a devouring and destructive creature (Alber 2011: 222).

3 The Apocalyptic Dawn of a New Ice Age in *The Day after Tomorrow*

In this section, we will show that Roland Emmerich's film *The Day after Tomorrow* – which received a $125 million budget from Twentieth Century Fox, a division of the conservative media conglomerate News Corporation (Livesey 2014: 72) – is a complex narrative in which progressive and reactionary ideologies are interwoven. The movie is about Jack Hall (Dennis Quaid), a paleoclimate scientist, who works for the National Oceanic and Atmospheric Administration (NOAA). Hall finds out that the world climate had changed in the past when water from the melting polar caps disturbed the saline mechanism of the Atlantic Meridional Overturning Circulation and caused severe cooling (see also Rahmstorf 2004 and Svoboda 2016: 48). In the film, Hall predicts that – due to a dramatic increase of carbon emissions at the beginning of the twenty-first century – this will happen again, and he turns out to be right: the only thing is that it happens much more quickly than he had initially predicted (namely within six or eight weeks).

How are different ideologies interwoven in the film? On the one hand, *The Day after Tomorrow* uses spectacular images of weather-related destruction – such as a hail storm in Tokyo, tornadoes in Los Angeles, and the flooding of New York City – to draw our attention to the actual problem of anthropogenic climate change.[1] In addition, the consistent use of 'realemes' (i.e., references to real-world people and actual environments in the sense of Even- Zohar [1980: 65]) makes it easier for the recipients "to feel moral allegiance with the victims of environmental injustice" (Weik von Mossner 2017: 79). In this connection, the movie explicitly critiques the administration of George W. Bush and Fox News for consistently denying the problem of climate change.[2] On the other hand, *The Day after Tomorrow* openly zooms in on the heroism of white, male, and heterosexual middle-class characters as well as their resilience in the face of global warming (see also Mc Greavy and Lindenfeld 2014; Salmose 2018: 1416). Furthermore, the ending downplays the severe consequences of climate change by representing it as a form of apocalyptic cleansing that ultimately leads to the renewal of the old order. Indeed, Niklas Salmose speaks of the affirmation of the sentiment "do not worry, everything will be as it has always been!" (2018: 1417).

In what follows, we will discuss the ideological implications of the most important segments of the film. During the opening credits, we are taken to the south pole. By means of a (simulated) high-angle tracking shot, the camera approaches the Larsen Ice Shelf of the Antarctic Peninsula, where Jack Hall and

---

[1] In the words of John Sanders, the film can be seen as a cinematic response to the global threat of climate change (2009: 18). Similarly, the climatologist Stefan Rahmstorf writes that "it is remarkable to what extent the film-makers have tried to include some realistic background." In particular, he considers the representation of the politics of climate change to be "chillingly realistic": Rahmstorf argues that "humans are indeed increasingly changing the climate and this is quite a dangerous experiment, including some risk of abrupt and unforeseen changes" (2004: no pag.).
[2] The title of the film alludes to Nicholas Meyer's film *The Day After* (1983), which allegedly made President Ronald Reagan sign the Intermediate-Range Nuclear Forces Treaty in 1987.

his colleagues Frank Harris (Jay O. Sanders) and Jason Evans (Dash Mihok) drill for ice-core samples. The opening sequence conveys a sense of the vastness and beauty of the ice masses. Moreover, the letters of the opening credits are white (like the ice of the melting polar caps), and they fly across the Ocean in a rather smooth manner. In addition, we see reflections of these flying letters in the water. Thus, already at the beginning, the film – quite realistically – establishes air traffic as one of the major causes of the increase of carbon emissions and thus global warming. In this context, the reflections of the 'flying' letters allude to the effects of air traffic on the Ocean and the rising sea-levels. We are then presented with a bird's eye-view of the NOAA drilling station, which diminishes the importance of the human characters: in the face of the global problem of climate change, individual humans become rather insignificant; they here look like small ants.[3] By means of an extreme close-up of the American flag, the film accentuates its focus on the specific ways in which the United States as a nation deals with climate change. The non-diegetic sad and melancholy song "The Day after Tomorrow" by Harald Kloser, finally, conveys a sense of the impending disaster.

In the first scene of the film, a large chunk of the Larsen Ice Shelf breaks off as a consequence of global warming. Evans almost falls into the opening crevasse but is saved by his colleagues. We are then confronted with a high-angle shot of the crack, which "increase[s] the amount and importance of space [. . .] and presents a privileged view of an environment" (Beaver 1994: 178). The fact that the crevasse dominates the screen as a whole conveys the seriousness of this development for humankind. In the words of Alexa Weik von Mossner, "the evocation of a spectacularly beautiful but suddenly also threatened environment cues awe for the sheer beauty of the images and sadness in relation to a vulnerable ecological space at risk" (2017: 155). The scene also foregrounds the heroic qualities of Hall, the film's major protagonist. As the shelf breaks apart, he jumps across the crevasse to save the data that the scientists have collected so far. When he jumps back, Hall also almost falls into the fissure but is saved by Harris and Evans. In a sense, the opening scene foreshadows the ending of the film: like humankind in the movie as a whole, Evans and Hall briefly face death but are ultimately saved. *The Day after Tomorrow* is apocalyptic because it does not end in total disaster (or with the complete disintegration of the

---

[3] This is an example of a distortion metaphor. In such cases, the image on the screen must represent an entity in such a way that our sense of what category it belongs to is affected (Alber 2011: 221). In this specific shot, the great distance between the scene and the camera deprives the characters of their humanity and turns them into insignificant ants.

planet) but with the hope for a renewal and the restoration of the traditional order.

Moreover, the film presents the scientist Hall as an eco-hero who reproduces the hypermasculinity (see also Murray and Heumann 2009: 6–10) of traditional cinematic heroes (such as the ones played by Clint Eastwood, Arnold Schwarzenegger, Sylvester Stallone, or Bruce Willis), albeit with a slightly nerdy touch. In the middle of the film, for instance, Hall goes on a heroic quest to save his seventeen-year-old son Sam (Jake Gyllenhaal), who is stranded in the New York Public Library (following an academic decathlon that he had joined because of his infatuation with Laura Chapman [Emmy Rossum]). More specifically, Hall, Harris, and Evans walk to Manhattan in a freezing and deadly snow storm. The events on the way – such as Harris's death and Evans's collapse – primarily serve to enhance Hall's masculinity and endurance. Generally speaking, the film reproduces and stabilizes ethnic and gender stereotypes: it concentrates on the hero-scientist Jack Hall and his son Sam, and thus on the white, male, and heterosexual middle class. With regard to the film's ideological underpinnings, it is significant that during the flooding of New York City, a French-speaking African family is saved by Laura, a white US-American woman, who in turn is saved by Sam, a white American man (Ingram 2005: 57). This character constellation clearly establishes a hierarchy among the figures in the movie.

The scientist Hall is surrounded by a few insignificant helpers such as his wife – Dr. Lucy Hall (Sela Ward) who becomes a surrogate mother as she looks after a young boy suffering from cancer – and the Asian-American NASA meteorologist Janet Tokado (Tamlyn Tomita). However, compared to our eco-hero, these characters are not particularly effective. The only proper helper is another member of the white and male middle class: Professor Terry Rapson (Ian Holm), an oceanographer at the Hedland Centre in Scotland whom Jack gets to know at the UN Conference on Global Warming in New Delhi, where Hall explains that "global warming can trigger a cooling trend." Since various buoys in the Atlantic Ocean document a drop of thirteen degrees, Rapson believes that Hall's theory about inevitable climate shift is correct. When a number of striking weather events occur, Hall is called to a meeting of fellow scientists, where he reports that the buoys maintained by his colleagues in Scotland have recorded several drops in Ocean temperature. Our hero concludes that "we've hit a critical desalinization point" and also that "we may be on the verge of a major climate shift."

Hall's heroic quest, i.e., his (almost superhuman) hike to New York City in sub-zero temperatures to save his son, is significant for two further reasons. First, it connotes resilience and hopefulness, i.e., the idea that something can still be done about climate change. As we have already said in our section on cli-fi, Stoknes argues that "when climate change is framed as an encroaching disaster that can only be addressed by loss, cost, and sacrifice, it creates a wish to avoid the topic." For him, climate fiction should be framed positively, and include, say, "preparedness and resilience" (Stoknes 2015: 82; 122), if it wants to have an impact. We feel that this is more or less what the film is doing. Second, Hall's journey is important with regard to the film's family subplot: it seems to argue that in the context of global warming, 'natural' family bonds have to be kept, cherished, or reinstated. *The Day after Tomorrow* posits an analogy between climate change on the one hand, and the separation of Sam from his parents on the other. The underlying idea seems to be that we will only survive if we also manage to hold our family structures together.

The most well-known scenes in *The Day after Tomorrow* are the powerful images of weather-related disaster connected with this climate shift. They reveal "the sublime power of wild nature: violent, chaotic, powerful beyond human control, and therefore exciting and seductive" (Ingram 2005: 55). The first of these apocalyptic scenes concerns the destruction of Los Angeles by a series of vicious tornadoes. In this scene, the tornadoes are so huge that they dominate the screen space. The fact that they are larger than the humans and their creations (including the Capitol Records building and the skyscrapers of L.A.) clearly matters: the weather (as a result of the changing world climate) is here represented as a destructive and uncontrollable force that constitutes an imminent threat for the human characters. However, the figures do not seem to recognize the danger they are in: they continue to watch, take pictures, and report although they might be blown away or even killed by the tornadoes. The camera twice describes a clockwise circular pan, which evokes feelings of instability. This is done in the context of a bird's-eye view of L.A., but also right before one of the reporting TV journalists is killed by a billboard advertising the model Angelyne. The sound effects underline the visual representation: the sounds created by the tornadoes are reminiscent of a howling monster,[4] while the unnerving non-diegetic string music is designed to make the viewers feel uncomfortable.

The second famous scene depicts the flooding of New York City. The destructive power of the towering flood waves is accentuated through an anticlockwise circular pan (typically used to highlight impending doom) of the Statue of Liberty, which almost disappears under the water mass. Niklas Salmose describes this shot as follows: "the camera, in one long, breathtaking shot, circles around the deluged and thunder-stricken Statue of Liberty to the sounds of lightning,

---

[4] This is an example of a film metaphor that is generated by the interplay between the auditory and the visual level (Alber 2011: 220). The destructive tornadoes can be seen on the screen, while the monstrous howls are present on the auditory level.

water, and sudden bursts of Bernard Hermann-like orchestral frenzies" (2018: 1423). Later on, we are also presented with a bird's-eye view of the city (and its skyscrapers) as it is being flooded. After the flooding of the New York Public Library, we witness another anticlockwise circular pan from above. As in the L.A. scene discussed above, size matters: the taxis and buses that we see are so small that they cannot possibly protect the characters from the enormously huge flood. In this scene, *The Day after Tomorrow* also ascribes agency to nature: when Sam urges Laura to enter the public library, we are presented with what looks like a POV-shot from the perspective of the towering flood wave – i.e., an inanimate entity – approaching the library building. The scene also foregrounds the alienation of the human characters from the environment. For example, we see a bus driver who prefers to rely on the radio news rather than his own eyes or ears. Like the three arrogant businessmen who bribe the driver by giving him 200$ to get to 'safety,' he only realizes that New York City is hit by a tidal wave when it is already too late: they all drown inside the vehicle.

The climate shift in the film is initiated by massive, hurricane-like ice storms that immediately freeze everything they pass over by (Svoboda 2016: 48). *The Day after Tomorrow* presents us with various images of instantaneous freezing. To begin with, their new friend J.D. (Austin Nichols) takes Sam, Laura, and Brian Parks (Arjay Smith) to New York's Natural History Museum, where they look at a perfectly preserved frozen mammoth "with food still in its mouth and stomach, indicating that it froze instantly while grazing." Later on, we see how Royal Air Force helicopter pilots actually freeze to death as Scotland is covered by a large ice sheet.[5] The freezing of the Empire State Building is also represented in rather dramatic fashion: in this scene, the camera literally follows the cold air that the storm systems in the film suck down from the stratosphere. This air is so cold that it freezes everything it touches, and the downward tilt of the camera follows the rapid freezing of the Empire State Building – starting from the stratosphere, continuing with the antenna, and ending with the first floor of the 102- story skyscraper.

Regarding these dramatic scenes of destruction, we agree with David Ingram's argument: he writes that regardless of whether the movie exaggerates the effects of climate change, it definitely uses

> [. . .] realist elements of climate science as a starting point for melodrama and fantasy, so that it can dwell on the spectacle of extreme weather [. . .] and also invite the audience's

---

[5] The film here seems to suggest that the disastrous images it presents us with might likewise become reality at some point.

> emotional engagement with the human-interest story that becomes the main focus of the narrative.
> (Ingram 2005: 55)

When Hall is asked to brief President Blake (Perry King) and Vice-President Becker (Kenneth Welsh) regarding the climate shift, he draws a horizontal line across a map of the United States. Hall claims that everyone south of the line must be evacuated and also that it is already "too late" for those in the north. *The Day after Tomorrow* uses 'realemes' (Zohar 1980), i.e., real-world references in fictional contexts, in a rather clever way. To begin with, Vice-President Becker looks almost exactly like Dick Cheney, who served as Vice-President under President George W. Bush (i.e., between 2001 and 2009). Furthermore, most of the news programs that are being watched in the film are broadcast by Fox News. These realemes are of course not coincidental: at the time, the Bush administration and Rupert Murdoch (who had founded the Fox News Channel, a 24-hour cable news station, in 1996) tried to systematically deny or play down the dangers of global warming.[6]

As more and more US-Americans from the southern states are evacuated into Mexico (in return for debt cancelation), Vice-President Becker apologizes for his ignorance regarding climate change in a TV address to the nation as follows:

> For years we operated under the belief that we could continue consuming our planet's resources without any consequences. We were wrong. I was wrong. The fact that my first address to you comes from a consulate on foreign soil is a testimony to our changed reality.

This part of the film is important for three reasons. First, Becker's speech involves "the greatest personal transformation and learning experience" (Weik von Mossner 2017: 157) in the film.[7] Second, this segment involves an explicit critique of the ineffectual Bush administration and its systematic denial of global warming. Third, the film reverses the hierarchical relationship between the United States and Mexico: in the actual world, many Mexicans try to flee to the United States, whereas in *The Day after Tomorrow*, US-American citizens are allowed to live as guests in Mexico.

Weik von Mossner also argues that climate fiction often uses an "insider" or an "outsider perspective" to introduce its recipients to environmental problems (2017: 79). One might argue that *The Day after Tomorrow* effectively combines the two. On the one hand, we are confronted with the perspective of Jack Hall, a scientific insider with regard to climate change. On the other hand, we are also

---

[6] Among many other things, they consistently argued in favor of the burning of fossil fuels, and in 2001, the Bush administration repudiated the 1997 Kyoto Protocol.

[7] Earlier on, Becker accused Hall for making "sensationalist claims," and he asked him who will pay "the price of the Kyoto Accord."

presented with the perspective of his son Sam, who is an outsider to science and gradually learns how serious climate change is: initial indicators are the severe turbulence on his flight into New York City and the masses of birds that cover the sky of New York City as they fly somewhere else. These phenomena might still be coincidental, but they cause him to reflect. Sam is finally sure that something is wrong when New York City is flooded. We are invited to empathize or identify with him: Sam is a dynamic character who moves from ignorance to knowledge, and this is what the audience is supposed to do as well.

At the end of the film, international space astronauts look down at the Earth in awe: the planet is now – suddenly and inexplicably – free of pollution and with new ice caps generated by the rapid superstorms, extending across the northern hemisphere. The planet seems to have healed itself as one of the astronauts points out that he has "never seen the air so clear." Hence, Phil Hammond and Hugh Ortega Breton argue that *The Day after Tomorrow* represents "climate change as positive [. . .]. Nature intervenes to rebalance and reorder the human world at the same time as it reorders the ecosystem" (2014: 314, fn 123). Indeed, after the scary apocalyptic threat, the ending involves a high degree of hopefulness and satisfaction – and notably first and foremost on the part of the white and male heterosexual middle class: Jack Hall has victoriously accomplished his quasi-superhuman mission to hold his family together, while Sam gets Laura so that a new white and heterosexual couple has been formed. At the same time, Manhattan is still intact and there are many additional survivors on the roofs of the skyscrapers. For Salmose, the film suggests "both a longing for past times and a strong desire to preserve what is imagined to be the essence of the Western world" (2018: 1426). *The Day after Tomorrow* suggests a new start that leaves the most important facets of western thinking – including the privileged position of the white, male, and heterosexual middle class – virtually untouched. In this context, the decision not to burn the Gutenberg Bible in the New York Public Library because it represents "the dawn of the age of reason" becomes emblematic: the film's new world nostalgically relates back to the old one, i.e., the world that produced the problem of climate change in the first place.

4 Conclusions

As we have shown, Emmerich's movie is an extremely ambivalent ideological phenomenon that negotiates global warming by combining progressive and conservative world views. In the words of Ingram, this ideological ambiguity probably has to do with the fact that the Hollywood industry seeks to "maximize profits by appealing to as wide and diverse an audience as possible by making movies which, ideologically speaking, seek to have it all ways at once" (2005: 53).

The following elements are expressive of a progressive ideology: the powerful images of weather-related disaster (which draw our attention to potential consequences of climate change); the many real-world references (to Los Angeles, New York City, Dick Cheney, and Fox News); the transformation of Vice-President Becker; and the reversal of the hierarchical relationship between the United States and Mexico. The following aspects, by contrast, can rather be associated with a conservative ideology: the film's focus on Jack and Sam Hall; the represented heroism and resilience of white, male, and heterosexual middle-class characters; the downplaying of the consequences of climate change at the end; and the nostalgic renewal of the old western order that could be seen as being the actual problem rather than a possible solution.

The film clearly argues in favor of science and rationality as well as the idea of learning "from our mistakes" as Hall once puts it. At the same time, however, it proposes a reactionary rather than a radical new start (Salmose 2018: 1426), while concentrating on an already privileged societal group whose supremacy it reproduces and stabilizes. Although progressive and reactionary ideologies virtually find themselves in a state of equilibrium in *The Day after Tomorrow*, it is perhaps worth noting that the reception studies that were conducted in the United States, Great Britain, Germany, and Japan all "demonstrated that the film itself had a significant impact on viewers' climate risk perceptions" (Weik von Mossner 2017: 159). In other words, even though the film oscillates between different and conflicting world views, it is still seen as depicting a possible future of ecological collapse that encourages its viewers to reflect about global warming.

Bibliography

Alber, Jan (2011) "Cinematic Carcerality: Prison Metaphors in Film," *The Journal of Popular Culture* 44.2, 217–232.

Alber, Jan (2019) "Introduction: The Ideological Ramifications of Narrative Strategies," *Storyworlds: A Journal of Narrative Studies* 9.1–2, 3–25.

Althusser, Louis (1970/2001) "Ideology and Ideological State Apparatuses," in *The Norton Anthology of Theory and Criticism*, ed. Vincent B. Leitch (New York: Norton), 1483–1509.

Beaver, Frank E. (1994) *Dictionary of Film Terms: The Aesthetic Companion to Film* (New York: Twayne Publishers).

The Day after Tomorrow (2004) Dir. Roland Emmerich. Twentieth-Century Fox.

Dennett, Daniel C. (1996) *Kinds of Minds: Towards an Understanding of Consciousness* (London: Weidenfeld and Nicolson).
Even-Zohar, Itamar (1980) "Constraints of Realeme Insertability in Narrative," *Poetics Today* 1.3, 65–74.
Genette, Gérard (1997 [1987]) *Paratexts: Thresholds of Interpretation* (Cambridge: Cambridge University Press).
Grodal, Torben Kragh (2005) "Film Narrative," in *Routledge Encyclopedia of Narrative Theory*, ed. David Hermann, Manfred Jahn and Marie-Laure Ryan (London: Routledge), 168–172.
Hammond, Phil and Hugh Ortega Breton (2014) "Bridging the Political Deficit: Loss, Morality, and Agency in Films Addressing Climate Change," *Communication, Culture, and Critique* 7, 303–319.
Heise, Ursula K. (2006) "The Hitchhiker's Guide to Ecocriticism," *PMLA* 121.2, 503–516.
Holt, Thomas (1992) *The Problem of Freedom: Race, Labor, and Politics in Jamaica and Britain, 1832–1938* (Baltimore: Johns Hopkins UP).
Ingram, David (2005) "Hollywood Cinema and Climate Change: *The Day after Tomorrow*," in *Words on Water: Literary and Cultural Representations*, ed. Maureen Devine and Christa Grewe-Volpp (Trier: WVT), 53–63.
Lanser, Susan Snaider (1992) *Fictions of Authority: Woman Writers and Narrative Voice* (Ithaca: Cornell UP).
Livesey, Sophie (2014) "Climate Change, Capitalism, 9/11, and *The Day after Tomorrow*." *Film Matters* 5.1, 71–75.
McGreavy, Bridie, and Laura Lindenfeld (2014) "Entertaining our Way to Engagement? Climate Change Films and Sustainable Development Values," *International Journal of Sustainable Development* 17, 123–136.
Mehnert, Antonia (2005) *Climate Change Fictions: Representations of Global Warming in American Literature* (London: Palgrave MacMillan).
Murray, Robin L., and Jospeh K. Heumann (2009) *Ecology and Popular Film: Cinema on the Edge* (Albany, NY: The State University of New York Press).
Rahmstorf, Stefan (2004) "*The Day after Tomorrow* – Some Comments on the Movie." <http://www.pik-potsdam.de/~stefan/tdat_review.html> (last accessed February 25, 2020).
Richardson, Brian (1994) "I etcetera: On the Poetics and Ideology of Multipersonal Narratives," *Style* 28.3, 312–328.
Salmose, Niklas (2018) "The Apocalyptic Sublime: Anthropocene Representation and Environmental Agency in Hollywood Action-Adventure Cli-Fi Films," *Journal of Popular Culture* 51.6, 1415–1433.
Sanders, John (2009) *Studying Disaster Movies* (Leighton Buzzard: Auteur).
Schmid, Wolf (2010) *Narratology: An Introduction* (Berlin: De Gruyter).
Schneider-Mayerson, Matthew (2018) "The Influence of Climate Fiction: An Empirical Survey of Readers," *Environmental Humanities* 10.2, 473–500.
Stoknes, Per Espen (2015) *What We Think About When We Try Not to Think About Global Warming: Toward a New Psychology of Climate Action* (White River Junction, VT: Chelsea Green Publishing).
Svoboda, Michael (2016) "Cli-Fi on the Screen(s): Patterns in the Representations of Climate Change," *WIREs Clim Change* 7, 43–64. https://doi.org/10.1002/wcc.381.
Weik von Mossner, Alexa (2017) *Affective Ecologies: Empathy, Emotion, and Environmental Narrative* (Columbus: The Ohio State University Press).
Whittock, Trevor (1990) *Metaphor and Film* (Cambridge: Cambridge University Press).

Biographical Information

Jan Alber is Professor of English Literature and Cognitive Studies at RWTH Aachen University (Germany) and Past President of the International Society for the Study of Narrative (ISSN). He received fellowships and research grants from the British Academy, the Exploratory Research Space (ERS) at RWTH Aachen University, the German Research Foundation (DFG), and the Humboldt Foundation. From 2014 to 2016, Alber worked as a Marie-Curie Fellow at the Aarhus Institute of Advanced Studies (AIAS) in Denmark.

Marco Caracciolo is Associate Professor of English and Literary Theory at Ghent University (Belgium). His work explores the phenomenology of narrative, or the structure of the experiences afforded by literary fiction and other narrative media. He is the author of five books, including most recently *Narrating the Mesh: Form and Story in the Anthropocene* (University of Virginia Press, 2021).

Diana Dimitrova is Professor of Hinduism and South Asian religions at the University of Montreal (Canada). She obtained her Ph.D. in Modern and Classical South Asian Studies, and English philology at the University of Heidelberg in Germany. She is the author of *Hinduism and Hindi Theatre* (Palgrave Macmillan, 2016), *Gender, Religion and Modern Hindu Drama* (McGill-Queen's University Press, 2008), *Western Tradition and Naturalistic Hindi Theatre* (Peter Lang, 2004), and the editor of various collections of essays. Her current research focusses on Hindu devotional and reform traditions (such as Radhasoami) and cultural identity and Hindi theatre.

Judith Eckenhoff is Research and Teaching Assistant at the Chair of Cognitive Literary Studies at RWTH Aachen University (Germany) and is currently working towards her PhD. In her thesis, she explores the ecological estrangement of imagined fictional futures and the genre hybridisation of twenty-first century postapocalyptic fiction. In 2018, she coordinated the interdisciplinary ERS project "The Apocalyptic Dimensions of Global Climate Change in Contemporary Models and Discourses" at RWTH Aachen University.

Jon Hegglund is Associate Professor of English at Washington State University, where he teaches courses in modernism, ecocriticism and environmental writing, and narrative theory. He has published on geography, spatiality, ecocriticism, and narrative in a number of places, including *ISLE*, *Twentieth-Century Literature*, and the recent edited collection, *Environment and Narrative*. His book, *World Views: Metageographies of Modernist Fiction* (Oxford UP, 2012) was nominated for an MLA First Book Prize, and he is the co-editor (with John McIntyre) of *Modernism and the Anthropocene* (Lexington Press, 2021). Currently, he is completing a book on anthropomorphism as an embodied mode of narrative cognition and serving as a faculty mentor for the *City Scripts* project, an interdisciplinary graduate research group based at Ruhr University in Bochum (Germany).

Steffen Jöris is Senior Lecturer of New Testament studies and early Christianity at RWTH Aachen University (Germany). He received his PhD from La Trobe University, Melbourne. His main research interests include ancient apocalyptic literature.

Gerbern S. Oegema studied Biblical Studies, Jewish Studies, and Religious Studies at the Vrije Universiteit in Amsterdam, the Hebrew University of Jerusalem, and the Freie Universität Berlin. He was an Assistant Professor and *Privatdozent* at the Universität Tübingen and a Scholar in Residence at the Center for Theological Inquiry in Princeton. He is currently Professor of Biblical Studies in the School of Religious Studies at McGill University in Montreal. In his research and teaching, he focuses on Second Temple Judaism and Christian origins. He is the author and co-editor of more than twenty books, editor of the Oxford Handbook of the Apocrypha, as well as the co-editor of several book series.

Wolfgang Römer is Extraordinary Professor at the Department of Geography at RWTH Aachen University (Germany). After studying geography and geology at the University of Munich and RWTH Aachen University, he worked in several research projects in South America, southern Africa, and Europe. The Association of Geographers at German Universities awarded him a prize for his PhD thesis in 1993/1994. After his *Habilitation*, he gave lectures at different universities in Germany, and he also worked as a consultant for many companies and in various projects. His major research areas are the analysis of the effects of climate change, structural and tectonic influences on hillslope processes, and the development of numerical process-response models of landscape development.

Carlos A. Segovia is Associate Professor of Religious Studies at Saint Louis University, Madrid Campus. He works on counter-dominant conceptual worlds and post-nihilism at the crossroads of contemporary philosophy, anthropological theory, and religious studies. He was visiting professor of philosophy and religious studies at the University of Aarhus (Denmark) and the Free University of Brussels (Belgium), and guest lecturer at the University of California Berkeley (USA), the European Research Council in Ghent (Belgium), the University of Lilongwe (Malawi), the Spanish National Research Council, the University of Seville (Spain), and the Complutense University of Madrid. He is series co-editor of "Apocalypticism: Cross-disciplinary Explorations" published by Peter Lang Academic Publishers, and member of various advisory boards, including the *Ghana Journal of Religion and Theology*, and learned societies, including the Early Islamic Studies Seminar: International Scholarship on the Qur'ān and Islamic Origins, which he co-directed between 2013 and 2020.

Axel Siegemund is Hemmerle-Professor for Interdisciplinary Research Areas of Theology, Natural Sciences, and Engineering at RWTH Aachen University (Germany). He studied Water Engineering in Germany and India and has practical experiences in Climate Adaptation and Education for Climate Awareness. Siegemund has worked for more than ten years in developmental cooperation. His PhD focusses on the ethics of technology (TU Dresden) and his *Habilitation* on intercultural questions of modernization (Leibniz-Univerity Hanover).

Zoë Takvorian holds a Master's degree in English and German literature and linguistics from RWTH Aachen University, where she worked as a research assistant for Jan Alber's Professorship of English Literature and Cognitive Studies as well as in English Linguistics. She is a recipient of a Fulbright Scholarship for American Studies at Humboldt University in Berlin (2016). During the winter term 2017–18, she studied Modern Literature at Maynooth University within the Erasmus Program. Currently, she is enrolled in a teacher training course in Aachen.

Subject Index

Acceptance 71–72, 75, 145
aesthetics 95, 105, 143–144
After Finitude 140–141, 143, 147
alienation 169
American President, The 161
Annihilation 7, 71–72, 74, 76, 101, 134
Anthropocene 66–67, 70, 88–89, 94, 102, 109, 126, 130
anthropocentrism (see also human exceptionalism) 8, 106, 110, 112, 145
anthropodenial 112
anthropomorphism 112–115, 117, 120–121
anti-Tehri dam movement 87
anxiety 56, 58, 60, 131
apocalypse 1, 5–6, 8–9, 49–55, 57–59, 65, 100–101, 126–127, 130, 133, 157
apocalyptic 1–3, 5–8, 43, 49–60, 63, 65, 71, 77, 81–85, 88–89, 96, 103, 105, 125–126, 130–134, 145, 157, 164–166, 168, 171
apocalypticism 6, 8, 49–59, 125–126, 129, 131–133
Arrival, The 161
Assessment of the Global Impact of 21st Century Land Use Change on Soil Erosion, An 25
Atlantic Meridional Overturning Circulation 165
ātman 83
Atmospheric Composition
atomic catastrophe 56
Authority 7, 71–72, 74
Avātara 81, 83–84

Back to the Garden 159
Bar Kockba Revolt 50
Beasts of the Southern Wild 160
belief system (see also ideology and worldview) 2, 5, 162–163
Beyond Nature and Culture 149
Bhagavadgītā 83–84
bhakti 84, 87
bhūmi pūjā 86

Big Bang theory 128
biopiracy 138
Book of Daniel 49, 52
boreal forests 17, 22, 28
brahman 83

Carbon Diaries, The 159
carbon emissions 101, 165–166
catastrophe 1, 7, 50, 56, 58–59, 63–65, 68, 70–72, 75–78, 105, 126, 134
Changes in Climate Extremes and Their Impacts on the Natural Physical Environment 27–28, 35–37
Chipko *andolan* 87
cinematic devices 157
cli-fi (see also climate fiction) 114, 121, 157–162, 164, 167
climate change 1–4, 6–9, 11–13, 16, 25, 27–33, 35–36, 41–43, 49–51, 56, 58–60, 64–68, 81–82, 84–86, 88–89, 93–96, 98–99, 103–105, 109–110, 121, 132, 138, 157–162, 165–172
climate fiction (see also cli-fi) 157–159, 168, 170
climate of history 88
Climate Tipping Points – Too Risky to Bet against 16–17, 20
Club of Rome 50, 56
coastal environments 11
Columbian exchange 88
comics 111
correlationism 140–141
Cosmological Perspectivism in Amazonia and Elsewhere 150–151
cosmopolitics 145, 151
Cosmopolitiques 146
cybernetics 138

Dasein 145
Day After Tomorrow, The 8, 126, 157, 160–161, 164–166, 168–172
Day the Earth Stood Still, The 161
Dead Sea Scrolls 50, 52, 56

delta erosion and subsidence 41
deltas 37, 40–41
Deltas at Risk 40
depression 36–37, 60
desertification 33, 35, 93, 103
Desertification and Land Degradation 33, 35
Devī 82–85
dharma, Hindu 85
diegetic (vs. non-diegetic) 164
disanthropic narration 115
disaster 8, 63–65, 68, 71, 81, 83–84, 93–95, 103, 105–106, 109, 126–127, 130, 132, 138, 159, 164, 166, 168, 172
disaster films 93, 105, 164
Doomsday 50, 57, 60, 126
drought 17, 20, 27–28, 33, 93–94, 103, 137, 159, 160–161
dynamic character (vs. static character) 171

Early Church 50
ecocriticism 7, 158
ecofeminism 7, 94–95, 97, 101
ecological conditions in Arctic areas 35
ecology 8, 24, 84, 125–127, 144, 146, 151
Ecology Without Nature 144
editing 96, 157, 163–164
embodiment 84, 105, 149–151
enactivism 69–70, 77
End of Nature, The 125–126
end of the world 56, 58, 65, 125–131, 144
enmeshment 7–8, 43, 72, 76–77, 110
entropy 129, 145
environmental change 3, 6, 11, 23, 27, 29–30, 43
extreme weather 105, 160–162, 169

Facing Gaia 146
flashbacks 72, 164
flat character (vs. round character) 164
Flight Behavior 159
Flood, The 160
flooding 24, 26–27, 32, 39–40, 160, 165, 167–169
fossil fuel 94–96, 99, 101, 170

Fury Road 7, 93–96, 101–103
Future Sea-Level Rise Contribution of Greenland's Glaciers and Ice Caps, The 18

Geostorm 161–162
glacial-isostatic rebound 37
global biogeochemical cycles 25
Global Metabolic Transition
global temperature increase 18
global warming 3–4, 12–13, 15–18, 20, 28, 31, 35–37, 59, 109, 157, 160, 165–168, 170–172
globalization 43, 146
God 2, 57, 81–86, 88–89, 103, 113, 125–127, 133–134, 145
Golden Age 57, 59
Greco-Roman 50
greenhouse gases 3, 12–17, 19–20, 28, 37, 41–42
green-house-effect 130
Greenland ice sheet 17–21
Gulf stream 17–18

Hebrew Bible 49, 51, 54
Here 7
Hinduism 51, 81, 83–87, 89
Hollywood 51, 157, 164, 172
human consumption of raw materials and fuels 42
Human Domination of Earth's Ecosystems 23–24
human exceptionalism (see also anthropocentrism) 110, 120–121
Human Impact on the Natural Environment 16, 24, 26, 28, 30, 35, 37–41
human interference 3, 11–12, 20, 23, 26, 29, 33–35, 38–39, 41–43
HYDE 3.1 Spatially Explicit Database of Human- Induced Global Land-Use Change over the Past 12,000 Years, The 24–25
hypermasculinity 167
hyperobjects 144

ice age 8, 30–32, 34, 37, 160–161, 164
ice storms 169
idealism 142–143
identification 84, 96, 159
ideology (see also belief system and worldview) 2, 162–163, 172
image schema 67
imagination 1, 3, 49–50, 64–65, 68–70, 73–74, 76, 78, 81–85, 89, 93–94, 112, 127
immanence 147
Impacts of 1.5°C Global Warming on Natural and Human Systems 18, 27
Inquiry into Modes of Existence, An 146
Interstellar 161
Into the Storm 160
iśvara 83

Jesus movement 50
Judeo-Christian 50, 57, 65, 126–127

land cover changes and transformation 16, 23, 27
land subsidence 24
Land Transformation by Humans 23–24
Last Winter, The 161
liberalism 139, 158, 160
limits of economic growth 56
logocentrism 147
Long-Lived Greenhouse Gases 13
Lost City Raiders 160

Maccabean Revolt 50
Mad Max
Mahābhārata 81, 83–84
materialism 146–147
mechanicism 149
melting polar caps 165–166
messianic age 57, 59
mise-en-scène 96, 103, 157, 163–164
Möbius strip 151
modernity 89, 140, 147–148, 151
Mokṣa 83, 88
monism 83, 142, 147
Mother Earth 81, 85–86, 89
Mother-Goddess 81
multinaturalism 150

narrative 1–2, 5–9, 51, 59, 63–65, 68–72, 76–77, 93–94, 99, 102–103, 105–106, 109–122, 137, 147, 158, 163–164, 170
narrative strategies (see also narrative techniques) 2, 163
narrative techniques (see also narrative strategies) 2, 163
National Oceanic and Atmospheric Administration 165
nature (vs. culture) 3, 7, 49, 51, 65, 68, 71, 73–75, 82, 86, 89, 93, 96–98, 105, 109, 125–130, 133, 138, 140–141, 144, 147, 149–150, 168–169, 171
Neganthropocene, The 145–146
New Formalism 64
new heaven and earth 59
New Testament 50
Nihil Unbound 143
Nihilism 140–141, 176
nitrogen in fertilizers 43
Noah 160
nonhuman 7, 65–68, 70, 72, 75–78, 96, 102–104, 109–113, 118, 145–146
nonlife 137
noumenon 143

Object-Oriented Ontology (OOO) 142–145, 147
ontology 145–146, 150–151
Orbis hypothesis 88
Order of Things, The 149
Otherness 87, 103, 148, 151

pañcabhūtas 86
paradise 59, 99
paratext 163
perception 63, 68–70, 76, 117, 127, 129–130, 132, 159, 172
permafrost 17–19, 21–22, 28, 31, 35–36
personhood 97, 149–150
perspectivism 150
phallocentrism 147
phenomenon. 1, 37, 50–51, 57, 103, 143–144, 171
Philosophische Briefe über Dogmatismus und Kritizismus 143
phosphorus influxes 26
planetary boundaries 137

pluriverse 146, 149, 151
postcolonialism 102, 146, 151
prakṛti 86
Primitive Culture 149
Prophecy 49, 52–53, 55–56
Pṛthvī 82
Purāṇas 81, 83–84

Rabbinic Judaism 50
Reading Capital 2, 140, 162
realemes 165, 170
realism 143
Recent Climate Change Impacts on the Boreal Forests of Alaska 17–18
Regional Patterns and Trends of Global Material Flows, 1950–2010, The 42
relationism 142
release of greenhouse gases 3, 12, 16, 19, 37, 42
Revelation of John 50, 52
Roman Empire 50

Safe Operating Space for Humanity, A 26, 43
saline mechanism 165
scarcity 94–95, 97, 103
science 3, 8, 56, 86, 93, 109, 112, 125, 128, 130–131, 133–134, 141, 143, 147, 149, 162, 169, 171–172, 176
sea level rise 11, 18, 20, 37, 39–41, 116, 159–160
socialism 139
soil erosion rates in cropland regions 5, 25–26
solastalgia 7, 94, 103, 105–106
Sorge 145
sound 105, 117–119, 157, 163–164, 168
species extinction 1, 8, 26, 97, 109, 120, 159
stereotypes 162, 167

steric effect 37
storyworlds 7, 64, 96–97, 106, 110–112, 114–119, 121
subaltern 148
subject (vs. object) 142–144
sublime 76, 93–94, 96, 103, 105, 137, 168

temporality, three registers of 116–117
terrestrial nitrogen fixation 24
texture 63–64, 66–70, 73–77, 119
thaw subsidence 36
Thaw, The 161
thermohaline circulation 17–21
Thousand Plateaus, A 143, 146
Three Ecologies, The 146
tipping points 16–17, 20
Tool-Being 143
tornadoes 165, 168
Totemism 149–150
trapping of sediments in dams 41
Twister 160

Untergang des Abendlandes 56
unworld 8, 137, 151
Upaniṣads 7, 81–83

Vedas 7, 81–82, 84
vitalism 146–147

wasteland 7, 93–96, 98, 100–104, 106
Waterworld 160
weird, the 71
When Species Meet 146
World of Tomorrow 7, 112, 114, 117–121
worlding 148–149, 151
worldview (see also belief system and ideology) 2, 5, 50–52, 56–58, 121, 144, 147

Name Index

Alber, Jan 1, 8, 157, 175–176
Althusser, Louis 2, 140, 162
Apostle Paul 50
Aristotle 143
Arrhenius, Svante 130
Augustine 127

Bacon, Francis 147
Bataille, Georges 144
Beaver, Frank
Beck, Ulrich 125
Becker, Patrick 51
Bennett, Jane 147
Bergson, Henri 142
Boccaccini, Gabriele 56
Brassier, Ray 140–141, 143, 147

Clastres, Pierre 148
Collins, John Joseph 49–52, 54–56
Crutzen, Paul 126

de Jardin, Teilhard 56
Deleuze, Gilles 146
Descola, Philippe 149–150
DiTommaso, Lorenzo 49

Edelman, Lee 119–120
Emmerich, Roland 8, 106, 157, 164, 171
Escobar, Arturo 151
Even-Zohar, Itamar 165

Fludernik, Monika 111
Foucault, Michel 149

Galilei, Galileo 146
Garrard, Greg 115
Ghosh, Amitav 109–110
Grant, Iain Hamilton 147
Grodal, Torben Kragh 164
Guattari, Felix 137, 146
Gunkel, Hermann 49, 53

Hallowell, Irving 150
Hanson, Paul D. 49, 52, 55

Haraway, Donna J. 146
Harman, Graham 142–143
Heidegger, Martin 138, 143, 145
Heise, Ursula 158
Hellholm, David 55
Herman, David 63, 65, 110, 121
Hertzfeldt, Don 7, 112, 118–120
Hilgenfeld, Adolf 49, 52
Holbraad, Martin 149
Holt, Thomas 162
Hooke, Roger LeB. 24
Hörl, Erich 146
Hume, David 142

Ingram, David 169, 171

Jambeshwar, Guru 86
Jesus of Nazareth 50
John the Baptist 50
Jöris, Steffen 1, 51, 175

Kant, Immanuel 137, 141, 143
Koch, Klaus 50, 54
Körtner, Ulrich 49, 56

Lanser, Susan 163
Latour, Bruno 117, 146
Lemaître, George 128
Lenton, Timothy M. 20
Levine, Caroline 64
Lévi-Strauss, Claude 149
Lovelock, James 146
Lücke, Friedrich 49, 52

Markley, Robert 116–117
Marx, Karl 145, 162
Massumi, Brian 147
McGuire, Richard 7, 112, 114–116, 118
McKibben, Bill 126
Mehnert, Antonia 158
Meillassoux, Quentin 140–141, 143, 147
Miller, George 95, 104
Morton, Timothy 67–68, 77, 110, 142, 144–145
Mowinckel, Sigmund 49

Name Index

Nietzsche, Friedrich 141

Oegema, Gerbern S. 6, 49–50, 176

Pascal, Blaise 140
Povinelli, Elizabeth A. 137

Rahner, Karl 134
Reuss, Eduard 49, 52
Richardson, Brian 163
Rowland, Christopher 49
Ryan, Marie-Laure 114

Salmose, Niklas 105–106, 157, 165, 168, 171
Scarry, Elaine 69–70, 73, 77
Schelling, Friedrich 143
Schmid, Wolf 163
Schmidt, Johann Michael 49, 52–54
Schneider-Mayerson, Matthew 158–160
Seneviratne, Sonia Isabelle 35
Siegemund, Axel 8, 49, 125, 176
Sloterdijk, Peter 145–146

Spengler, Oswald 56
Spinoza, Baruch 147
Stengers, Isabelle 145–146
Stiegler, Bertrand 145–146
Stockwell, Peter 64, 76, 111
Stoknes, Per Espen 159, 167
Svoboda, Michael 160–162
Syvitski, Jaia 41

Thompson, Evan 69
Tillich, Paul 133–134
Tylor, Edward Burnett 149

Urquiza-Haas, Esmerelda, and Kurt Kotrschal 113

VanderMeer, Jeff 7, 70–71, 73, 77–78
Vitousek, Peter M. 23
Viveiros de Castro, Eduardo 149–151

Weik von Mossner, Alexa 166, 170
Wood, Aylish 119–120

www.ingramcontent.com/pod-product-compliance
Lightning Source LLC
Chambersburg PA
CBHW062103080426
42734CB00012B/2738